TREASURY
OF
COOKING
HEALTHY
GREAT-TASTING · LOW-FAT RECIPES

Pictured on the front cover: Florida Grapefruit Marinated Shrimp *(page 316)*.
Pictured on the back cover *(clockwise from top right):* Shrimp Toast *(page 58)*, Honey Glazed Pork *(page 202)*, Cherry Cornmeal Cobbler *(page 538)* and Southwestern Beef and Bean Lasagna *(page 394)*.

ISBN: 0-7853-0795-8

Library of Congress Catalog Card Number: 94-69613

Manufactured in U.S.A.

8   7   6   5   4   3   2   1

Microwave Cooking: Microwave ovens vary in wattage. The microwave cooking times given in this publication are approximate. Use the cooking times as guidelines and check for doneness before adding more time. Consult manufacturer's instructions for suitable microwave-safe cooking dishes.

The publishers would like to thank the following companies and organizations for the use of their recipes in this publication: American Celery Council, American Lamb Council, Almond Board of California, California Apricot Advisory Board, California Cling Peach Advisory Board, California Tree Fruit Agreement, Florida Department of Citrus, Minnesota Cultivated Wild Rice Council, National Dairy Board, National Live Stock & Meat Board, National Pork Producers Council, New York Apple Growers, Pacific Coast Canned Pear Service and Wisconsin Milk Marketing Board.

TREASURY
OF
COOKING
HEALTHY
GREAT-TASTING ◆ LOW-FAT RECIPES

PUBLICATIONS INTERNATIONAL, LTD.

CONTENTS

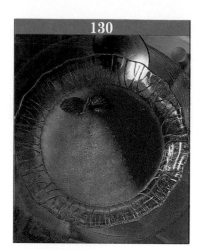

CONTENTS

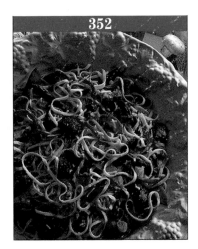

INTRODUCTION

Today, people everywhere are more aware than ever before about the importance of maintaining a healthful lifestyle. In addition to proper exercise, this includes eating foods that are lower in fat, sodium and cholesterol. The goal of Cooking Healthy is to provide today's cook with easy-to-prepare recipes that taste great, yet easily fit into your dietary goals. Eating well is a matter of making smarter choices about the foods you eat. Preparing the recipes in Cooking Healthy is your first step toward making smart choices a delicious reality.

A Balanced Diet

The U.S. Department of Agriculture and the Department of Health and Human Services have developed a Food Guide Pyramid to illustrate how easy it is to eat a healthier diet. It is not a rigid prescription, but rather a general guide that lets you choose a healthful diet that's right for you. It calls for eating a wide variety of foods to get the nutrients you need and, at the same time, the right amount of calories to maintain a healthy weight.

Food Guide Pyramid

A Guide to Daily Food Choices

Fats, Oils, & Sweets
Use Sparingly
(Also found in other
groups; see text.)

KEY
•Fat (naturally occurring ▼Sugar
and added)   (added)
These symbols show fats, oils, and
added sugars in foods.

Milk, Yogurt,
& Cheese
Group
2–3 Servings

Meat, Poultry, Fish,
Dry Beans, Eggs,
& Nuts Group
2–3 Servings

Vegetable Group
3–5 Servings

Fruit Group
2–4 Servings

Bread, Cereal,
Rice, & Pasta
Group
6–11
Servings

The number of servings, and consequently, the number of calories a person can eat each day, is determined by a number of factors, including age, weight, height, activity level and gender. Sedentary women and some older adults need about 1,600 calories each day. For most children, teenage girls, active women and many sedentary men, 2,000 calories is about right. Teenage boys, active men and some very active women use about 2,800 calories each day. Use the chart below to determine how many servings you need for your calorie level.

Personalized Food Group Servings for Different Calorie Levels*			
	1,600	2,000	2,800
Bread Group Servings	6	8	11
Vegetable Group Servings	3	4	5
Fruit Group Servings	2	3	4
Milk Group Servings	2-3**	2-3**	2-3**
Meat Group Servings (ounces)	5	6	7

* Numbers may be rounded.
**Women who are pregnant or breast-feeding, teenagers and young adults to age 24 need 3 or more servings.

Lower Fat for Healthier Living

It is widely known that most Americans' diets are too high in fat. A low fat diet reduces your risk of getting certain diseases and helps you maintain a healthy weight. Studies have shown that eating more than the recommended amount of fat (especially saturated fat) is associated with increased blood cholesterol levels in some adults. A high blood cholesterol level is associated with increased risk for heart disease. A high fat diet may also increase your chances for obesity and some types of cancer.

Nutrition experts recommend diets that contain 30% or less of total daily calories from fat. The "30% calories from fat" goal applies to a total diet over time, not to a single food, serving of a recipe or meal. To find the approximate percentage of calories from fat use this easy 3-step process:

1 Multiply the grams of fat per serving by 9 (there are 9 calories in each gram of fat), to give you the number of calories from fat per serving.

2 Divide by the total number of calories per serving.

3 Multiply by 100%.

For example, imagine a 200 calorie sandwich that has 10 grams of fat. To find the percentage of calories from fat, first multiply the grams of fat by 9:

$$10 \times 9 = 90$$

Then, divide by the total number of calories in a serving:

$$90 \div 200 = .45$$

Multiply by 100% to get the percentage of calories from fat:

$$.45 \times 100\% = 45\%$$

You may find doing all this math tiresome, so an easier way to keep track of the fat in your diet is to calculate the total *grams* of fat appropriate to your caloric intake, then keep a running count of fat grams over the course of a day. The Nutrition Reference Chart on page 11 lists recommended daily fat intakes based on calorie level.

Defining "Fat-Free"

It is important to take the time to read food labels carefully. For example, you'll find many food products on the grocery store shelves making claims such as "97% fat free." This does not necessarily mean that 97% of the *calories* are free from fat (or that only 3 percent of calories come from fat). Often these numbers are calculated by weight. This means that out of 100 grams of this food, 3 grams are fat. Depending on what else is in the food, the percentage of calories from fat can be quite high. You may find that the percent of calories *from fat* can be as high as 50%.

Daily Values

Fat has become the focus of many diets and eating plans. This is because most Americans' diets are too high in fat. However, there are other important nutrients to be aware of, including saturated fat, sodium, cholesterol, protein, carbohydrates and several vitamins and minerals. Daily values for these nutrients have been established by the government and reflect current nutritional recommendations for a 2,000 calorie reference diet. They are appropriate for most adults and children (age 4 or older) and provide excellent guidelines for an overall healthy diet. The chart on page 11 gives the daily values for the nutrients listed in this publication.

Nutritional Analysis

Every recipe in *Cooking Healthy* is followed by a nutritional analysis block that lists certain nutrient values for a single serving.

■ The analysis of each recipe includes all the ingredients that are listed in that recipe, *except* ingredients labeled as "optional" or "for garnish."

■ If a range is given in the yield of a recipe ("Makes 6 to 8 servings" for example), the *lower* yield was used to calculate the per serving information.

■ If a range is offered for an ingredient ("¼ to ⅛ teaspoon" for example), the *first* amount given was used to calculate the nutrition information.

■ If an ingredient is presented with an option ("2 cups hot cooked rice or noodles" for example), the *first* item listed was used to calculate the nutritional information.

■ Foods shown in photographs on the same serving plate and offered as "serve with" suggestions at the end of a recipe are *not* included in the recipe analysis unless they are listed in the ingredient list.

■ Meat should be trimmed of all visible fat since this is reflected in the nutritional analysis.

■ In recipes calling for cooked rice or noodles, the analysis was based on rice or noodles that were prepared without added salt or fat unless otherwise mentioned in the recipe.

The nutrition information that appears with each recipe was calculated by an independent nutrition consulting firm. Every effort has been made to check the accuracy of these numbers. However, because numerous variables account for a wide range of values in certain foods, all analyses that appear in this book should be considered approximate.

The recipes in this publication are *not* intended as a medically therapeutic program, nor as a substitute for medically approved diet plans for people on fat, cholesterol or sodium restricted diets. You should consult your physician before beginning any diet plan. The recipes offered here can be a part of a healthy lifestyle that meets recognized dietary guidelines. A healthy lifestyle includes not only eating a balanced diet, but engaging in proper exercise as well.

All the ingredients called for in these recipes are generally available in large supermarkets, so there is no need to go to specialty or health food stores. You'll also see an ever-increasing amount of reduced fat and nonfat products available in local markets. Take advantage of these items to reduce your daily fat intake even more.

Cooking Healthier

When cooking great-tasting low fat meals, you will find some techniques or ingredients are different from traditional cooking. Fat, in the form of oil, butter, margarine and shortening is used in nearly every type of recipe. Because fat plays an important role in cooking and baking, it is difficult to merely omit it. It acts as a flavor enhancer and gives food a distinctive and desirable texture. So, instead of taking it out completely, several techniques are employed to make up for the loss of flavor and texture. These techniques include:

■ Investing in nonstick bakeware and using nonstick cooking spray to reduce the need for added oil.

■ Incorporating applesauce or other puréed fruit into baked goods to create a texture similar to high-fat foods.

■ "Sautéing" vegetables a small amount of broth to further reduce the need for oil.

■ Using herbs, spices and flavorful vegetables in a variety of combinations to highlight the natural flavor of food, making up for the lack of fat.

■ Choosing alternative protein sources, such as dried beans or tofu in recipes. Often, meat is included in a recipe as an accent flavor rather that the star attraction.

These methods for reducing fat can benefit recipes in two ways: 1) by reducing the overall amount of fat in the recipe and 2) by boosting the nutritional content of the recipe when fruits and vegetables replace high fat ingredients. These are all simple changes that you can easily make when you start cooking healthy!

Personalized Nutrition Reference for Different Calorie Levels*

Daily Calorie Level	1,600	2,000	2,200	2,800
Total Fat	53 g	65 g	73 g	93 g
% of Calories from Fat	30%	30%	30%	30%
Saturated Fat	18 g	20 g	24 g	31 g
Carbohydrate	240 g	300 g	330 g	420 g
Protein	46 g**	50 g	55 g	70 g
Dietary Fiber	20 g***	25 g	25 g	32 g
Cholesterol	300 mg	300 mg	300 mg	300 mg
Sodium	2,400 mg	2,400 mg	2,400 mg	2,400 mg
Calcium	1,000 mg	1,000 mg	1,000 mg	1,000 mg
Iron	18 mg	18 mg	18 mg	18 mg
Vitamin A	1,000 RE	1,000 RE	1,000 RE	1,000 RE
Vitamin C	60 mg	60 mg	60 mg	60 mg

  * Numbers may be rounded
 ** 46 g is the minimum amount of protein recommended for all calorie levels below 1,800.
*** 20 g is the minimum amount of fiber recommended for all calorie levels below 2,000.

Note: These calorie levels may not apply to children or adolescents, who have varying calorie requirements. For specific advice concerning calorie levels, please consult a registered dietitian, qualified health professional or pediatrician.

APPETIZERS

PEPPY SNACK MIX

If you are closely watching the sodium in your diet, make this recipe with unsalted rice cakes and no-salt pretzels.

3 plain rice cakes, broken into
    bite-size pieces
1½ cups bite-size frosted shredded
    wheat biscuit cereal
¾ cup pretzel sticks, halved
3 tablespoons reduced calorie
    margarine, melted

2 teaspoons low sodium
    Worcestershire sauce
¾ teaspoon chili powder
⅛ to ¼ teaspoon ground red
    pepper

1 Preheat oven to 300°F.

2 Combine rice cakes, wheat biscuits and pretzels in 13×9-inch baking pan; mix well.

3 Combine margarine, Worcestershire, chili powder and pepper in small bowl. Drizzle over cereal mixture; toss to combine.

4 Bake 20 minutes, stirring after 10 minutes.   *Makes 6 servings*

Nutrients per Serving:

½ cup snack mix

Calories	118 (25% of calories from fat)				
Total Fat	3 g	Carbohydrate	20 g	Iron	1 mg
Saturated Fat	1 g	Dietary Fiber	1 g	Vitamin A	266 RE
Cholesterol	0 mg	Protein	2 g	Vitamin C	11 mg
Sodium	156 mg	Calcium	12 mg		

DIETARY EXCHANGES: 1½ Starch/Bread, ½ Fat

FRESH FRUIT WITH CREAMY LIME DIPPING SAUCE

A delicious, refreshing and healthy alternative to salty, high fat snacks, fruits and vegetables also help protect the body from most kinds of cancer. This is a good start toward fulfilling your minimum five servings per day.

Creamy Lime Dipping Sauce
(recipe follows)
2 tablespoons lime juice
1 small jicama, peeled, cut into
½-inch-thick strips 3 to 4
inches long
2 pounds watermelon, rind
removed, fruit cut into
½-inch-thick wedges 2 to
3 inches wide

½ small pineapple, peeled, halved
lengthwise, cut crosswise
into wedges
1 ripe papaya, peeled, seeded,
sliced crosswise

1 Prepare Creamy Lime Dipping Sauce; set aside. Combine lime juice and jicama in large bowl; toss. Drain. Arrange jicama, watermelon, pineapple and papaya on large serving platter. Serve with Creamy Lime Dipping Sauce.

Makes 12 servings

CREAMY LIME DIPPING SAUCE

1 container (6 ounces) nonfat
vanilla yogurt
2 tablespoons minced fresh
cilantro

2 tablespoons lime juice
1 tablespoon minced jalapeño
pepper*

1 Combine all ingredients in small bowl; mix well to combine.

Makes about 1 cup

*Jalapeño peppers can sting and irritate the skin; wear rubber gloves when handling peppers and do not touch eyes. Wash hands after handling.

Nutrients per Serving:					
Calories	65 (5% of calories from fat)				
Total Fat	<1 g	Carbohydrate	15 g	Iron	<1 mg
Saturated Fat	0 g	Dietary Fiber	1 g	Vitamin A	28 RE
Cholesterol	<1 mg	Protein	1 g	Vitamin C	38 mg
Sodium	23 mg	Calcium	42 mg		

DIETARY EXCHANGES: 1 Fruit

ROASTED EGGPLANT SPREAD WITH FOCACCIA

This no cholesterol appetizer is perfect for any Italian meal!

Focaccia (page 158)
1 eggplant (1 pound)
1 medium tomato
1 tablespoon lemon juice
1 tablespoon chopped fresh basil
   or 1 teaspoon dried basil
   leaves

2 teaspoons chopped fresh
   thyme *or* ¾ teaspoon dried
   thyme leaves
1 clove garlic, minced
¼ teaspoon salt
1 tablespoon extra virgin olive oil

1 Prepare Focaccia; set aside. Preheat oven to 400°F. Poke holes in several places in eggplant with fork. Cut stem end from tomato and place in small baking pan. Place eggplant on oven rack; bake 10 minutes. Place tomato in oven with eggplant. Bake vegetables 40 minutes.

2 Cool vegetables slightly, then peel. Cut eggplant into large slices. Place tomato and eggplant in food processor or blender. Add lemon juice, basil, thyme, garlic and salt; process until well blended. Slowly drizzle oil through feed tube and process until mixture is well blended. Refrigerate 3 hours or overnight.

3 To serve, spread 1 tablespoon on each focaccia wedge. Garnish with cherry tomato wedges and additional fresh basil, if desired.

Makes 10 servings

Nutrients per Serving:

3 tablespoons eggplant spread with 3 wedges focaccia

Calories	127 (21% of calories from fat)				
Total Fat	3 g	Carbohydrate	22 g	Iron	1 mg
Saturated Fat	<1 g	Dietary Fiber	3 g	Vitamin A	12 RE
Cholesterol	0 mg	Protein	4 g	Vitamin C	4 mg
Sodium	267 mg	Calcium	15 mg		

DIETARY EXCHANGES: 1½ Starch, ½ Fat

ORIENTAL SALSA

Easy Wonton Chips (recipe
follows) or assorted fresh
vegetables
1 cup diced cucumber
½ cup chopped red bell pepper
½ cup thinly sliced green onions
⅓ cup coarsely chopped fresh
cilantro

1 clove garlic, minced
1 tablespoon rice vinegar
½ teaspoon Oriental sesame oil
2 tablespoons low sodium soy
sauce
¼ teaspoon crushed red pepper

1 Prepare Easy Wonton Chips; set aside. Combine cucumber, bell pepper, onions, cilantro, garlic, rice vinegar, oil, soy sauce and crushed red pepper in medium bowl until well blended.

2 Cover and refrigerate until ready to serve. Serve with Easy Wonton Chips or assorted fresh vegetables for dipping. Or, use as an accompaniment to broiled fish, chicken or pork.

Makes 6 servings

EASY WONTON CHIPS

1 tablespoon soy sauce
2 teaspoons vegetable oil
½ teaspoon sugar

¼ teaspoon garlic salt
12 wonton wrappers

1 Preheat oven to 375°F. Combine soy sauce, oil, sugar and garlic salt in small bowl; mix well.

2 Cut each wonton wrapper diagonally in half. Place on 15×10-inch jelly-roll pan coated with nonstick cooking spray. Brush soy mixture lightly but evenly over both sides of wrappers.

3 Bake 4 to 6 minutes or until crisp and lightly browned, turning after 3 minutes. Transfer to cooling rack; cool completely.

Makes 2 dozen chips

Nutrients per Serving:
¼ cup salsa plus 4 chips

Calories	77 (29% of calories from fat)				
Total Fat	3 g	Carbohydrate	16 g	Iron	1 mg
Saturated Fat	<1 g	Dietary Fiber	1 g	Vitamin A	15 RE
Cholesterol	11 mg	Protein	4 g	Vitamin C	5 mg
Sodium	361 mg	Calcium	4 mg		

DIETARY EXCHANGES: ½ Starch/Bread, ½ Fat

GREEN PEA GUACAMOLE WITH AVOCADO AND TOMATO

If you simply cannot get by without the smooth rich taste of the real McCoy, savor the avocado's flavor in a few chunks. Though most of the avocado's calories come from fat, it is primarily monounsaturated (the kind not associated with heart disease) and contains no cholesterol. So enjoy those tender morsels!

Baked Tortilla Chips (page 22)
(optional)
½ cup diced ripe California
avocado*
3 tablespoons lemon juice,
divided
1 package (16 ounces) frozen
petite peas, thawed

4 green onions
½ cup lightly packed fresh
cilantro
1 jalapeño pepper, seeded**
1 medium tomato, diced

1 Prepare Baked Tortilla Chips; set aside. Combine avocado and 1 tablespoon lemon juice in medium bowl.

2 Combine peas, onions, cilantro, remaining 2 tablespoons lemon juice and jalapeño in food processor or blender; process until smooth. Add avocado and tomato; gently stir to combine. Garnish with additional cilantro or tomato wedges, if desired. Serve with Baked Tortilla Chips.   *Makes 8 servings*

*To lower fat content, omit avocado.

**Jalapeño peppers can sting and irritate the skin; wear rubber gloves when handling peppers and do not touch eyes. Wash hands after handling.

Nutrients per Serving:

Calories	100 (28% of calories from fat)				
Total Fat	3 g	Carbohydrate	15 g	Iron	2 mg
Saturated Fat	1 g	Dietary Fiber	4 g	Vitamin A	124 RE
Cholesterol	0 mg	Protein	5 g	Vitamin C	23 mg
Sodium	141 mg	Calcium	32 mg		

DIETARY EXCHANGES: 1 Starch/Bread, ½ Fat

BAKED TORTILLA CHIPS

Traditional tortilla chips bubble and crisp in hot oil, sending their fat content soaring. Baking is easier and keeps fat to a minimum. Plus, these chips (pictured on page 21) have no added salt.

BAKED FLOUR OR CORN TORTILLA CHIPS

6 (7- to 8-inch) flour tortillas *or*
6 (6-inch) corn tortillas

Paprika, chili powder or
ground red pepper

1 Preheat oven to 375°F. Sprinkle 1 tortilla with water to dampen; shake off excess water. Lightly sprinkle top with paprika. Repeat with remaining tortillas. Cut each flour tortilla into 8 wedges, each corn tortilla into 6 wedges.

2 Arrange as many wedges as fit in single layer on baking sheet (edges may overlap slightly). Bake 4 minutes. Rotate sheet. Bake 2 to 4 minutes or until chips are firm and flour tortillas are spotted with light golden color. Do not let corn tortillas brown. Transfer to cooling rack; cool completely. Repeat with remaining wedges.

Makes 6 servings

Nutrients per Serving:

Calories	67 (15% of calories from fat)				
Total Fat	1 g	Carbohydrate	13 g	Iron	1 mg
Saturated Fat	<1 g	Dietary Fiber	2 g	Vitamin A	5 RE
Cholesterol	0 mg	Protein	2 g	Vitamin C	0 mg
Sodium	53 mg	Calcium	42 mg		

DIETARY EXCHANGES: 1 Starch/Bread

PARMESAN CHIPS

1 Prepare Baked Tortilla Chips as directed above, omitting paprika. Sprinkle each tortilla with 1 tablespoon grated Parmesan cheese and ¼ teaspoon dried oregano leaves.

Makes 6 servings

Nutrients per Serving:

Calories	97 (28% of calories from fat)				
Total Fat	3 g	Carbohydrate	13 g	Iron	1 mg
Saturated Fat	1 g	Dietary Fiber	2 g	Vitamin A	21 RE
Cholesterol	5 mg	Protein	5 g	Vitamin C	0 mg
Sodium	170 mg	Calcium	134 mg		

DIETARY EXCHANGES: 1 Starch/Bread, ½ Fat

SWEET TORTILLA CHIPS

1 tablespoon margarine
1½ teaspoons water

¼ cup firmly packed brown sugar
6 (6- to 7-inch) flour tortillas

1 Microwave margarine and water at HIGH in small microwavable bowl for 15 seconds or until margarine melts. Stir in brown sugar until smooth.

2 Spread equal amount of sugar mixture over top of each tortilla, leaving ½-inch border. Cut as directed for Baked Flour Tortilla Chips (page 22). Bake 7 to 9 minutes or until sugar melts and bubbles and chips feel firm.

Makes 6 servings

CINNAMON–SUGAR CHIPS

1 tablespoon margarine
1½ teaspoons water
¼ cup firmly packed brown sugar

1½ teaspoons ground cinnamon
6 (6- to 7-inch) flour tortillas

1 Prepare chips as directed above. Add cinnamon to sugar mixture before spreading over tortillas.

Makes 6 servings

FIERY SWEET CHIPS

1 tablespoon margarine
1½ teaspoons water
¼ cup firmly packed brown sugar

6 (6- to 7-inch) flour tortillas
Ground red pepper

1 Prepare chips as directed above. Lightly sprinkle chips with red pepper before baking.

Makes 6 servings

Nutrients per Serving:

Sweet Tortilla, Cinnamon-Sugar or Fiery Sweet Chips

Calories	118 (22% of calories from fat)				
Total Fat	3 g	Carbohydrate	22 g	Iron	1 mg
Saturated Fat	<1 g	Dietary Fiber	2 g	Vitamin A	28 RE
Cholesterol	0 mg	Protein	2 g	Vitamin C	0 mg
Sodium	78 mg	Calcium	50 mg		

DIETARY EXCHANGES: 1 Starch/Bread, ½ Fruit, ½ Fat

CROSTINI

These tasty little Tuscan treats are colorful and easy to make. Crostini are wonderful for last minute parties or unexpected guests because they can be made in minutes.

¼ loaf whole wheat baguette (4 ounces)
4 plum tomatoes
1 cup (4 ounces) shredded part-skim mozzarella cheese

3 tablespoons prepared pesto sauce

1 Preheat oven to 400°F. Slice baguette diagonally into 16 very thin slices. Slice each tomato vertically into four ¼-inch slices.

2 Place baguette slices on nonstick baking sheet. Top each with 1 tablespoon cheese, then 1 slice tomato. Bake about 8 minutes or until bread is lightly toasted and cheese is melted. Remove from oven; top each crostini with about ½ teaspoon pesto sauce. Garnish with fresh basil, if desired. Serve warm.

Makes 8 servings

Nutrients per Serving:

2 crostini

Calories	83 (34% of calories from fat)				
Total Fat	3 g	Carbohydrate	9 g	Iron	1 mg
Saturated Fat	2 g	Dietary Fiber	<1 g	Vitamin A	51 RE
Cholesterol	9 mg	Protein	5 g	Vitamin C	7 mg
Sodium	159 mg	Calcium	121 mg		

DIETARY EXCHANGES: ½ Starch/Bread, ½ Lean Meat, ½ Fat

TINY SEAFOOD TOSTADAS WITH BLACK BEAN DIP

Instead of making tiny round tortilla chips, you may cut the tortillas with cookie cutters into other shapes for special holidays, such as hearts for Valentine's Day or shamrocks for St. Patrick's Day. For vegetarian tostadas, omit the shrimp and add a bit more cheese.

4 (8-inch) whole wheat or flour tortillas, cut into 32 (2½-inch) rounds
Nonstick cooking spray
1 cup Black Bean Dip (page 28)
1 cup washed and shredded fresh spinach

¾ cup tiny cooked or canned shrimp, rinsed and drained
¾ cup salsa
½ cup (2 ounces) shredded reduced fat Monterey Jack cheese
¼ cup low fat sour cream

1 Preheat oven to 350°F. Spray baking sheet with nonstick cooking spray. Place tortilla rounds evenly on prepared baking sheet. Lightly spray tortillas with cooking spray and bake 10 minutes. Turn over and spray again; bake 3 minutes more. Meanwhile, prepare Black Bean Dip.

2 To prepare tostadas, spread each toasted tortilla with 1½ teaspoons Black Bean Dip. Layer each with 1½ teaspoons shredded spinach, 1 teaspoon shrimp, 1 teaspoon salsa, a sprinkle of cheese and a small amount of sour cream. Garnish with thin green chili strips or fresh cilantro, if desired. Serve immediately.

Makes 8 servings

Nutrients per Serving:					
4 tostadas					
Calories	157 (20% of calories from fat)				
Total Fat	4 g	Carbohydrate	23 g	Iron	1 mg
Saturated Fat	1 g	Dietary Fiber	4 g	Vitamin A	148 RE
Cholesterol	31 mg	Protein	12 g	Vitamin C	21 mg
Sodium	747 mg	Calcium	117 mg		

DIETARY EXCHANGES: 1 Starch/Bread, 1 Lean Meat, 1 Vegetable

BLACK BEAN DIP

This bean dip is an essential ingredient in the Tiny Seafood Tostadas (page 26), but it is also a superb dip for Corn Tortilla Chips (page 22) or with raw jicama sticks. Recipe pictured on page 27.

1 can (15 ounces) black beans, undrained
1 teaspoon chili powder
¼ teaspoon salt
¼ teaspoon ground black pepper
¼ teaspoon ground cumin

2 drops hot pepper sauce
¾ cup minced onion
2 cloves garlic, minced
1 can (4 ounces) diced green chilies, drained

1 Drain beans, reserving 2 tablespoons liquid. Combine drained beans, reserved liquid, chili powder, salt, black pepper, cumin and hot pepper sauce in food processor or blender; process until smooth.

2 Combine onion and garlic in nonstick skillet or saucepan; cover and cook over low heat until onion is soft and translucent. Uncover and cook until slightly browned. Add chilies and cook 3 minutes more. Add bean mixture and mix well. Garnish with pepper strips, if desired. Serve hot or cold.

Makes about 24 servings

Nutrients per Serving:					
1 tablespoon dip					
Calories	18 (7% of calories from fat)				
Total Fat	<1 g	Carbohydrate	4 g	Iron	1 mg
Saturated Fat	<1 g	Dietary Fiber	1 g	Vitamin A	7 RE
Cholesterol	0 mg	Protein	2 g	Vitamin C	4 mg
Sodium	134 mg	Calcium	3 mg		

DIETARY EXCHANGES: ½ Starch/Bread

PETITE PIZZAS

½ cup warm water (110° to
   115°F)
¾ teaspoon active dry yeast
½ teaspoon sugar
¾ cup bread flour*
¾ cup whole wheat flour
¼ teaspoon salt
1½ teaspoons extra virgin olive oil
   Pizza Sauce (page 30)
¼ cup finely chopped green bell
   pepper

¼ cup minced onion
2 ounces Italian turkey sausage,
   crumbled and cooked
⅔ cup sliced mushrooms, cooked
   until tender
¼ cup freshly grated Parmesan
   cheese
¼ cup (1 ounce) shredded part-
   skim mozzarella cheese

1 To prepare crust, place water in small bowl. Sprinkle yeast and sugar on top; stir to combine. Let stand 10 minutes or until bubbly. Combine flours and salt in medium bowl. Stir in oil and yeast mixture; mix until smooth. Turn dough onto lightly floured surface. Knead 5 minutes or until dough is smooth and elastic. Place dough in medium bowl sprayed with nonstick cooking spray. Turn dough so all sides are coated; cover with towel.

2 Let rise in warm place 45 minutes or until doubled in bulk. Punch down dough; place on lightly floured surface and knead 2 minutes more. Cover with towel and let rise 20 minutes more. Roll out to ¼-inch thickness and cut into 32 circles with 2-inch cookie or biscuit cutter. Place on baking sheet sprayed with cooking spray. (Combine scraps of dough and roll out again to obtain 32 circles, if necessary.)

3 Prepare Pizza Sauce. Place about ½ teaspoon sauce on each dough round. Spread sauce gently, leaving a small border of crust.

4 Preheat oven to 400°F. Combine bell pepper and onion in small bowl. Evenly sprinkle on top of sauce. Place sausage on half the pizzas and 1 or 2 mushroom slices on each of remaining pizzas. Evenly sprinkle cheeses on pizzas. Bake 10 minutes or until cheese melts. Serve immediately. (To reheat, warm pizzas in 250°F oven 10 minutes.) Garnish with fresh basil, if desired. *Makes 8 appetizer servings*

*You may substitute all-purpose flour for bread flour; however, bread flour works better with yeast since it contains more gluten. It also contains more vitamin C and potassium.

(continued on page 30)

Petite Pizzas, continued

PIZZA SAUCE

½ teaspoon extra virgin olive oil
1 clove garlic, minced
1 can (8 ounces) tomato sauce
1 tablespoon chopped fresh basil
    or 1 teaspoon dried basil
    leaves

½ teaspoon dried oregano leaves
    Dash salt and ground black
    pepper

1 Heat oil in small saucepan over medium heat. Add garlic; cook and stir 1 minute, being careful not to brown garlic. Add tomato sauce, basil and oregano; simmer 20 minutes. Stir in salt and black pepper.

Nutrients per Serving:

2 sausage pizzas and 2 mushroom pizzas

Calories	148 (25% of calories from fat)				
Total Fat	4 g	Carbohydrate	22 g	Iron	2 mg
Saturated Fat	1 g	Dietary Fiber	2 g	Vitamin A	47 RE
Cholesterol	9 mg	Protein	7 g	Vitamin C	9 mg
Sodium	357 mg	Calcium	88 mg		

DIETARY EXCHANGES: 1 Starch/Bread, ½ Lean Meat, ½ Vegetable, ½ Fat

Health Note

These tasty tidbits are not only packed with flavor, the dough uses whole wheat flour which contains wheat germ and adds fiber.

PITA PIZZAS

Pita, or pocket bread, is a flat bread served throughout the Middle East, either as an accompaniment to meals, stuffed to form sandwiches, or cut into wedges to serve as dippers. Using whole wheat pita breads as the chewy crust for these mini-pizzas provides an extra boost of vitamins, minerals and fiber.

Nonstick cooking spray
½ pound boneless skinless chicken breasts, cut into ½-inch cubes
½ cup thinly sliced red bell pepper
½ cup thinly sliced mushrooms
½ cup thinly sliced red onion
2 cloves garlic, minced

1 teaspoon dried basil leaves
½ teaspoon dried oregano leaves
1 cup washed and torn fresh spinach leaves
6 mini whole wheat pita breads
½ cup (2 ounces) shredded part-skim mozzarella cheese
1 tablespoon freshly grated Parmesan cheese

1 Preheat oven to 375°F. Spray medium nonstick skillet with cooking spray; heat over medium heat until hot. Add chicken; cook and stir 6 minutes or until browned and no longer pink in center. Remove chicken from skillet.

2 Spray same nonstick skillet again with cooking spray; add bell pepper, mushrooms, onion, garlic, basil and oregano. Cook and stir over medium heat 5 to 7 minutes or until vegetables are crisp-tender. Return chicken to skillet; stir well.

3 Place spinach on top of pita breads. Divide chicken and vegetable mixture evenly; spoon over spinach. Sprinkle evenly with mozzarella and Parmesan cheese. Bake, uncovered, 7 to 10 minutes or until cheese is melted.

Makes 6 servings

Nutrients per Serving:

Calories	158 (17% of calories from fat)				
Total Fat	3 g	Carbohydrate	19 g	Iron	2 mg
Saturated Fat	2 g	Dietary Fiber	4 g	Vitamin A	99 RE
Cholesterol	125 mg	Protein	14 g	Vitamin C	21 mg
Sodium	198 mg	Calcium	119 mg		

DIETARY EXCHANGES: 1 Starch/Bread, 1½ Lean Meat, ½ Vegetable

TORTILLA PIZZA WEDGES

Not only are these pizza wedges great tasting but they're high in complex carbohydrates as well.

Nonstick cooking spray
1 cup frozen whole kernel corn, thawed, drained
1 cup thinly sliced mushrooms
4 (6-inch) corn tortillas
¼ cup low sodium spaghetti sauce
1 to 2 teaspoons chopped jalapeño pepper*

¼ teaspoon dried oregano leaves
¼ teaspoon dried marjoram leaves
½ cup (2 ounces) shredded part-skim mozzarella cheese

1 Preheat oven to 450°F.

2 Spray large skillet with cooking spray; heat over medium heat. Add corn and mushrooms. Cook and stir 4 to 5 minutes or until vegetables are tender.

3 Place tortillas on baking sheet. Bake about 4 minutes or until edges start to brown.

4 Combine spaghetti sauce, jalapeño, oregano and marjoram in small bowl. Spread over tortillas. Arrange corn and mushrooms on top of tortillas. Sprinkle with cheese. Bake 4 to 5 minutes or until cheese melts and pizzas are heated through. Cut into wedges. *Makes 4 servings*

*Jalapeño peppers can sting and irritate the skin; wear rubber gloves when handling peppers and do not touch eyes. Wash hands after handling.

Nutrients per Serving:

Calories	155 (23% of calories from fat)				
Total Fat	4 g	Carbohydrate	24 g	Iron	1 mg
Saturated Fat	2 g	Dietary Fiber	3 g	Vitamin A	80 RE
Cholesterol	8 mg	Protein	7 g	Vitamin C	4 mg
Sodium	136 mg	Calcium	143 mg		

DIETARY EXCHANGES: 1½ Starch/Bread, ½ Lean Meat

NACHOS

These nachos combine beans, corn and cheese to create a complete protein equal to that in meat—but without the fat.

8 (6-inch) corn tortillas
   Nonstick cooking spray
1 cup chopped onion
1 tablespoon chili powder
2 teaspoons dried oregano leaves
1 can (15 ounces) pinto beans or
   black beans, rinsed and
   drained
1¼ cups (5 ounces) shredded
   reduced fat Monterey Jack
   cheese

¾ cup frozen whole kernel corn,
   thawed, drained
1 jar (2 ounces) pimientos,
   drained
3 tablespoons ripe olive slices
2 to 3 tablespoons pickled
   jalapeño pepper slices,
   drained

1 Preheat oven to 375°F. Bake corn tortillas according to directions for Baked Tortilla Chips (page 22), baking 8 tortillas instead of 6. Arrange chips on baking sheet or in two 9-inch pie plates. Set aside.

2 Spray medium saucepan with cooking spray. Heat over medium-high heat. Add onion; cook and stir 8 to 10 minutes or until onion is tender and beginning to brown. Add chili powder and oregano; cook and stir 1 minute.

3 Remove from heat. Add beans and 2 tablespoons water; mash with fork or potato masher until blended yet chunky. Return to heat. Cover; cook beans, stirring occasionally, 6 to 8 minutes or until bubbly. Stir in additional water if beans become dry. Remove from heat. Set beans aside.

4 Sprinkle cheese evenly over chips. Spoon beans over chips. Combine corn and pimientos in small bowl; spoon over beans. Bake about 8 minutes or until cheese melts. Sprinkle with olives and jalapeños. Serve immediately.

Makes 8 servings

Nutrients per Serving:

Calories	202 (21% of calories from fat)				
Total Fat	5 g	Carbohydrate	29 g	Iron	1 mg
Saturated Fat	1 g	Dietary Fiber	6 g	Vitamin A	103 RE
Cholesterol	6 mg	Protein	13 g	Vitamin C	9 mg
Sodium	455 mg	Calcium	246 mg		

DIETARY EXCHANGES: 1½ Starch/Bread, 1 Lean Meat, 1 Vegetable, ½ Fat

CHILE-CHEESE QUESADILLAS WITH SALSA CRUDA

Salsa Cruda (recipe follows)
2 tablespoons part-skim ricotta cheese
6 (6-inch) corn tortillas

½ cup (2 ounces) shredded reduced fat Monterey Jack cheese
2 tablespoons diced mild green chilies
Nonstick cooking spray

1 Prepare Salsa Cruda; set aside. To make 1 quesadilla, spread 2 teaspoons ricotta over tortilla. Sprinkle with heaping tablespoonful Monterey Jack cheese and 2 teaspoons diced chilies. Top with 1 tortilla. Repeat to make 2 more quesadillas.

2 Spray small nonstick skillet with cooking spray. Heat over medium-high heat. Add 1 quesadilla; cook 2 minutes or until bottom is golden. Turn quesadilla over; cook 2 minutes. Remove from heat. Cut into 4 wedges. Repeat with remaining quesadillas. Serve warm with Salsa Cruda.

Makes 4 servings

SALSA CRUDA

1 cup chopped tomato
2 tablespoons minced onion
2 tablespoons minced fresh cilantro (optional)

2 tablespoons lime juice
½ jalapeño pepper, seeded, minced*
1 clove garlic, minced

1 Combine tomato, onion, cilantro, lime juice, jalapeño and garlic in small bowl. Stir to combine.

Makes 4 servings

*Jalapeño peppers can sting and irritate the skin; wear rubber gloves when handling peppers and do not touch eyes. Wash hands after handling.

Nutrients per Serving:

Calories	167 (21% of calories from fat)					
Total Fat	4 g	Carbohydrate	25 g	Iron		1 mg
Saturated Fat	1 g	Dietary Fiber	3 g	Vitamin A		87 RE
Cholesterol	7 mg	Protein	10 g	Vitamin C		25 mg
Sodium	172 mg	Calcium	242 mg			

DIETARY EXCHANGES: 1½ Starch/Bread, ½ Lean Meat, ½ Vegetable

BUFFALO CHICKEN TENDERS

3 tablespoons hot pepper sauce
½ teaspoon paprika
¼ teaspoon ground red pepper
1 pound chicken tenders
½ cup fat free blue cheese
   dressing
¼ cup reduced fat sour cream
2 tablespoons crumbled blue
   cheese
1 medium red bell pepper, cut
   into ½-inch slices

1 Preheat oven to 375°F.

2 Combine pepper sauce, paprika and ground red pepper in small bowl; brush on all surfaces of chicken. Place chicken in 11×7-inch baking pan coated with nonstick cooking spray. Cover; marinate in refrigerator 30 minutes.

3 Bake, uncovered, about 15 minutes or until chicken is no longer pink in center.

4 Combine blue cheese dressing, sour cream and crumbled blue cheese in small serving bowl. Garnish as desired. Serve with chicken and bell pepper for dipping.

Makes 10 servings

Nutrients per Serving:

Calories	83 (27% of calories from fat)				
Total Fat	2 g	Carbohydrate	5 g	Iron	<1 mg
Saturated Fat	1 g	Dietary Fiber	0 g	Vitamin A	19 RE
Cholesterol	27 mg	Protein	9 g	Vitamin C	7 mg
Sodium	180 mg	Calcium	14 mg		

DIETARY EXCHANGES: ½ Starch/Bread, 1 Lean Meat

LEMON AND FENNEL MARINATED VEGETABLES

Although most vegetables lose vitamins during cooking, carrots are an exception. Cooking breaks down cell walls in carrots, releasing far more beta-carotene (a precursor of vitamin A) than raw carrots.

1 cup water
2 medium carrots, diagonally
    sliced ½ inch thick
1 cup small whole mushrooms
1 small red or green bell pepper,
    cut into ¾-inch pieces
3 tablespoons lemon juice

1 tablespoon sugar
1 tablespoon olive oil
1 clove garlic, minced
½ teaspoon fennel seeds, crushed
½ teaspoon dried basil leaves
¼ teaspoon ground black pepper

1 Bring water to a boil over high heat in small saucepan. Add carrots. Return to a boil; reduce heat to medium-low. Cover and simmer about 5 minutes or until carrots are crisp-tender. Drain and cool.

2 Place carrots, mushrooms and bell pepper in large resealable plastic food storage bag. Combine lemon juice, sugar, oil, garlic, fennel, basil and black pepper in small bowl. Pour over vegetables. Close bag securely; turn to coat. Marinate in refrigerator 8 hours or overnight, turning occasionally.

3 Drain vegetables; discard marinade. Place vegetables in serving dish. Serve with toothpicks.

Makes 4 servings

Nutrients per Serving:

Calories	47 (24% of calories from fat)				
Total Fat	1 g	Carbohydrate	9 g	Iron	1 mg
Saturated Fat	<1 g	Dietary Fiber	2 g	Vitamin A	1,058 RE
Cholesterol	0 mg	Protein	1 g	Vitamin C	44 mg
Sodium	15 mg	Calcium	18 mg		

DIETARY EXCHANGES: 2 Vegetable

HERBED STUFFED TOMATOES

The fat content of cottage cheese varies widely. Creamed cottage cheese can have as much as 4% fat, low fat cottage cheese ranges from 1% to 2% fat and dry curd cottage cheese, made without added cream, has less than ½% fat. In this recipe the 1% cottage cheese adds a little richness to the filling without adding a lot of fat.

15 cherry tomatoes
½ cup 1% low fat cottage cheese
1 tablespoon thinly sliced green onion
1 teaspoon chopped fresh chervil *or* ¼ teaspoon dried chervil leaves, crushed

½ teaspoon chopped fresh dill *or* ⅛ teaspoon dried dill weed
⅛ teaspoon lemon pepper

1 Cut thin slice off bottom of each tomato. Scoop out pulp with small spoon; discard pulp. Invert tomatoes on paper towels to drain.

2 Combine cottage cheese, green onion, chervil, dill and lemon pepper in small bowl. Spoon into tomatoes. Serve at once or cover and refrigerate up to 8 hours.

Makes 5 servings

Nutrients per Serving:
3 tomatoes

Calories	27 (12% of calories from fat)				
Total Fat	<1 g	Carbohydrate	3 g	Iron	<1 mg
Saturated Fat	<1 g	Dietary Fiber	<1 g	Vitamin A	39 RE
Cholesterol	1 mg	Protein	3 g	Vitamin C	9 mg
Sodium	96 mg	Calcium	18 mg		

DIETARY EXCHANGES: ½ Vegetable

CHINATOWN STUFFED MUSHROOMS

Lean ground turkey replaces the usual ground beef in this popular appetizer. A hint of soy and ginger gives the mushrooms a pleasant Oriental flavor.

24 large mushrooms
½ pound ground turkey
1 clove garlic, minced
¼ cup fine dry bread crumbs
¼ cup thinly sliced green onions
3 tablespoons low sodium soy
    sauce, divided

1 teaspoon minced fresh ginger
1 egg white, slightly beaten
⅛ teaspoon crushed red pepper
    (optional)
24 pieces of Melba toast

1 Remove stems from mushrooms; finely chop enough stems to equal 1 cup. Reserve remaining stems for use in salads, soups or stews, if desired.

2 Combine turkey, chopped stems and garlic in medium skillet. Cook over medium-high heat until turkey is no longer pink, stirring to break up turkey. Spoon off any fat; discard.

3 Stir in bread crumbs, onions, 2 tablespoons soy sauce, ginger, egg white and crushed red pepper; mix well.

4 Brush mushrooms lightly on all sides with remaining 1 tablespoon soy sauce; spoon about 2 teaspoons stuffing into each mushroom.* Place stuffed mushrooms on rack of foil-lined broiler pan. Broil 4 to 5 inches from heat 5 to 6 minutes or until hot. Serve with Melba toast.   *Makes 8 servings*

* Mushrooms may be made ahead to this point; cover and refrigerate up to 24 hours. Add 1 to 2 minutes to broiling time for chilled mushrooms.

Nutrients per Serving:
3 mushrooms with Melba toast

Calories	37 (29% of calories from fat)				
Total Fat	1 g	Carbohydrate	14 g	Iron	1 mg
Saturated Fat	1 g	Dietary Fiber	2 g	Vitamin A	13 RE
Cholesterol	11 mg	Protein	9 g	Vitamin C	3 mg
Sodium	332 mg	Calcium	13 mg		

DIETARY EXCHANGES: 1 Starch/Bread, 1 Vegetable

POLENTA TRIANGLES

This recipe uses corn grits rather than cornmeal because corn grits give the polenta a heartier texture. Yellow grits have a nice golden color; however, white corn grits are more readily available and may be substituted. You can find grits in most supermarket cereal aisles.

½ cup yellow corn grits
1½ cups chicken broth, divided
2 cloves garlic, minced
½ cup (2 ounces) crumbled feta cheese

1 red bell pepper, roasted,*
  peeled and finely chopped
Nonstick cooking spray

1 Combine grits and ½ cup chicken broth; mix well. Set aside. Pour remaining 1 cup chicken broth into heavy large saucepan; bring to a boil. Add garlic and moistened grits; mix well and return to a boil. Reduce heat to low; cover and cook 20 minutes. Remove from heat. Add feta cheese and stir until cheese is completely melted. Add bell pepper; mix well.

2 Spray 8-inch square pan with cooking spray. Spoon grits mixture into prepared pan. Press grits evenly into pan with wet fingertips. Refrigerate until cold.

3 Preheat broiler. Turn polenta out onto cutting board and cut into 2-inch squares. Cut each square diagonally into 2 triangles. Spray baking sheet with cooking spray. Place polenta triangles on prepared baking sheet and spray tops lightly with cooking spray. Place under broiler until lightly browned. Turn triangles over and broil until browned and crisp. Serve warm or at room temperature. Garnish with fresh oregano and chives, if desired.

Makes 8 servings

*Place pepper on foil-lined broiler pan; broil 15 minutes or until blackened on all sides, turning every 5 minutes. Place pepper in paper bag; close bag and let stand 15 minutes before peeling.

Nutrients per Serving:				
6 triangles				
Calories	62 (26% of calories from fat)			
Total Fat	2 g	Carbohydrate	9 g	Iron	1 mg
Saturated Fat	1 g	Dietary Fiber	<1 g	Vitamin A	26 RE
Cholesterol	6 mg	Protein	3 g	Vitamin C	7 mg
Sodium	142 mg	Calcium	37 mg		

DIETARY EXCHANGES: 1 Starch/Bread

PINWHEEL APPETIZERS

These delicious appetizers can be made way ahead; the longer they sit in the refrigerator, the more the flavors will blend.

3 cups cooked wild rice
1 package (8 ounces) fat free cream cheese
⅓ cup freshly grated Parmesan cheese
1 teaspoon dried parsley flakes
½ teaspoon garlic powder
½ teaspoon Dijon mustard

2 to 3 drops hot pepper sauce (optional)
3 (12-inch) soft flour tortillas
2½ ounces thinly sliced corned beef
9 fresh spinach leaves, washed and patted dry

1 Combine rice, cream cheese, Parmesan cheese, parsley, garlic powder, mustard and pepper sauce in large bowl.

2 Spread evenly over tortillas, leaving ½-inch border on one side of each tortilla.

3 Place single layer corned beef over rice and cheese mixture. Top with layer of spinach. Roll each tortilla tightly toward ½-inch border. Moisten border of tortilla with water; press to seal roll. Wrap tightly in plastic wrap. Refrigerate several hours or overnight. Cut into 1-inch slices.

Makes 36 servings

Nutrients per Serving:

Calories	37 (21% of calories from fat)				
Total Fat	1 g	Carbohydrate	5 g	Iron	<1 mg
Saturated Fat	<1 g	Dietary Fiber	<1 g	Vitamin A	19 RE
Cholesterol	4 mg	Protein	2 g	Vitamin C	1 mg
Sodium	91 mg	Calcium	20 mg		

DIETARY EXCHANGES: ½ Starch/Bread

SPRING ROLLS

*Flour tortillas and preshredded cabbage make these no-cook spring rolls
a breeze to prepare. Assemble them the day before serving for even
more convenience.*

1 cup preshredded cabbage or
    coleslaw mix
½ cup finely chopped cooked ham
¼ cup finely chopped water
    chestnuts
¼ cup sliced green onions

3 tablespoons plum sauce,
    divided
1 teaspoon Oriental sesame oil
3 (6-inch) flour tortillas

1 Combine cabbage, ham, water chestnuts, onions, 2 tablespoons plum
sauce and oil in medium bowl; mix well.

2 Spread remaining 1 tablespoon plum sauce evenly over tortillas. Spread
about ½ cup cabbage mixture on each tortilla, leaving ¼ inch border; roll up.

3 Wrap each tortilla tightly in plastic wrap. Refrigerate at least 1 hour or up
to 24 hours before serving.

4 Cut each tortilla into 4 pieces.   *Makes 12 servings*

Nutrients per Serving:

Calories	44 (24% of calories from fat)					
Total Fat	1 g	Carbohydrate	7 g	Iron	<1 mg
Saturated Fat	<1 g	Dietary Fiber	<1 g	Vitamin A	10 RE
Cholesterol	3 mg	Protein	2 g	Vitamin C	6 mg
Sodium	101 mg	Calcium	17 mg		

DIETARY EXCHANGES: ½ Starch/Bread, ½ Vegetable

GINGERED CHICKEN POT STICKERS

These tidbits are also great on steamed rice as an entrée. For a meatless dish, use tempeh, found in Asian markets, instead of chicken.

3 cups finely shredded cabbage
1 egg white, lightly beaten
1 tablespoon light soy sauce
¼ teaspoon crushed red pepper
1 tablespoon minced fresh ginger
4 green onions with tops, finely chopped
¼ pound ground chicken breast, cooked and drained

24 wonton wrappers, at room temperature
Cornstarch
½ cup water
1 tablespoon oyster sauce
½ teaspoon honey
⅛ teaspoon crushed red pepper
2 teaspoons grated lemon peel
1 tablespoon peanut oil

1 Steam cabbage 5 minutes; cool to room temperature. Squeeze out any excess moisture; set aside. To prepare filling, combine egg white, soy sauce, ¼ teaspoon red pepper, ginger and onions in large bowl; blend well. Stir in cabbage and chicken.

2 To prepare pot stickers, place 1 tablespoon filling in center of 1 wonton wrapper. Gather edges around filling, pressing firmly at top to seal. Repeat with remaining wrappers and filling.

3 Place pot stickers on large baking sheet dusted with cornstarch. Refrigerate 1 hour or until cold. Meanwhile, to prepare sauce, combine remaining ingredients except oil in small bowl; mix well. Set aside.

4 Heat oil in large nonstick skillet over high heat. Add pot stickers and cook until bottoms are golden brown. Pour sauce over top. Cover and cook 3 minutes. Uncover and cook until all liquid is absorbed. Serve warm on tray as finger food or on small plates with chopsticks as first course.

Makes 8 servings

Nutrients per Serving:					
3 pot stickers					
Calories	111 (20% of calories from fat)				
Total Fat	2 g	Carbohydrate	6 g	Iron	1 mg
Saturated Fat	<1 g	Dietary Fiber	<1 g	Vitamin A	20 RE
Cholesterol	11 mg	Protein	6 g	Vitamin C	12 mg
Sodium	303 mg	Calcium	27 mg		

DIETARY EXCHANGES: 1 Starch/Bread, ½ Lean Meat

CRAB CAKES CANTON

These tasty seafood cakes are a good source of copper, a trace mineral that helps your body form red blood cells and absorb iron.

7 ounces frozen cooked
　　crabmeat, thawed and
　　drained or imitation
　　crabmeat, drained and
　　flaked
1½ cups fresh whole wheat bread
　　crumbs
¼ cup thinly sliced green onions

1 clove garlic, minced
1 teaspoon minced fresh ginger
2 egg whites, slightly beaten
1 tablespoon teriyaki sauce
2 teaspoons vegetable oil,
　　divided
Prepared sweet and sour sauce
　　(optional)

1 Combine crabmeat, bread crumbs, onions, garlic and ginger in medium bowl; mix well. Add egg whites and teriyaki sauce; mix well.

2 Shape into patties about ½ inch thick and 2 inches in diameter.* Heat 1 teaspoon oil in large nonstick skillet over medium heat until hot.

3 Add about half of crab cakes to hot oil. Cook 2 minutes per side or until golden brown. Remove to warm serving plate; keep warm. Repeat with remaining 1 teaspoon oil and crab cakes. Serve with sweet and sour sauce. Garnish with cherry tomatoes and fresh herbs, if desired.

Makes 6 servings

*Crab cakes may be made ahead to this point; cover and refrigerate up to 24 hours before cooking.

Nutrients per Serving:

2 crab cakes

Calories	84 (27% of calories from fat)				
Total Fat	2 g	Carbohydrate	6 g	Iron	1 mg
Saturated Fat	<1 g	Dietary Fiber	<1 g	Vitamin A	20 RE
Cholesterol	18 mg	Protein	9 g	Vitamin C	4 mg
Sodium	480 mg	Calcium	38 mg		

DIETARY EXCHANGES: ½ Lean Meat, ½ Vegetable

SHRIMP TOAST

Shrimp toast is a perennial favorite, turning up on the menus of most Chinese restaurants. With this delicious recipe, you can now easily prepare a healthier, lower fat version at home.

½ pound shrimp, peeled and deveined

2 tablespoons chopped green onions

2 tablespoons finely chopped water chestnuts

2 tablespoons low sodium soy sauce

1 teaspoon Oriental sesame oil

1 egg white, slightly beaten

6 slices whole wheat sandwich bread, crusts removed

1 Finely chop shrimp.

2 Combine shrimp, onions, water chestnuts, soy sauce and oil in medium bowl; mix well. Stir in egg white; mix well.*

3 Toast bread lightly on both sides. Cut toast diagonally into quarters. Spread shrimp mixture evenly over toast to edges.

4 Place toast on foil-lined baking sheet or broiler pan. Broil 6 inches from heat 4 minutes or until lightly browned. Garnish with red and yellow peppers, if desired.

Makes 12 servings

*The filling may be made ahead to this point; cover and refrigerate filling up to 24 hours. Proceed as directed in step 3.

Nutrients per Serving:

2 pieces

Calories	26 (17% of calories from fat)				
Total Fat	<1 g	Carbohydrate	3 g	Iron	<1 mg
Saturated Fat	<1 g	Dietary Fiber	<1 g	Vitamin A	8 RE
Cholesterol	15 mg	Protein	2 g	Vitamin C	<1 mg
Sodium	92 mg	Calcium	11 mg		

DIETARY EXCHANGES: 1 Vegetable

CHILLED SHRIMP WITH CHINESE MUSTARD SAUCE

A quick and easy recipe, the shrimp can be prepared up to one day in advance. If you are unable to find hot Chinese mustard or simply want a sauce with less heat, substitute a spicy brown or Dijon mustard.

1 cup water
½ cup dry white wine
2 tablespoons low sodium soy sauce
½ teaspoon Szechuan or black peppercorns

1 pound large shrimp, peeled and deveined
¼ cup prepared sweet and sour sauce
2 teaspoons hot Chinese mustard

1 Combine water, wine, soy sauce and peppercorns in medium saucepan. Bring to a boil over high heat. Add shrimp; reduce heat to medium. Cover and simmer 2 to 3 minutes or until shrimp turn pink and opaque. Remove from heat; drain well. Cover and refrigerate until chilled.

2 Combine sweet and sour sauce and mustard in small bowl; mix well. Serve as a dipping sauce for shrimp.

Makes 6 servings

Nutrients per Serving:

Calories	92 (7% of calories from fat)				
Total Fat	1 g	Carbohydrate	5 g	Iron	2 mg
Saturated Fat	<1 g	Dietary Fiber	<1 g	Vitamin A	50 RE
Cholesterol	116 mg	Protein	13 g	Vitamin C	3 mg
Sodium	365 mg	Calcium	29 mg		

DIETARY EXCHANGES: 1½ Lean Meat

Health Note

Shellfish, such as shrimp, is an excellent source of low calorie, low fat protein. It's also rich in the minerals iron, copper and zinc, yet low in sodium.

MARINATED ARTICHOKES & SHRIMP IN CITRUS VINAIGRETTE

Poaching the shrimp in orange juice adds a subtle and complementary flavor to the marinated artichoke hearts. This unique appetizer has only 2 grams of fat per serving and is high in vitamin C.

VINAIGRETTE

1 large seedless orange, peeled and sectioned

3 tablespoons red wine vinegar

3 tablespoons fat free mayonnaise

1 teaspoon fresh thyme *or* ¼ teaspoon dried thyme leaves

2 teaspoons extra virgin olive oil

SALAD

1 package (9 ounces) frozen artichoke hearts, thawed

12 large shrimp (12 ounces)

1 cup orange juice

1 To prepare vinaigrette, combine all vinaigrette ingredients except oil in food processor or blender; process until smooth. Pour mixture into medium nonmetallic bowl and whisk in oil until blended. Fold artichoke hearts into vinaigrette. Cover and refrigerate several hours or overnight.

2 Peel shrimp, leaving tails attached. Devein and butterfly shrimp. Bring orange juice to a boil in medium saucepan. Add shrimp and cook about 2 minutes or just until shrimp turn pink and opaque.

3 To serve, place about 3 artichoke hearts on each of 6 plates. Top each serving with 2 shrimp. Drizzle vinaigrette over top. Garnish with fresh Italian parsley, if desired.

Makes 6 servings

Nutrients per Serving:

Calories	135 (14% of calories from fat)				
Total Fat	2 g	Carbohydrate	19 g	Iron	2 mg
Saturated Fat	<1 g	Dietary Fiber	4 g	Vitamin A	66 RE
Cholesterol	87 mg	Protein	12 g	Vitamin C	61 mg
Sodium	236 mg	Calcium	69 mg		

DIETARY EXCHANGES: 1 Lean Meat, 1 Fruit, 1 Vegetable

GRILLED SCALLOP CEVICHE

Scallops are extremely lean. One sea scallop (about one ounce) contains just half a gram of fat, yet provides about one-fifth of your daily protein.

6 to 7 ounces sea scallops, 1 to
    2 inches in diameter
¼ cup lime juice, divided
¼ teaspoon chili powder or
    paprika
½ large honeydew melon
1 ripe medium papaya or mango,
    or ½ large cantaloupe

¼ cup minced onion
1 to 2 fresh jalapeño or serrano
    peppers, seeded, minced*
3 tablespoons minced fresh mint
    or fresh basil
1 teaspoon honey (optional)

1 Rinse scallops and pat dry. Place scallops, 2 tablespoons lime juice and chili powder in large resealable food storage bag. Press air from bag and seal. Marinate scallops in refrigerator 30 minutes to 1 hour.

2 Scoop seeds from melon. Remove fruit from rind with melon baller or cut melon into ¾-inch wedges; remove rind and cut fruit into cubes. Halve papaya, scoop out seeds, remove peel with knife; cut fruit into cubes. Place fruit into nonmetallic bowl. Stir in remaining 2 tablespoons lime juice, onion and jalapeño. Cover and refrigerate.

3 To prevent sticking, spray grill with nonstick cooking spray. Prepare coals for grilling.

4 Drain scallops; discard marinade. Thread scallops onto 10- to 12-inch metal skewers. Grill skewers 3 minutes or until marks are established. Turn skewers over; grill 3 minutes more or until scallops are opaque.

5 Remove scallops from skewers; cut into quarters. Stir into fruit mixture. Refrigerate until thoroughly chilled, about 30 minutes or up to 24 hours. Stir in mint and honey.   *Makes 6 servings*

*Jalapeño peppers can sting and irritate the skin; wear rubber gloves when handling peppers and do not touch eyes. Wash hands after handling.

Nutrients per Serving:

Calories	120 (5% of calories from fat)				
Total Fat	1 g	Carbohydrate	23 g	Iron	1 mg
Saturated Fat	0 g	Dietary Fiber	3 g	Vitamin A	40 RE
Cholesterol	15 mg	Protein	8 g	Vitamin C	80 mg
Sodium	164 mg	Calcium	64 mg		

DIETARY EXCHANGES: 1 Lean Meat, 1½ Fruit

GRILLED SPICED HALIBUT, PINEAPPLE AND PEPPER SKEWERS

You will get a large dose of your daily requirement of vitamin C from the pineapple and peppers on just two of these tasty skewers. You will also get only one gram of fat from the halibut, which is among the fish lowest in fat and cholesterol.

2 tablespoons lemon juice or
    lime juice
1 teaspoon minced garlic
1 teaspoon chili powder
½ teaspoon ground cumin
¼ teaspoon ground cinnamon
⅛ teaspoon ground cloves

½ pound boneless skinless
    halibut steak, about 1 inch
    thick
½ small pineapple, peeled, halved
    vertically, cut into 24 pieces
1 large green or red bell pepper,
    cut into 24 squares

1 Combine lemon juice, garlic, chili powder, cumin, cinnamon and cloves in large resealable food storage bag; knead until blended.

2 Rinse fish and pat dry. Cut into 12 cubes about 1 to 1¼ inch square. Add fish to bag; press out air and seal. Turn bag gently to coat fish with marinade. Refrigerate halibut 30 minutes to 1 hour. Soak 12 (6- to 8- inch) bamboo skewers in water while fish marinates.

3 Alternately thread 2 pieces pineapple, 2 pieces pepper and 1 piece fish onto each skewer.

4 To prevent sticking, spray grill with nonstick cooking spray. Prepare coals for grilling. Place skewers on grill, cover if possible (or tent with foil) and grill 3 to 4 minutes or until marks are established on bottom. Turn and grill skewers 3 to 4 minutes or until fish is opaque and flakes easily when tested with fork.

Makes 6 servings

Nutrients per Serving:

Calories	64 (15% of calories from fat)					
Total Fat	1 g	Carbohydrate	6 g	Iron	1 mg
Saturated Fat	<1 g	Dietary Fiber	1 g	Vitamin A	30 RE
Cholesterol	12 mg	Protein	8 g	Vitamin C	18 mg
Sodium	23 mg	Calcium	23 mg		

DIETARY EXCHANGES: 1 Lean Meat, ½ Vegetable

MINI MARINATED BEEF SKEWERS

Marinating these beef kabobs makes them tender, flavorful and easy to make ahead of time. If desired, add the cherry tomato topper to give a splash of color and additional vitamin C.

1 pound lean beef round tip, cut 1-inch thick

2 tablespoons low sodium soy sauce

1 tablespoon dry sherry

1 teaspoon Oriental sesame oil

2 cloves garlic, minced

18 cherry tomatoes (optional)

1 Cut beef across the grain into ⅛-inch slices. Place in large resealable food storage bag. Combine soy sauce, sherry, oil and garlic in cup; pour over steak. Close bag securely; turn to coat. Marinate in refrigerator at least 30 minutes or up to 2 hours.

2 Soak 18 (6-inch) bamboo skewers in water to cover 20 minutes.

3 Drain steak; discard marinade. Weave beef accordion-style onto skewers. Spray rack of broiler pan with nonstick cooking spray. Place skewers on rack.

4 Broil 4 to 5 inches from heat 4 minutes or until beef is barely pink in center, turning occasionally.

5 If desired, garnish each skewer with 1 cherry tomato. Place skewers on lettuce-lined platter. Serve warm or at room temperature.

Makes 6 servings

Nutrients per Serving:					
3 skewers					
Calories	120 (30% of calories from fat)				
Total Fat	4 g	Carbohydrate	2 g	Iron	2 mg
Saturated Fat	1 g	Dietary Fiber	<1 g	Vitamin A	<1 RE
Cholesterol	60 mg	Protein	20 g	Vitamin C	<1 mg
Sodium	99 mg	Calcium	5 mg		

DIETARY EXCHANGES: 3 Lean Meat

SALADS

JAMAICAN SEAFOOD SALAD

You can almost feel the tropical breezes as you savor each bite of this delicate seafood and pasta salad.

6 ounces uncooked vermicelli noodles

6 ounces fresh or imitation crabmeat

4 ounces cooked medium shrimp

1 cup diagonally sliced yellow squash

1 cup diagonally sliced zucchini

1 tablespoon rice wine vinegar

1 tablespoon reduced sodium soy sauce

1 tablespoon minced fresh cilantro

1 tablespoon lime juice

2 teaspoons Oriental sesame oil

2 teaspoons grated fresh ginger

1 teaspoon grated lime peel

⅛ teaspoon ground cinnamon

1 Cook noodles according to package directions, omitting salt. Drain and rinse well under cold water until pasta is cool.

2 Combine crabmeat, shrimp, yellow squash and zucchini in medium bowl.

3 Combine vinegar, soy sauce, cilantro, lime juice, sesame oil, ginger, lime peel and cinnamon in small bowl; pour over vegetable mixture.

4 Toss to coat evenly. Serve over noodles, chilled or at room temperature.

Makes 6 (1-cup) servings

Nutrients per Serving:

Calories	136 (15% of calories from fat)				
Total Fat	3 g	Carbohydrate	19 g	Iron	2 mg
Saturated Fat	<1 g	Dietary Fiber	1 g	Vitamin A	36 RE
Cholesterol	56 mg	Protein	9 g	Vitamin C	7 mg
Sodium	269 mg	Calcium	54 mg		

DIETARY EXCHANGES: 1 Starch/Bread, 1 Lean Meat, ½ Vegetable

CRAB SPINACH SALAD WITH TARRAGON DRESSING

Scientists urge us to eat more spinach because it's such a rich source of beta-carotene.

12 ounces coarsely flaked cooked crabmeat *or* 2 packages (6 ounces each) frozen crabmeat, thawed and drained
1 cup chopped tomato
1 cup sliced cucumber
⅓ cup sliced red onion
¼ cup nonfat salad dressing or mayonnaise

¼ cup low fat sour cream
¼ cup chopped fresh parsley
2 tablespoons skim milk
2 teaspoons chopped fresh tarragon *or* ½ teaspoon dried tarragon leaves
1 clove garlic, minced
¼ teaspoon hot pepper sauce
8 cups washed and torn spinach leaves

1 Combine crabmeat, tomato, cucumber and onion in medium bowl.

2 Combine salad dressing, sour cream, parsley, milk, tarragon, garlic and hot pepper sauce in small bowl.

3 Line four salad plates with spinach. Place crabmeat mixture on spinach; drizzle with dressing.   *Makes 4 servings*

Nutrients per Serving:					
Calories	170 (18% of calories from fat)				
Total Fat	4 g	Carbohydrate	14 g	Iron	4 mg
Saturated Fat	<1 g	Dietary Fiber	4 g	Vitamin A	816 RE
Cholesterol	91 mg	Protein	22 g	Vitamin C	51 mg
Sodium	481 mg	Calcium	226 mg		

DIETARY EXCHANGES: 2½ Meat, 2 Vegetable

SPINACH SALAD WITH ORANGE-CHILI GLAZED SHRIMP

Orange-Chili Glazed Shrimp
(recipe follows)
2 teaspoons sesame seeds
¼ cup orange juice
1 tablespoon cider vinegar
1 clove garlic, minced
1 teaspoon grated orange peel
1 teaspoon olive oil

½ teaspoon honey
⅛ teaspoon crushed red pepper
1 ripe large mango or ripe
medium papaya
12 cups washed and torn spinach
leaves
½ cup (2 ounces) crumbled feta
cheese

1 Prepare Orange-Chili Glazed Shrimp; set aside. Heat small nonstick skillet over medium heat. Add sesame seeds and cook, stirring often, about 4 minutes or until golden. Pour into small bowl. Add orange juice, vinegar, garlic, orange peel, oil, honey and red pepper; stir to combine. Set aside.

2 Peel mango. Cut fruit away from pit; cut fruit into cubes. Place spinach into large bowl and toss with dressing. Top with mango, cheese and shrimp.

Makes 4 servings

ORANGE–CHILI GLAZED SHRIMP

½ cup orange juice
4 cloves garlic, minced
1 teaspoon chili powder

8 ounces large shrimp, peeled
and deveined

1 Combine juice, garlic and chili powder in large nonstick skillet. Bring to a boil over high heat. Boil 3 minutes or until mixture just coats bottom of pan. Reduce heat to medium. Add shrimp; cook and stir 2 minutes or until shrimp turn pink and opaque and juice mixture coats shrimp. (Add orange juice or water to keep shrimp moist, if necessary.)

Makes 4 servings

Nutrients per Serving:						
Calories	177 (29% of calories from fat)					
Total Fat	6 g	Carbohydrate	19 g	Iron		3 mg
Saturated Fat	3 g	Dietary Fiber	3 g	Vitamin A		671 RE
Cholesterol	100 mg	Protein	14 g	Vitamin C		57 mg
Sodium	311 mg	Calcium	165 mg			

DIETARY EXCHANGES: 1½ Lean Meat, 1 Fruit, 1 Vegetable

CHILI-CRUSTED GRILLED CHICKEN CAESAR SALAD

Not only is this salad low in fat, it is also full of B-vitamins and folic acid, a nutrient linked with the prevention of some birth defects.

Parmesan Chips (page 22)
(optional)
1 to 2 lemons
1 tablespoon minced garlic, divided
1½ teaspoons dried oregano leaves, divided
1 teaspoon chili powder
1 pound boneless skinless chicken breasts

1 tablespoon olive oil
2 anchovy fillets, minced
1 large head romaine lettuce, cut into 1-inch strips
¼ cup freshly grated Parmesan cheese
4 whole wheat rolls

1 Prepare Parmesan Chips; set asie. Grate lemon peel; measure 1 to 2 teaspoons. Juice lemon; measure ¼ cup. Combine lemon peel and 1 tablespoon juice in small bowl. Set ¼ teaspoon garlic aside. Add remaining garlic, 1 teaspoon oregano and chili powder to bowl; stir to combine. Rub chicken completely with chili mixture.

2 Combine remaining 3 tablespoons lemon juice, reserved ¼ teaspoon garlic, remaining ½ teaspoon oregano, oil and anchovy in large bowl. Add lettuce to bowl; toss to coat with dressing. Sprinkle with cheese; toss.

3 To prevent sticking, spray grill with nonstick cooking spray. Prepare coals for grilling.

4 Place chicken on grill, 4 to 6 inches from medium coals. Grill 10 to 12 minutes or until chicken is no longer pink in center, turning occasionally.

5 Arrange salad on 4 large plates. Slice chicken; fan on each salad. Serve with whole wheat rolls. Garnish with Parmesan Tortilla Chips, if desired.

Makes 4 servings

Nutrients per Serving:				
Calories	301 (28% of calories from fat)			
Total Fat	9 g	Carbohydrate	25 g	Iron	4 mg
Saturated Fat	3 g	Dietary Fiber	5 g	Vitamin A	483 RE
Cholesterol	64 mg	Protein	31 g	Vitamin C	49 mg
Sodium	457 mg	Calcium	211 mg		

DIETARY EXCHANGES: 1½ Starch/Bread, 3 Lean Meat, 1 Vegetable

TAOS CHICKEN SALAD

Lime Vinaigrette (recipe follows)

3 flour or corn tortillas, cut into ¼-inch strips

Nonstick cooking spray

1 pound boneless skinless chicken thighs, cut into strips

6 cups washed and torn assorted salad greens

2 oranges, peeled and cut into segments

2 cups peeled jicama strips

1 can (15½ ounces) pinto beans, drained and rinsed

1 cup cubed red bell pepper

½ cup sliced celery

½ cup sliced green onions with tops

1 Prepare Lime Vinaigrette; set aside. Preheat oven to 350°F. Spray tortilla strips lightly with cooking spray; place in 15×10-inch jelly-roll pan. Bake about 10 minutes or until browned, stirring occasionally. Cool to room temperature.

2 Spray medium nonstick skillet with cooking spray; heat over medium heat until hot. Add chicken; cook and stir about 15 minutes or until no longer pink in center. Refrigerate until chilled.

3 Combine greens, oranges, jicama, beans, bell pepper, celery and green onions in large bowl; add chicken. Drizzle with Lime Vinaigrette; toss to coat. Serve immediately; garnish with tortilla strips. *Makes 6 servings*

LIME VINAIGRETTE

3 tablespoons finely chopped fresh cilantro or parsley

3 tablespoons plain low fat yogurt

3 tablespoons orange juice

2 tablespoons lime juice

2 tablespoons white wine vinegar

2 tablespoons water

1 tablespoon sugar

1 teaspoon chili powder

½ teaspoon onion powder

½ teaspoon ground cumin

1 Combine all ingredients in small jar with tight-fitting lid; shake well. Refrigerate until ready to use; shake before using. *Makes about ¾ cup*

Nutrients per Serving:

Calories	258 (19% of calories from fat)					
Total Fat	6 g	Carbohydrate	36 g	Iron	4 mg
Saturated Fat	1 g	Dietary Fiber	6 g	Vitamin A	281 RE
Cholesterol	37 mg	Protein	18 g	Vitamin C	100 mg
Sodium	437 mg	Calcium	143 mg		

DIETARY EXCHANGES: 1½ Starch/Bread, 1½ Lean Meat, ½ Fruit, 1 Vegetable

CHICKEN SALAD NIÇOISE

Herb and Mustard Dressing
(recipe follows)
Nonstick cooking spray
1 pound chicken tenders
½ cup red onion wedges
(about 1 small)
Spinach leaves, washed
(optional)

2 cups whole green beans,
cooked and chilled
2 cups cubed red potatoes,
cooked and chilled
2 cups halved cherry tomatoes
1 can (15½ ounces) Great
Northern beans, rinsed and
drained

1 Prepare Herb and Mustard Dressing; set aside. Spray medium nonstick skillet with cooking spray; heat over medium heat until hot. Add chicken; cook and stir 7 to 10 minutes or until chicken is browned and no longer pink in center. Cool slightly; refrigerate until chilled.

2 Spray small nonstick skillet with cooking spray; heat over medium heat until hot. Add onion; cook and stir over low heat about 15 minutes or until onions are caramelized. Cool to room temperature.

3 Place spinach on plates. Top with chicken, onion, green beans, potatoes, tomatoes and Great Northern beans. Drizzle with Herb and Mustard Dressing. Serve immediately.

Makes 6 servings

HERB AND MUSTARD DRESSING

¼ cup water
3 tablespoons balsamic or cider
vinegar
1½ tablespoons Dijon mustard
1 tablespoon olive oil

1 teaspoon dried basil leaves
1 teaspoon dried thyme leaves
1 teaspoon dried rosemary,
crushed
1 small clove garlic, minced

1 Combine all ingredients in small jar with tight-fitting lid; shake well. Refrigerate until ready to use; shake before using.

Makes about ⅔ cup

Nutrients per Serving:					
Calories	301 (16% of calories from fat)				
Total Fat	5 g	Carbohydrate	42 g	Iron	4 mg
Saturated Fat	1 g	Dietary Fiber	3 g	Vitamin A	85 RE
Cholesterol	40 mg	Protein	23 g	Vitamin C	27 mg
Sodium	103 mg	Calcium	104 mg		

DIETARY EXCHANGES: 2 Starch/Bread, 2 Lean Meat, 1½ Vegetable

CHICKEN AND COUSCOUS SALAD

A staple of North African cuisine, couscous is a quick-cooking grain with many uses. It can be served with milk as a cereal, in casseroles or stuffings, or tossed with dressing for a salad, as it is here.

1 can (14½ ounces) ⅓-less-salt chicken broth
½ teaspoon ground cinnamon
¼ teaspoon ground nutmeg
¼ teaspoon curry powder
1 cup uncooked couscous
1½ pounds boneless skinless chicken breasts, cooked
2 cups cubed fresh pineapple
2 cups cubed seeded cucumber
2 cups cubed red bell pepper

2 cups cubed yellow bell pepper
1 cup sliced celery
½ cup sliced green onions with tops
3 tablespoons apple cider vinegar
3 tablespoons water
2 tablespoons vegetable oil
1 tablespoon fresh mint *or*
   1 teaspoon dried mint leaves
Lettuce leaves

1 Combine chicken broth, cinnamon, nutmeg and curry powder in nonstick Dutch oven or large nonstick saucepan. Bring to a boil over high heat. Stir in couscous; remove pan from heat and let stand, covered, 5 minutes. Fluff couscous with fork; cool to room temperature.

2 Cut chicken into ½-inch pieces. Add chicken, pineapple, cucumber, bell peppers, celery and green onions to couscous; toss to combine.

3 Combine vinegar, water, oil and mint in small jar with tight-fitting lid; shake well. Pour over couscous mixture; toss to coat. Serve immediately in lettuce-lined bowl. Garnish as desired.

Makes 6 servings

Nutrients per Serving:

Calories	348 (20% of calories from fat)				
Total Fat	8 g	Carbohydrate	43 g	Iron	2 mg
Saturated Fat	1 g	Dietary Fiber	9 g	Vitamin A	143 RE
Cholesterol	58 mg	Protein	27 g	Vitamin C	150 mg
Sodium	85 mg	Calcium	59 mg		

DIETARY EXCHANGES: 1½ Starch/Bread, 2½ Lean Meat, ½ Fruit, 1 Vegetable

BLACKENED CHICKEN SALAD

A cool and creamy yet low fat ranch salad dressing, along with chunks of crisp zucchini and cucumber, provides a refreshing contrast to spicy strips of skinless chicken.

Ranch Salad Dressing
    (page 86)
2 cups cubed sourdough or
    French bread
  Nonstick cooking spray
1 tablespoon paprika
1 teaspoon onion powder
1 teaspoon garlic powder
½ teaspoon dried oregano leaves
½ teaspoon dried thyme leaves
½ teaspoon white pepper
½ teaspoon ground red pepper
½ teaspoon ground black pepper

1 pound boneless skinless
    chicken breasts
4 cups washed and torn spinach
    leaves
2 cups washed and torn romaine
    lettuce
2 cups cubed zucchini
2 cups cubed seeded cucumber
½ cup sliced green onions with
    tops
1 medium tomato, cut into 8
    wedges

1 Prepare Ranch Salad Dressing; set aside. Preheat oven to 375°F. To make croutons, spray bread cubes lightly with cooking spray; place in 15×10-inch jelly-roll pan. Bake 10 to 15 minutes or until browned, stirring occasionally.

2 Combine paprika, onion powder, garlic powder, oregano, thyme, white pepper, red pepper and black pepper in small bowl; rub on all surfaces of chicken. Place chicken on grill over medium-hot coals. Grill 20 minutes or until chicken is no longer pink in center, turning occasionally. Or, place chicken on rack of broiler pan coated with cooking spray. Broil 6 inches from heat, 7 to 8 minutes on each side or until chicken is no longer pink in center. Cool slightly. Cut chicken into thin strips.

3 Combine warm chicken, greens, zucchini, cucumber, green onions, tomato and croutons in large bowl. Drizzle with Ranch Salad Dressing; toss to coat. Serve immediately.

Makes 4 servings

(continued on page 86)

Blackened Chicken Salad, continued

RANCH SALAD DRESSING

¼ cup water

3 tablespoons reduced calorie cucumber-ranch salad dressing

1 tablespoon reduced fat mayonnaise or salad dressing

1 tablespoon lemon juice

2 teaspoons minced fresh parsley

⅛ teaspoon salt

⅛ teaspoon ground black pepper

 Combine all ingredients in small jar with tight-fitting lid; shake well. Refrigerate until ready to use; shake before using.   *Makes about ½ cup*

Nutrients per Serving:				
includes Ranch Salad Dressing				
Calories	249 (25% of calories from fat)			
Total Fat	7 g	Carbohydrate	21 g	Iron	5 mg
Saturated Fat	1 g	Dietary Fiber	5 g	Vitamin A	664 RE
Cholesterol	59 mg	Protein	27 g	Vitamin C	45 mg
Sodium	369 mg	Calcium	137 mg		

DIETARY EXCHANGES: 1 Starch/Bread, 2½ Lean Meat, 2 Vegetable

❖

Cook's Tip

Cooking methods often turn low fat food into a high fat dish simply by using oil for cooking or to prevent sticking to the pan. Naturally low in fat, skinless chicken breasts remain that way by broiling or grilling.

❖

CHICKEN, TORTELLINI AND ROASTED VEGETABLE SALAD

Roasting vegetables at high heat gives them a wonderful new flavor complexity without adding any fat. Combine them with low fat tortellini and tender chicken to make this a vitamin-rich salad.

Sun-Dried Tomato and Basil
   Dressing (page 88)
3 cups whole medium
   mushrooms
2 cups cubed zucchini
2 cups cubed eggplant
¾ cup red onion wedges
   (about 1 medium)
   Olive oil flavored nonstick
   cooking spray

1½ packages (9-ounce size)
   reduced fat cheese tortellini
6 cups washed and torn leaf
   lettuce and arugula
1 pound boneless skinless
   chicken breasts, cooked and
   cut into 1½-inch pieces

1 Prepare Sun-Dried Tomato and Basil Dressing; set aside. Heat oven to 425°F. Place mushrooms, zucchini, eggplant and onion in 15×10-inch jelly-roll pan. Spray generously with cooking spray; toss to coat. Bake 20 to 25 minutes or until vegetables are browned. Cool to room temperature.

2 Cook tortellini according to package directions; drain. Cool to room temperature.

3 Combine roasted vegetables, tortellini, lettuce and chicken in large bowl. Drizzle with Sun-Dried Tomato and Basil Vinaigrette; toss to coat. Serve immediately.   *Makes 8 servings*

(continued on page 88)

Chicken, Tortellini and Roasted Vegetable Salad, continued

SUN–DRIED TOMATO AND BASIL DRESSING

4 sun-dried tomato halves, not packed in oil

Hot water

½ cup ½-less-salt chicken broth

2 tablespoons finely chopped fresh basil *or* 2 teaspoons dried basil leaves

2 tablespoons olive oil

2 tablespoons lemon juice

2 tablespoons water

1 clove garlic, minced

¼ teaspoon salt

¼ teaspoon ground black pepper

 Place sun-dried tomatoes in small bowl. Pour hot water over tomatoes to cover. Let stand 10 to 15 minutes or until tomatoes are soft. Drain well; chop tomatoes.

 Combine tomatoes and remaining ingredients in small jar with tight-fitting lid; shake well. Refrigerate until ready to use; shake before using.

Makes about 1 cup

Nutrients per Serving:
includes Sun-Dried Tomato and Basil Dressing

Calories	210 (27% of calories from fat)				
Total Fat	7 g	Carbohydrate	24 g	Iron	4 mg
Saturated Fat	1 g	Dietary Fiber	3 g	Vitamin A	851 RE
Cholesterol	31 mg	Protein	16 g	Vitamin C	53 mg
Sodium	219 mg	Calcium	137 mg		

DIETARY EXCHANGES: 1 Starch/Bread, 1½ Lean Meat, 2 Vegetable, ½ Fat

❖

Cook's Tip
Look for firm eggplant with smooth skin and uniform color. Usually the smaller the eggplant, the softer and more tender it is. Store at room temperature for two days or refrigerate in a plastic bag up to four days.

❖

SZECHUAN CHICKEN SALAD

*Traditional Chinese seasonings give an exciting new taste to this salad,
served over napa cabbage.*

1 package (5 ounces) Chinese-
style rice noodles
Nonstick cooking spray
1 pound boneless skinless
chicken breasts, cut into
2½-inch pieces
3 cups snow peas
2 cups small broccoli flowerets
2 cups matchstick size carrot
strips
2 cups sliced mushrooms

1 teaspoon cornstarch
3 tablespoons reduced sodium
soy sauce
3 to 4 teaspoons rice wine
vinegar
1 tablespoon Oriental sesame oil
1 tablespoon Szechuan hot and
spicy all-purpose sauce
½ teaspoon five-spice powder
3 cups coarsely chopped napa
cabbage

1 Cook noodles according to package directions, omitting salt; cool to room
temperature.

2 Spray wok or large nonstick skillet with cooking spray; heat over medium-
high heat until hot. Add chicken; stir-fry 5 to 7 minutes or until browned and
no longer pink in center. Remove chicken from wok.

3 Add snow peas, broccoli, carrots, mushrooms and 2 tablespoons water to
wok; cook, covered, 2 minutes. Uncover; stir-fry about 5 minutes or until
vegetables are crisp-tender. Remove vegetables from wok.

4 Combine remaining ¼ cup water and cornstarch in small bowl; stir in soy
sauce, vinegar, oil, hot and spicy sauce and five-spice powder. Add to wok;
heat to a boil. Cook 1 minute, stirring constantly. Return chicken and
vegetables to wok; toss to coat with cornstarch mixture.

5 Divide cabbage among 6 serving plates; arrange noodles over cabbage.
Top with warm chicken mixture. Serve immediately.   *Makes 6 servings*

Nutrients per Serving:

Calories	261 (15% of calories from fat)				
Total Fat	4 g	Carbohydrate	37 g	Iron	4 mg
Saturated Fat	1 g	Dietary Fiber	5 g	Vitamin A	1,098 RE
Cholesterol	37 mg	Protein	19 g	Vitamin C	67 mg
Sodium	377 mg	Calcium	104 mg		

DIETARY EXCHANGES: 1½ Starch/Bread, 2 Lean Meat, 1½ Vegetable, ½ Fat

HOT CHINESE CHICKEN SALAD

The "hot" in this recipe stands for temperature and level of spice. If the amount of crushed red pepper is too much for you, simply lower the quantity to satisfy your tastebuds.

8 ounces fresh or steamed Chinese egg noodles
¼ cup ⅓-less-salt chicken broth
2 tablespoons reduced sodium soy sauce
2 tablespoons rice wine vinegar
1 tablespoon rice wine or dry sherry
1 teaspoon sugar
½ teaspoon crushed red pepper
1 tablespoon vegetable oil, divided

1 clove garlic, minced
1½ cups fresh pea pods, sliced diagonally
1 cup thinly sliced green or red bell pepper
1 pound boneless skinless chicken breasts, cut into ½-inch pieces
1 cup thinly sliced red or green cabbage
2 green onions, thinly sliced

1 Cook noodles in boiling water 4 to 5 minutes or until tender. Drain and set aside.

2 Combine chicken broth, soy sauce, vinegar, rice wine, sugar and crushed red pepper in small bowl; set aside.

3 Heat 1 teaspoon oil in large nonstick skillet or wok. Add garlic, pea pods and bell pepper. Cook 1 to 2 minutes or until vegetables are crisp-tender; set aside.

4 Heat remaining 2 teaspoons oil in skillet. Add chicken and cook 3 to 4 minutes or until chicken is no longer pink. Add cabbage, cooked vegetables and noodles. Stir in sauce; toss to coat evenly. Cook and stir 1 to 2 minutes or until heated through. Sprinkle with green onions before serving.

Makes 6 (1⅓-cup) servings

Nutrients per Serving:

Calories	164 (30% of calories from fat)				
Total Fat	6 g	Carbohydrate	12 g	Iron	2 mg
Saturated Fat	1 g	Dietary Fiber	2 g	Vitamin A	81 RE
Cholesterol	45 mg	Protein	17 g	Vitamin C	55 mg
Sodium	353 mg	Calcium	34 mg		

DIETARY EXCHANGES: ½ Starch/Bread, 2 Lean Meat, 1 Vegetable, ½ Fat

SINGAPORE RICE SALAD

The fresh, sweet taste of pineapple mingles with rice and vegetables in this sprightly salad. It's perfect on its own as a luncheon entrée or as an accompaniment to Honey Lime Glazed Chicken (page 230).

1 can (8 ounces) pineapple tidbits or chunks in pineapple juice, undrained
3 cups chilled cooked white rice, prepared in salted water
1 cup diced cucumber
1 red bell pepper, diced
1 cup shredded carrots
½ cup sliced green onions

2 tablespoons lime juice
2 tablespoons dry sherry
1 tablespoon rice wine vinegar
1 teaspoon minced fresh ginger
2 tablespoons chopped fresh cilantro
1 tablespoon chopped unsalted peanuts

1 Drain pineapple, reserving 3 tablespoons juice. Combine rice, cucumber, bell pepper, carrots, onions and pineapple in large bowl.

2 Combine lime juice, sherry, vinegar, ginger and reserved pineapple juice in small bowl; mix well. Pour over rice mixture; toss to coat.

3 Cover and refrigerate at least 2 hours or up to 12 hours. Sprinkle with cilantro and peanuts before serving. Garnish with cucumber slices, if desired.

Makes 6 servings

Nutrients per Serving:					
Calories	188 (6% of calories from fat)				
Total Fat	1 g	Carbohydrate	40 g	Iron	2 mg
Saturated Fat	<1 g	Dietary Fiber	3 g	Vitamin A	566 RE
Cholesterol	0 mg	Protein	4 g	Vitamin C	23 mg
Sodium	367 mg	Calcium	33 mg		

DIETARY EXCHANGES: 2 Starch/Bread, ½ Vegetable, ½ Fruit

SPICY BEEF AND RICE SALAD

Beef is very dense in its concentration of nutrients, it's loaded with iron, zinc and B vitamins.

2 teaspoons Spicy Seasoning Mix
   (recipe follows), divided
2 cups Spicy Cooked Rice (recipe
   follows)
1 pound boneless beef top sirloin
   steak, cut 1 inch thick

Salt (optional)
1 medium red apple, cored and
   cut into pieces
2 to 3 green onions, thinly sliced
¼ cup coarsely chopped walnuts,
   toasted

1 Prepare Spicy Seasoning Mix and Spicy Cooked Rice; set aside.

2 Heat large nonstick skillet over medium heat 5 minutes.

3 Meanwhile, rub 1 teaspoon Spicy Seasoning Mix into sides of steak. Place steak in skillet and cook 12 to 14 minutes, turning once. Season with salt.

4 Meanwhile, combine rice, apple, onions and walnuts. Carve steak into thin slices; arrange over rice mixture. Garnish with leaf lettuce and apple, if desired.

Makes 4 servings

SPICY SEASONING MIX

3 tablespoons chili powder
2 teaspoons ground cumin
1½ teaspoons garlic powder

¾ teaspoon dried oregano leaves
½ teaspoon ground red pepper

1 Combine all ingredients. Store, covered, in airtight container. Shake before using.

Makes about ⅓ cup

Spicy Cooked Rice: Prepare ⅔ cup rice according to package directions; add 1 teaspoon Spicy Seasoning Mix to water before cooking.

Nutrients per Serving:					
Calories	379 (25% of calories from fat)				
Total Fat	10 g	Carbohydrate	35 g	Iron	5 mg
Saturated Fat	3 g	Dietary Fiber	2 g	Vitamin A	17 RE
Cholesterol	72 mg	Protein	35 g	Vitamin C	3 mg
Sodium	68 mg	Calcium	31 mg		

DIETARY EXCHANGES: 2 Starch/Bread, 3 Lean Meat, ½ Fat

ARTICHOKE WILD RICE SALAD

Artichokes are a member of the thistle family. They are higher in protein than most vegetables and are delicious to eat.

1 jar (6 ounces) marinated
   artichoke hearts
2 cups cooked wild rice
1 cup frozen peas, thawed
1 can (8 ounces) sliced water
   chestnuts, drained
4 ounces shredded part-skim
   mozzarella cheese (optional)

1 jar (2 ounces) diced pimiento,
   drained
2 tablespoons canola oil
1 tablespoon balsamic vinegar
½ teaspoon dried tarragon leaves
½ teaspoon Dijon mustard
2 to 3 drops hot pepper sauce
   (or to taste)

1 Drain artichokes, reserving 2 tablespoons liquid.

2 Combine artichokes, rice, peas, water chestnuts, cheese and pimiento in large bowl.

3 In small bowl, combine oil, reserved liquid from artichokes, vinegar, tarragon, mustard and pepper sauce; pour over salad and toss to coat. Refrigerate 4 hours or overnight to allow flavors to blend.

Makes 8 servings

Nutrients per Serving:

Calories	129 (22% of calories from fat)				
Total Fat	4 g	Carbohydrate	22 g	Iron	1 mg
Saturated Fat	<1 g	Dietary Fiber	3 g	Vitamin A	37 RE
Cholesterol	0 mg	Protein	4 g	Vitamin C	11 mg
Sodium	48 mg	Calcium	21 mg		

DIETARY EXCHANGES: 1 Starch/Bread, ½ Vegetable, 1 Fat

TABBOULEH SALAD

Bulgur wheat, a good source of fiber, is made from the whole wheat kernel that has been soaked, steamed and dried. Then, part of the bran layer is removed and the kernel is cracked into pieces.

¾ cup bulgur wheat, cooked
¾ cup chopped green bell pepper
½ cup chopped fresh parsley
2 tablespoons thinly sliced green onion
¼ cup lemon juice
2 tablespoons water
4 teaspoons vegetable oil

2 teaspoons chopped fresh dill *or* ½ teaspoon dried dill weed
1 teaspoon sugar
¼ teaspoon salt
Lettuce leaves
½ cup coarsely chopped seeded tomato

1 Place bulgur in colander. Rinse under cold water; drain. Combine bulgur, bell pepper, parsley and onion in medium bowl.

2 Combine lemon juice, water, oil, dill, sugar and salt in jar with tight-fitting lid. Cover; shake well. Add to bulgur mixture; toss to combine. Cover and refrigerate at least 4 hours or up to 24 hours.

3 Line salad bowl with lettuce. Add bulgur mixture. Arrange tomato on top.

Makes 4 servings

Nutrients per Serving:

Calories	158 (27% of calories from fat)				
Total Fat	5 g	Carbohydrate	27 g	Iron	2 mg
Saturated Fat	<1 g	Dietary Fiber	8 g	Vitamin A	98 RE
Cholesterol	0 mg	Protein	4 g	Vitamin C	58 mg
Sodium	145 mg	Calcium	30 mg		

DIETARY EXCHANGES: 1½ Starch/Bread, ½ Vegetable, 1 Fat

SALMON AND GREEN BEAN SALAD WITH PASTA

All types of salmon are high in protein, the B-vitamins, vitamin A and are also a rich source of OMEGA-3 oils, which studies show protect against heart disease.

1 can (6¼ ounces) salmon
8 ounces small whole wheat or
    regular pasta shells
¾ cup fresh green beans, cut into
    2-inch pieces
⅔ cup finely chopped carrots
½ cup nonfat cottage cheese

3 tablespoons plain nonfat
    yogurt
1½ tablespoons lemon juice
1 tablespoon fresh dill
2 teaspoons grated onion
1 teaspoon prepared mustard

1 Drain salmon and separate into chunks; set aside.

2 Cook pasta according to package directions, including ¼ teaspoon salt; add green beans during last 3 minutes of cooking. Drain and rinse well under cold water until pasta and green beans are cool.

3 Combine pasta, green beans, carrots and salmon in medium bowl.

4 Place cottage cheese, yogurt, lemon juice, dill, onion and mustard in blender or food processor; process until smooth. Pour over pasta mixture; toss to coat evenly. Garnish as desired. *Makes 6 (1-cup) servings*

Nutrients per Serving:

Calories	210 (15% of calories from fat)				
Total Fat	3 g	Carbohydrate	29 g	Iron	2 mg
Saturated Fat	1 g	Dietary Fiber	2 g	Vitamin A	383 RE
Cholesterol	15 mg	Protein	16 g	Vitamin C	5 mg
Sodium	223 mg	Calcium	118 mg		

DIETARY EXCHANGES: 1½ Starch/Bread, 1½ Lean Meat, ½ Vegetable

SMOKED TURKEY PASTA SALAD

This simple and fast pasta salad can be prepared in advance and refrigerated until ready to serve. The smoked turkey gives it an imaginative flair.

8 ounces uncooked ditalini pasta (small tubes)

6 ounces boneless skinless smoked turkey or chicken breast, cut into strips

1 can (15 ounces) light kidney beans, rinsed and drained

½ cup thinly sliced celery

¼ cup chopped red onion

⅓ cup reduced fat mayonnaise

2 tablespoons balsamic vinegar

2 tablespoons chopped fresh chives or green onion

1 tablespoon fresh tarragon *or* 1½ teaspoons dried tarragon leaves

1 teaspoon Dijon mustard

1 clove garlic, minced

¼ teaspoon ground black pepper

Lettuce leaves (optional)

1 Cook pasta according to package directions, omitting salt. Drain and rinse well under cold water until pasta is cool.

2 Combine pasta with turkey, beans, celery and onion in medium bowl. Combine mayonnaise, vinegar, chives, tarragon, mustard, garlic and pepper in small bowl. Pour over pasta mixture; toss to coat evenly. Serve on lettuce leaves.

Makes 7 (1-cup) servings

Nutrients per Serving:					
Calories	233 (19% of calories from fat)				
Total Fat	5 g	Carbohydrate	34 g	Iron	2 mg
Saturated Fat	1 g	Dietary Fiber	5 g	Vitamin A	12 RE
Cholesterol	12 mg	Protein	13 g	Vitamin C	4 mg
Sodium	249 mg	Calcium	34 mg		

DIETARY EXCHANGES: 2 Starch/Bread, 1 Lean Meat, ½ Vegetable, ½ Fat

GARBANZO PASTA SALAD

Garbanzo beans can be purchased dried or, for simplicity, canned as they are in this recipe. They are known for their high vegetable protein content. To get the optimum use of the protein, combine this salad with meats and dairy foods.

4 ounces uncooked spinach rotini or fusilli
1 can (15 ounces) garbanzo beans (chickpeas), rinsed and drained
⅓ cup finely chopped carrot
⅓ cup chopped celery
½ cup chopped red bell pepper
2 green onions with tops, chopped

3 tablespoons balsamic vinegar
2 tablespoons reduced calorie mayonnaise
2 teaspoons prepared whole-grain mustard
½ teaspoon ground black pepper
¼ teaspoon Italian seasoning Leaf lettuce

1 Cook pasta according to directions, omitting salt. Drain and rinse well under cold water until pasta is cool.

2 Combine pasta, garbanzo beans, carrot, celery, bell pepper and onions in medium bowl.

3 Whisk together vinegar, mayonnaise, mustard, black pepper and Italian seasoning in small bowl until blended. Pour over salad; toss to coat evenly. Cover and refrigerate up to 8 hours.

4 Arrange lettuce on individual plates. Spoon salad over lettuce and garnish with cherry tomatoes, if desired. *Makes 8 (½-cup) servings*

Note: This can also be served as a vegetarian main-dish salad.

Nutrients per Serving:

Calories	129 (16% of calories from fat)				
Total Fat	2 g	Carbohydrate	22 g	Iron	2 mg
Saturated Fat	<1 g	Dietary Fiber	3 g	Vitamin A	146 RE
Cholesterol	1 mg	Protein	5 g	Vitamin C	18 mg
Sodium	242 mg	Calcium	29 mg		

DIETARY EXCHANGES: 1 Starch/Bread, ½ Vegetable, ½ Fat

SWEET AND SOUR BROCCOLI PASTA SALAD

If you have shied away from sweet and sour dishes because of the high fat content, then this dish is for you! Apple juice, cider vinegar, mustard, honey and nonfat yogurt provide the taste sensations in this nutritious salad.

8 ounces uncooked pasta twists
2 cups broccoli flowerets
⅔ cup shredded carrots
1 medium Red or Golden
    Delicious apple, cored,
    seeded and chopped
⅓ cup plain nonfat yogurt

⅓ cup apple juice
3 tablespoons cider vinegar
1 tablespoon olive oil
1 tablespoon Dijon mustard
1 teaspoon honey
½ teaspoon dried thyme leaves
    Lettuce leaves

1 Cook pasta according to package directions, omitting salt and adding broccoli during the last 2 minutes of cooking. Drain and rinse well under cold water until pasta and broccoli are cool.

2 Place pasta, broccoli, carrots and apple in medium bowl.

3 Combine yogurt, apple juice, cider vinegar, oil, mustard, honey, and thyme in small bowl and pour over pasta mixture; toss to coat evenly.

4 Serve on individual dishes lined with lettuce. Garnish with apple slices, if desired.

Makes 6 (1-cup) servings

Nutrients per Serving:

Calories	198 (15% of calories from fat)				
Total Fat	3 g	Carbohydrate	36 g	Iron	2 mg
Saturated Fat	1 g	Dietary Fiber	3 g	Vitamin A	389 RE
Cholesterol	<1 mg	Protein	7 g	Vitamin C	31 mg
Sodium	57 mg	Calcium	55 mg		

DIETARY EXCHANGES: 2 Starch/Bread, ½ Fruit, ½ Vegetable, ½ Fat

GREEK PASTA AND VEGETABLE SALAD

Everyone knows you should eat your spinach, but why? Spinach is a wonderful source of vitamin A, phosphorus and calcium.

⅔ cup corkscrew macaroni
⅓ cup lime juice
2 tablespoons honey
1 tablespoon olive oil
1 clove garlic, minced
4 cups washed and torn spinach leaves

1 cup sliced cucumber
½ cup thinly sliced carrot
¼ cup sliced green onions
2 tablespoons crumbled feta cheese
2 tablespoons sliced ripe olives

1 Prepare pasta according to package directions, omitting salt. Drain and rinse well under cold water until pasta is cool.

2 Combine lime juice, honey, oil and garlic in large bowl. Stir in pasta. Cover; marinate in refrigerator 2 to 24 hours.

3 Combine spinach, cucumber, carrot, onions, cheese and olives in large bowl. Add pasta mixture to salad; toss to combine.

Makes 4 servings

Nutrients per Serving:

Calories	188 (28% of calories from fat)				
Total Fat	6 g	Carbohydrate	30 g	Iron	3 mg
Saturated Fat	1 g	Dietary Fiber	2 g	Vitamin A	794 RE
Cholesterol	3 mg	Protein	5 g	Vitamin C	27 mg
Sodium	230 mg	Calcium	94 mg		

DIETARY EXCHANGES: 1 Starch/Bread, 2 Vegetable, 1 Fat

FRUIT SALAD WITH JALAPEÑO-CITRUS DRESSING

On an average day, 1 out of 10 adults eats no fruit at all. Here is a striking salad that will entice everyone to indulge, packing away lots of vitamins B and C, folic acid and fiber.

Jalapeño-Citrus Dressing (recipe follows)
½ small honeydew melon
1 ripe large papaya, peeled, seeded, cubed

1 pint strawberries, stemmed, halved
1 can (8 ounces) pineapple chunks, drained

1 Prepare Jalapeño-Citrus Dressing; set aside. Scoop seeds from melon. Remove fruit from rind with melon baller or cut melon into ¾-inch wedges; remove rind and cut fruit into cubes. Place in large bowl.

2 Add papaya, strawberries, pineapple and Jalapeño-Citrus Dressing; gently toss to combine. Serve immediately or cover and refrigerate up to 3 hours. Garnish with mint leaves, if desired. *Makes 6 servings*

JALAPEÑO-CITRUS DRESSING

⅓ cup orange juice
3 tablespoons lime juice
3 tablespoons minced fresh mint, basil or cilantro (optional)

2 jalapeño peppers, seeded, minced*
1 tablespoon sugar or honey

1 Combine orange juice, lime juice, mint, jalapeños and sugar in small bowl; mix well. *Makes 6 servings*

*Jalapeño peppers can sting and irritate the skin; wear rubber gloves when handling peppers and do not touch eyes. Wash hands after handling.

Nutrients per Serving:

Calories	127 (3% of calories from fat)				
Total Fat	<1 g	Carbohydrate	31 g	Iron	1 mg
Saturated Fat	0 g	Dietary Fiber	4 g	Vitamin A	39 RE
Cholesterol	0 mg	Protein	1 g	Vitamin C	115 mg
Sodium	153 mg	Calcium	42 mg		

DIETARY EXCHANGES: 2 Fruit

JICAMA SLAW

Studies indicate that people who eat lots of foods belonging to the Brassica family, such as cabbage, have a reduced risk of various cancers, thanks to fiber and antioxidants such as vitamin A and C.

2 to 3 large oranges
½ cup minced red onion
½ cup lightly packed fresh cilantro, coarsely chopped plus additional cilantro for garnish
⅓ cup reduced calorie mayonnaise

2 tablespoons frozen orange juice concentrate, thawed
1 tablespoon sugar
1 jalapeño or serrano pepper, seeded, minced*
4 cups shredded jicama**
3 cups shredded green cabbage

1 Grate orange peel with grater or zester; measure 1 tablespoon. Place in large bowl; set aside. Cut away remaining white pith from oranges, working over bowl to collect juices. Cut between membranes to separate orange segments; set segments aside. Squeeze membranes with hand to remove additional juice.

2 Add onion, cilantro, mayonnaise, orange juice concentrate, sugar and jalapeño.

3 Add jicama and cabbage; stir to combine. Reserve several orange segments for garnish; cut remaining segments in half and stir into slaw. Transfer slaw to serving bowl and garnish with orange curls and cilantro, if desired.

Makes 6 servings

*Jalapeño peppers can sting and irritate the skin; wear rubber glves when handling peppers and do not touch eyes. Wash hands after handling.

**Peel jicama with sharp knife, removing brown outer skin and thin coarse layer of flesh underneath. Shred jicama in food processor.

Nutrients per Serving:

Calories	108 (30% of calories from fat)				
Total Fat	4 g	Carbohydrate	18 g	Iron	1 mg
Saturated Fat	<1 g	Dietary Fiber	3 g	Vitamin A	49 RE
Cholesterol	4 mg	Protein	2 g	Vitamin C	73 mg
Sodium	94 mg	Calcium	54 mg		

DIETARY EXCHANGES: 1 Fruit, 1 Vegetable, ½ Fat

ROASTED PEPPER, CORN AND BEAN SALAD

Sweet and hot peppers have gained immense popularity with nutritionists worldwide. One red bell pepper has 16 times the beta carotene and nearly twice the vitamin C of one orange.

Cumin Dressing (recipe
    follows)
1 large red bell pepper
2 cans (15 ounces each) black
    turtle beans, garbanzo
    beans, pinto or kidney beans,
    rinsed and drained

1 cup frozen whole kernel corn,
    thawed, drained
1 can (4 ounces) diced mild
    green chilies
2 green onions, thinly sliced

1 Prepare Cumin Dressing; set aside. Place pepper on rack of broiler pan coated with nonstick cooking spray. Broil 2 inches from heat, 15 to 18 minutes, turning pepper as each side becomes charred. Invert bowl over pepper (or place in resealable food storage bag) until cool. Rub charred skin from pepper (all skin need not come off). Working over large bowl, cut stem from pepper; let juice run into bowl. Quarter pepper lengthwise; discard seeds. Slice crosswise; add to bowl.

2 Add beans, corn, chilies, onions and Cumin Dressing to pepper; stir. Cover and refrigerate 1 hour or up to 24 hours. Serve on lettuce-lined plate garnished with green onion fans, if desired.

Makes 8 servings

CUMIN DRESSING

2 tablespoons white wine vinegar
    or cider vinegar
2 tablespoons lemon juice

1 teaspoon grated lemon peel
1 clove garlic, minced
½ teaspoon ground cumin

1 Combine all ingredients in small bowl; mix well.

Makes 8 servings

Nutrients per Serving:				
Calories	128 (10% of calories from fat)			
Total Fat	2 g	Carbohydrate	26 g	Iron	2 mg
Saturated Fat	<1 g	Dietary Fiber	7 g	Vitamin A	35 RE
Cholesterol	0 mg	Protein	8 g	Vitamin C	54 mg
Sodium	380 mg	Calcium	30 mg		

DIETARY EXCHANGES: 1 Starch/Bread, 1 Vegetable

GRILLED RATATOUILLE

The uniqueness of this marinated salad lies in the grilling of the vegetables before serving.

3 tablespoons red wine vinegar
1 tablespoon olive oil
2 teaspoons fresh thyme
½ teaspoon ground black pepper
4 small Japanese eggplants, cut lengthwise into ½-inch-thick slices
2 small zucchini, cut in half lengthwise
1 medium red onion, quartered
1 red bell pepper, halved and seeded

1 yellow bell pepper, halved and seeded
6 ounces uncooked ziti or penne pasta
½ cup ⅓-less-salt chicken broth
1 tablespoon honey
1 tablespoon Dijon mustard
½ teaspoon Italian seasoning
¼ teaspoon salt
1 cup cherry tomato halves

1 Combine vinegar, oil, thyme and black pepper in shallow bowl. Add eggplants, zucchini, onion and bell peppers; toss to coat evenly. Let stand at room temperature 1 hour or cover and refrigerate overnight.

2 Cook pasta according to package directions, omitting salt. Drain and rinse well under cold water; set aside.

3 Remove vegetables from marinade; reserve marinade. Grill vegetables over medium-hot coals until tender, about 3 to 4 minutes per side. Cool vegetables; cut into 1-inch pieces. Combine vegetables and pasta in large bowl. Add chicken broth, honey, mustard, Italian seasoning and salt to reserved vegetable marinade; whisk to combine. Pour over vegetable-pasta mixture. Gently stir in tomato halves. Serve chilled or at room temperature.

Makes 9 (1-cup) servings

Nutrients per Serving:

Calories	115 (18% of calories from fat)					
Total Fat	2 g	Carbohydrate	21 g	Iron	1 mg
Saturated Fat	<1 g	Dietary Fiber	3 g	Vitamin A	41 RE
Cholesterol	0 mg	Protein	4 g	Vitamin C	23 mg
Sodium	91 mg	Calcium	21 mg		

DIETARY EXCHANGES: ½ Starch/Bread, 1 Vegetable, ½ Fat

LAYERED MEXICAN SALAD

No sense denying yourself favorites simply because they do not fall into the guidelines of a low fat diet. Nonfat mayonnaise and reduced fat cheese replace their regular counterparts in this delightful layered salad.

Salsa Cruda (page 38)
⅔ cup dried black beans *or* 1 can (15 ounces) black beans, rinsed and drained
1 small head romaine lettuce, washed, cored
1 cup frozen whole kernel corn, thawed, drained
1 large cucumber, peeled
1 can (2¼ ounces) sliced ripe olives, drained

1 large lemon
¾ cup nonfat mayonnaise
3 tablespoons plain nonfat yogurt
2 to 3 cloves garlic, minced
½ cup (2 ounces) shredded low fat Cheddar cheese
1 green onion, thinly sliced

1 Prepare Salsa Cruda; set aside. Rinse and sort beans. Place in medium saucepan with 2 cups water. Bring to a boil over high heat. Reduce heat to medium-low; simmer 5 minutes. Remove from heat; cover and let stand 1 to 2 hours. Drain. Return beans to pan with 2 cups fresh water. Bring to a boil. Reduce heat to medium-low; cover and simmer 1 to 2 hours or until tender. Drain and rinse.

2 Layer romaine leaves and slice crosswise into ½-inch strips. Place half of lettuce in large serving bowl. Layer Salsa Cruda, beans and corn over lettuce.

3 Halve cucumber lengthwise; scoop out and discard seeds. Slice thinly. Place cucumber over corn, sprinkle with olives and top with remaining lettuce.

4 Grate lemon peel; combine with mayonnaise, yogurt and garlic. Juice lemon; stir 3 to 4 tablespoons juice into dressing. Spread dressing evenly over top of salad. Sprinkle with cheese and onion. Cover salad and refrigerate 2 hours or up to 1 day.

Makes 12 servings

Nutrients per Serving:					
Calories	117 (22% of calories from fat)				
Total Fat	3 g	Carbohydrate	19 g	Iron	2 mg
Saturated Fat	1 g	Dietary Fiber	3 g	Vitamin A	121 RE
Cholesterol	3 mg	Protein	6 g	Vitamin C	18 mg
Sodium	349 mg	Calcium	77 mg		

DIETARY EXCHANGES: ½ Starch/Bread, 1 Vegetable, 1 Fat

MARINATED TOMATO SALAD

This uniquely different salad takes full advantage of the colorful array of tomatoes available in summer. During other seasons, you can make this salad with readily available plum tomatoes. The subtly seasoned marinade enhances the fabulous flavor of truly ripe tomatoes without masking it. This salad should be served at room temperature. Refrigerating tomatoes destroys their natural flavor and texture.

MARINADE

1½ cups tarragon or white wine vinegar
½ teaspoon salt
¼ cup finely chopped shallots
2 tablespoons finely chopped chives

2 tablespoons fresh lemon juice
¼ teaspoon ground white pepper
2 tablespoons extra virgin olive oil

SALAD

6 plum tomatoes, quartered
2 large yellow tomatoes, sliced horizontally into ½-inch slices

16 red cherry tomatoes, halved
16 small yellow pear tomatoes, halved

1 To prepare marinade, combine vinegar and salt in large bowl; stir until salt is completely dissolved. Add shallots, chives, lemon juice and pepper; mix well. Slowly whisk in oil until well blended.

2 Add tomatoes to marinade; toss well. Cover and let stand at room temperature 2 to 3 hours.

3 To serve, place 3 plum tomato quarters on each of 8 salad plates. Add 2 slices yellow tomato, 4 cherry tomato halves and 4 pear tomato halves. Garnish each plate with sunflower sprouts, if desired. (Or, place all marinated tomatoes on large serving platter.)

Makes 8 servings

Nutrients per Serving:

Calories	56 (24% of calories from fat)				
Total Fat	2 g	Carbohydrate	10 g	Iron	1 mg
Saturated Fat	<1 g	Dietary Fiber	2 g	Vitamin A	145 RE
Cholesterol	0 mg	Protein	2 g	Vitamin C	40 mg
Sodium	64 mg	Calcium	15 mg		

DIETARY EXCHANGES: 2 Vegetable

GAZPACHO SALAD

This colorful and spicy salad features the same combination of tastes and textures found in the famous cold Mexican soup. Try it with freshly toasted Corn Tortilla Chips (page 22).

1½ cups peeled and coarsely chopped tomatoes*
1 cup peeled, seeded and diced cucumber
¾ cup chopped onion
½ cup chopped red bell pepper
½ cup fresh corn kernels, cooked and drained or frozen corn kernels, thawed and drained
1 tablespoon lime juice

1 tablespoon red wine vinegar
2 teaspoons water
1 teaspoon extra virgin olive oil
1 teaspoon minced garlic
¼ teaspoon salt
¼ teaspoon ground black pepper
Pinch ground red pepper
1 medium head romaine lettuce, washed and torn
1 cup peeled and diced jicama

1 Combine tomatoes, cucumber, onion, bell pepper and corn in large bowl. Combine lime juice, vinegar, water, oil, garlic, salt, black pepper and ground red pepper in small bowl; whisk until well blended. Pour over tomato mixture; toss well. Cover and refrigerate several hours to allow flavors to blend.

2 Toss together lettuce, jicama and cilantro in another large bowl. Divide lettuce mixture evenly among 6 plates. Place ⅔ cup chilled tomato mixture on top of lettuce, spreading to edges. *Makes 6 servings*

*To peel tomatoes easily, blanch in boiling water 30 seconds; immediately transfer to bowl of cold water, then peel.

Nutrients per Serving:					
Calories	71 (14% of calories from fat)				
Total Fat	1 g	Carbohydrate	14 g	Iron	2 mg
Saturated Fat	<1 g	Dietary Fiber	3 g	Vitamin A	287 RE
Cholesterol	0 mg	Protein	3 g	Vitamin C	52 mg
Sodium	105 mg	Calcium	51 mg		

DIETARY EXCHANGES: 3 Vegetable

GARDEN GREENS WITH FENNEL DRESSING

The pine nuts add only 1 gram of fat to this salad. However, if you prefer to have only 23% of the calories from fat, omit the nuts.

DRESSING

½ teaspoon unflavored gelatin
2 tablespoons cold water
¼ cup boiling water
½ teaspoon salt
½ teaspoon sugar
¼ teaspoon dry mustard

⅛ teaspoon ground black pepper
¼ teaspoon anise extract or
   ground fennel seeds
1 tablespoon lemon juice
¼ cup raspberry or wine vinegar
1¼ teaspoons walnut or canola oil

SALAD

1 head Bibb lettuce, torn into
   bite-sized pieces
1 head radicchio, washed and
   torn
1 bunch arugula, washed and
   torn

1 cup mache or spinach leaves,
   washed and torn
1 fennel bulb, finely chopped
   (reserve fern for garnish)
1 tablespoon pine nuts, toasted

1 To prepare dressing, sprinkle gelatin over cold water in small bowl; let stand 1 minute to soften. Add boiling water; stir 2 minutes or until gelatin is completely dissolved. Add salt and sugar; stir until sugar is completely dissolved. Add all remaining dressing ingredients except oil; mix well. Slowly whisk in oil until well blended. Cover and refrigerate 2 hours or overnight. Shake well before using.

2 To prepare salad, place all salad ingredients except pine nuts in large bowl. Add dressing; toss until all leaves glisten. Divide salad among 6 chilled salad plates. Top each salad with ½ teaspoon pine nuts. Garnish with sprig of fennel fern, if desired.

Makes 6 servings

Nutrients per Serving:

Calories	60 (30% of calories from fat)				
Total Fat	2 g	Carbohydrate	9 g	Iron	1 mg
Saturated Fat	<1 g	Dietary Fiber	1 g	Vitamin A	191 RE
Cholesterol	0 mg	Protein	3 g	Vitamin C	21 mg
Sodium	226 mg	Calcium	94 mg		

DIETARY EXCHANGES: 1½ Vegetable, ½ Fat

STILTON SALAD DRESSING

In this salad dressing, most of the cholesterol usually found in cheese dressings is missing by using tofu for texture and low fat cottage cheese for the lumps associated with the higher fat Stilton. Toasting the walnuts enhances their flavor enormously so that you can use fewer of them. Although the walnuts add 4 grams of fat per serving, they add a wonderful flavor.

½ cup buttermilk
¼ cup silken firm tofu
2 ounces Stilton cheese
1 teaspoon lemon juice
½ clove garlic, peeled
¼ teaspoon salt
⅛ teaspoon ground black pepper

2 tablespoons 1% low fat cottage cheese
Romaine lettuce hearts, washed and torn (optional)
Toasted chopped walnuts (optional)

 Place buttermilk, tofu, Stilton cheese, lemon juice, garlic, salt and pepper in food processor or blender; process until smooth. Pour mixture into small bowl and fold in cottage cheese. Store in airtight container and refrigerate 3 hours or overnight. Serve with Romaine lettuce and toasted walnuts, if desired.

Makes 6 servings

Nutrients per Serving:

Calories	51 (55% of calories from fat)				
Total Fat	3 g	Carbohydrate	2 g	Iron	<1 mg
Saturated Fat	2 g	Dietary Fiber	<1 g	Vitamin A	23 RE
Cholesterol	8 mg	Protein	4 g	Vitamin C	1 mg
Sodium	265 mg	Calcium	80 mg		

DIETARY EXCHANGES: ½ Lean Meat, ½ Fat

Cook's Tip

To toast walnuts, spread on baking sheet in a single layer. Bake in a preheated 350°F oven 5 to 10 minutes until lightly browned and fragrant. Watch carefully to avoid burning.

❖

SOUPS & BREADS

MINTED MELON SOUP

1 tablespoon sugar
1½ cups fresh mint, including
    stems
2 fresh basil leaves

1½ cups diced cantaloupe
4 teaspoons lemon juice, divided
1½ cups diced and seeded
    watermelon

1 Combine 1 cup water and sugar in small saucepan; mix well. Bring to a boil over medium heat. Add mint and basil; simmer 10 minutes or until reduced by two-thirds. Remove from heat; cover and let stand at least 2 hours or until cool. Strain liquid; set aside.

2 Place cantaloupe in food processor or blender; process until smooth. Add 2 tablespoons mint syrup and 2 teaspoons lemon juice. Blend to mix well. Pour into airtight container. Cover and refrigerate until cold. Repeat procedure with watermelon, 2 teaspoons mint syrup and remaining 2 teaspoons lemon juice. Discard any remaining mint syrup.

3 To serve, simultaneously pour ¼ cup of each melon soup, side by side, into a serving bowl. Place 1 mint sprig in center for garnish, if desired. Repeat with remaining soup.

Makes 4 servings

Nutrients per Serving:

Calories	48 (7% of calories from fat)					
Total Fat	<1 g	Carbohydrate	11 g	Iron	<1 mg
Saturated Fat	0 g	Dietary Fiber	1 g	Vitamin A	216 RE
Cholesterol	0 mg	Protein	1 g	Vitamin C	33 mg
Sodium	7 mg	Calcium	12 mg		

DIETARY EXCHANGES: 1 Fruit

GAZPACHO

Cool and crisp, this chilled soup of Spanish origin is a refreshing way to get lots of vegetables and fiber. Peppers and tomatoes are a great source of vitamin C—more in just a small bowl than in an orange.

2 large cucumbers, peeled, seeded, divided

12 roma tomatoes, divided

1 cup chopped yellow or green bell pepper, divided

⅓ cup green onions, sliced, divided

1 cup ⅓-less-salt chicken broth

½ cup low sodium vegetable juice cocktail

½ teaspoon dried thyme leaves

3 tablespoons red wine vinegar

¼ to ½ teaspoon hot pepper sauce

1 can (2¼ ounces) sliced ripe olives

3 tablespoons crumbled feta cheese (optional)

2 teaspoons drained capers (optional)

6 whole wheat rolls

1 Chop 1 cucumber and 9 tomatoes. Combine chopped cucumber, tomatoes, ½ cup pepper, 2 tablespoons green onions, chicken broth, vegetable juice and thyme in food processor or blender; process until puréed. (If necessary, do in 2 batches.) Pour into fine wire strainer set over large bowl. Rub back of spoon over bottom of strainer until all that remains are vegetable skins and seeds; discard. Skim foam from juice. Add vinegar and pepper sauce.

2 Chop remaining cucumber and 3 tomatoes. Combine with remaining ½ cup pepper and green onions. Add vegetables to puréed mixture. Cover and chill thoroughly 2 hours or up to 24 hours. Top with olives. Garnish with cheese and capers, if desired. Serve with whole wheat rolls.

Makes 6 servings

Nutrients per Serving:

Calories	209 (23% of calories from fat)				
Total Fat	6 g	Carbohydrate	37 g	Iron	3 mg
Saturated Fat	1 g	Dietary Fiber	6 g	Vitamin A	257 RE
Cholesterol	0 mg	Protein	7 g	Vitamin C	93 mg
Sodium	583 mg	Calcium	83 mg		

DIETARY EXCHANGES: 1½ Starch/Bread, 2 Vegetable, 1 Fat

GREEN CHILE SOUP
WITH SPICY BAKED WONTONS

½ teaspoon chili powder

⅛ teaspoon garlic powder

⅛ teaspoon onion powder

1 teaspoon vegetable oil

12 fresh or frozen, thawed wonton skins

1 tablespoon reduced calorie margarine

1 leek (white part only) thinly sliced

1 cup chopped celery

2 cloves garlic, minced

½ can (7 ounces) ⅓-less-salt chicken broth

1 cup water

2 cans (4 ounces each) diced green chilies, drained and rinsed

2 cups skim milk

3 tablespoons all-purpose flour

½ teaspoon ground cumin

1 Preheat oven to 375°F. In small bowl, combine chili powder, garlic powder and onion powder. Stir in 1 teaspoon water and oil.

2 Cut wonton skins in half diagonally and place on large ungreased baking sheet. Brush wontons with chili powder mixture. Bake 5 to 6 minutes or until crisp. Cool completely on wire rack.

3 Heat margarine in medium saucepan. Add leek, celery and garlic; cook 4 minutes or until softened, stirring occasionally. Stir in chicken broth, 1 teaspoon water and chilies. Heat to boiling.

4 Whisk together milk, flour and cumin until smooth. Add milk mixture to saucepan and cook until thickened, stirring constantly, about 4 minutes.

5 Ladle into individual soup bowls. Serve with wontons. Garnish with fresh cilantro, if desired.

Makes 4 (1-cup) servings

Nutrients per Serving:

Calories	150 (24% of calories from fat)				
Total Fat	4 g	Carbohydrate	32 g	Iron	2 mg
Saturated Fat	1 g	Dietary Fiber	2 g	Vitamin A	159 RE
Cholesterol	5 mg	Protein	5 g	Vitamin C	44 mg
Sodium	605 mg	Calcium	199 mg		

DIETARY EXCHANGES: 1½ Starch/Bread, ½ Milk, 1 Vegetable, ½ Fat

COUNTRY BEAN SOUP

Dried beans are full of protein, complex carbohydrates, fiber and B vitamins, which makes them a nutritious addition to any diet.

1¼ cups dried navy beans or lima
    beans, rinsed and drained
4 ounces salt pork or fully
    cooked ham, chopped
¼ cup chopped onion
½ teaspoon dried oregano leaves

¼ teaspoon salt
¼ teaspoon ground ginger
¼ teaspoon dried sage
¼ teaspoon ground black pepper
2 cups skim milk
2 tablespoons butter

1 Place navy beans in large saucepan; add enough water to cover beans. Bring to a boil; reduce heat and simmer 2 minutes. Remove from heat; cover and let stand for 1 hour. (Or, cover beans with water and soak overnight.)

2 Drain beans and return to saucepan. Stir in 2½ cups water, salt pork, onion, oregano, salt, ginger, sage and pepper. Bring to a boil; reduce heat. Cover and simmer 2 to 2½ hours or until beans are tender. (If necessary, add more water during cooking.) Add milk and butter, stirring until mixture is heated through and butter is melted. Season with additional salt and pepper, if desired.

Makes 6 servings

Nutrients per Serving:

Calories	230 (27% of calories from fat)					
Total Fat	7 g	Carbohydrate	27 g	Iron		2 mg
Saturated Fat	4 g	Dietary Fiber	<1 g	Vitamin A		86 RE
Cholesterol	27 mg	Protein	15 g	Vitamin C		2 mg
Sodium	420 mg	Calcium	167 mg			

DIETARY EXCHANGES: 1½ Starch/Bread, 1 Meat, ½ Milk, 1 Fat

WHITE BEAN CHILI

In addition to being an excellent source of fiber, legumes (beans, lentils and peas) are also beneficial in lowering blood cholesterol and protecting against colon cancer. Rinse and drain canned beans before using to eliminate excess sodium.

Nonstick cooking spray
1 pound ground chicken
3 cups coarsely chopped celery
1½ cups coarsely chopped onions
3 cloves garlic, minced
4 teaspoons chili powder
1½ teaspoons ground cumin
¾ teaspoon ground allspice
¾ teaspoon ground cinnamon
½ teaspoon ground black pepper
1 can (16 ounces) whole tomatoes, undrained and coarsely chopped
1 can (15½ ounces) Great Northern beans, rinsed and drained
2 cups ⅓-less-salt chicken broth

1 Spray large nonstick skillet with cooking spray; heat over medium heat until hot. Add chicken; cook and stir until browned, breaking into pieces with fork. Remove chicken from skillet. Drain fat from skillet; discard.

2 Add celery, onions and garlic to skillet; cook and stir over medium heat 5 to 7 minutes or until tender. Sprinkle with chili powder, cumin, allspice, cinnamon and pepper; cook and stir 1 minute.

3 Return chicken to skillet. Stir in tomatoes with juice, beans and chicken broth; heat to a boil. Reduce heat to low and simmer, uncovered, 15 minutes. Garnish as desired.

Makes 6 servings

Nutrients per Serving:

Calories	232 (22% of calories from fat)				
Total Fat	6 g	Carbohydrate	26 g	Iron	3 mg
Saturated Fat	1 g	Dietary Fiber	3 g	Vitamin A	128 RE
Cholesterol	36 mg	Protein	20 g	Vitamin C	21 mg
Sodium	241 mg	Calcium	117 mg		

DIETARY EXCHANGES: 1 Starch/Bread, 2 Lean Meat, 2 Vegetable

SPICY LENTIL AND PASTA SOUP

Lentils, a popular meat substitute, have a fair amount of calcium and vitamins A and B, and are a good source of iron and phosphorus.

2 medium onions, thinly sliced
½ cup chopped carrot
½ cup chopped celery
½ cup peeled and chopped turnip
1 small jalapeño pepper, finely chopped*
2 cans (14½ ounces each) clear vegetable broth
1 can (14½ ounces) no-salt-added stewed tomatoes

2 cups water
8 ounces dried lentils
2 teaspoons chili powder
½ teaspoon dried oregano
3 ounces uncooked whole wheat spaghetti, broken
¼ cup minced fresh cilantro

1 Spray large nonstick saucepan with nonstick cooking spray. Add onions, carrot, celery, turnip and jalapeño. Cook over medium heat 10 minutes or until vegetables are crisp-tender.

2 Add vegetable broth, tomatoes, water, lentils, chili powder and oregano. Bring to a boil. Reduce heat; cover and simmer 20 to 30 minutes or until lentils are tender.

3 Add pasta and cook 10 minutes or until tender.

4 Ladle soup into bowls; sprinkle with cilantro.

Makes 6 (1¼-cup) servings

*Jalapeño peppers can sting and irritate the skin; wear rubber gloves when handling peppers and do not touch eyes. Wash hands after handling.

Nutrients per Serving:

Calories	261 (7% of calories from fat)				
Total Fat	2 g	Carbohydrate	49 g	Iron	6 mg
Saturated Fat	<1 g	Dietary Fiber	5 g	Vitamin A	475 RE
Cholesterol	1 mg	Protein	15 g	Vitamin C	27 mg
Sodium	771 mg	Calcium	65 mg		

DIETARY EXCHANGES: 3 Starch/Bread, ½ Vegetable

ZESTY LENTIL STEW

Dried legumes, such as lentils, beans and black-eyed peas are good sources of iron, thiamine, riboflavin, niacin, potassium and phosphorus.

1 cup dried lentils
2 cups chopped peeled potatoes
1 can (14½ ounces) ⅓-less-salt
　chicken broth
1⅔ cups water
1½ cups chopped seeded tomatoes
1 can (11½ ounces) no-salt-
　added spicy vegetable juice
　cocktail
1 cup chopped onion
½ cup chopped carrot

½ cup chopped celery
2 tablespoons chopped fresh
　basil *or* 2 teaspoons dried
　basil leaves
2 tablespoons chopped fresh
　oregano *or* 2 teaspoons dried
　oregano leaves
1 to 2 tablespoons finely chopped
　jalapeño pepper*
¼ teaspoon salt

1 Rinse lentils under cold water; drain.

2 Combine lentils, potatoes, chicken broth, water, tomatoes, vegetable juice cocktail, onion, carrot, celery, basil, oregano, jalapeño and salt in 3-quart saucepan. Bring to a boil over high heat. Reduce heat to medium-low. Cover; simmer 45 to 50 minutes or until lentils are tender, stirring occasionally.

Makes 4 servings

*Jalapeño peppers can sting and irritate the skin; wear rubber gloves when handling peppers and do not touch eyes. Wash hands after handling.

Nutrients per Serving:

Calories	369 (3% of calories from fat)				
Total Fat	1 g	Carbohydrate	72 g	Iron	8 mg
Saturated Fat	<1 g	Dietary Fiber	7 g	Vitamin A	604 RE
Cholesterol	0 mg	Protein	19 g	Vitamin C	58 mg
Sodium	620 mg	Calcium	104 mg		

DIETARY EXCHANGES: 4 Starch/Bread, 3 Vegetable

CHICKEN AND CORN CHOWDER

This hearty chowder is thickened in a healthful way. A portion of the ingredients are processed in a blender until finely chopped, then added to the rest of the chowder. As a result, milk can be used instead of heavy cream to finish the soup, saving over 30 grams of fat per serving.

Nonstick cooking spray
1 pound boneless skinless
    chicken breasts, cut into
    ½-inch pieces
3 cups frozen whole kernel corn,
    thawed
¾ cup coarsely chopped onion
1 to 2 tablespoons water

1 cup diced carrots
2 tablespoons finely chopped
    jalapeño pepper*
½ teaspoon dried oregano leaves
¼ teaspoon dried thyme leaves
3 cups ⅓-less-salt chicken broth
1½ cups 2% low fat milk
½ teaspoon salt

1 Spray large nonstick saucepan with cooking spray; heat over medium heat until hot. Add chicken; cook and stir about 10 minutes or until browned and no longer pink in center. Remove chicken from saucepan.

2 Add corn and onion to saucepan; cook and stir about 5 minutes or until onion is tender. Place 1 cup corn mixture in food processor or blender. Process until finely chopped, adding 1 to 2 tablespoons water; reserve.

3 Add carrots, jalapeño, oregano and thyme to saucepan; cook and stir about 5 minutes or until corn begins to brown. Return chicken to saucepan. Stir in chicken broth, milk, reserved corn mixture and salt; heat to a boil. Reduce heat to low and simmer, covered, 15 to 20 minutes.

Makes 4 servings

*Jalapeño peppers can sting and irritate the skin; wear rubber gloves when handling peppers and do not touch eyes. Wash hands after handling.

Nutrients per Serving:

Calories	292 (14% of calories from fat)				
Total Fat	5 g	Carbohydrate	36 g	Iron	2 mg
Saturated Fat	2 g	Dietary Fiber	4 g	Vitamin A	874 RE
Cholesterol	65 mg	Protein	29 g	Vitamin C	9 mg
Sodium	465 mg	Calcium	151 mg		

DIETARY EXCHANGES: 1½ Starch/Bread, 2½ Lean Meat, ½ Milk ½ Vegetable

MEXICAN TORTILLA SOUP

Fresh cilantro is used extensively in Mexican cooking. Also called fresh coriander or Chinese parsley, this pungent herb is similar in appearance to flat-leaf parsley.

Nonstick cooking spray
2 pounds boneless skinless
   chicken breasts, cut into
   ½-inch strips
4 cups diced carrots
2 cups sliced celery
1 cup chopped green bell pepper
1 cup chopped onion
4 cloves garlic, minced
1 teaspoon dried oregano leaves
½ teaspoon ground cumin

1 jalapeño pepper, sliced and
   seeded*
8 cups ⅓-less-salt chicken broth
1 large tomato, seeded and
   chopped
4 to 5 tablespoons lime juice
2 (6-inch) corn tortillas, cut into
   ¼-inch strips
Salt (optional)
3 tablespoons finely chopped
   fresh cilantro

1 Preheat oven to 350°F. Spray large nonstick saucepan with cooking spray; heat over medium heat until hot. Add chicken; cook and stir about 10 minutes or until browned and no longer pink in center. Add carrots, celery, bell pepper, onion, garlic, oregano, cumin and jalapeño; cook and stir over medium heat 5 minutes.

2 Stir in chicken broth, tomato and lime juice; heat to a boil. Reduce heat to low; cover and simmer 15 to 20 minutes.

3 Meanwhile, spray tortilla strips lightly with cooking spray; sprinkle very lightly with salt. Place on baking sheet. Bake about 10 minutes or until browned and crisp, stirring occasionally.

4 Stir cilantro into soup. Ladle soup into bowls; top with tortilla strips.

Makes 8 servings

*Jalapeño peppers can sting and irritate the skin; wear rubber gloves when handling peppers and do not touch eyes. Wash hands after handling.

Nutrients per Serving:

Calories	184 (15% of calories from fat)				
Total Fat	3 g	Carbohydrate	16 g	Iron	2 mg
Saturated Fat	1 g	Dietary Fiber	4 g	Vitamin A	1,595 RE
Cholesterol	58 mg	Protein	23 g	Vitamin C	41 mg
Sodium	132 mg	Calcium	66 mg		

DIETARY EXCHANGES: 2½ Starch/Bread, 2 Vegetable

VEGETABLE-CHICKEN NOODLE SOUP

If chicken soup is famous for making you feel better, then this soup should keep you feeling great! Loaded with vegetables, this noodle soup is a wonderful start to any meal.

1 cup chopped celery
½ cup thinly sliced leek
  (white part only)
½ cup chopped carrot
½ cup chopped turnip
6 cups ⅓-less-salt chicken broth,
  divided
1 tablespoon minced fresh
  parsley
1 teaspoon balsamic vinegar

1½ teaspoons fresh thyme *or*
  ½ teaspoon dried thyme
  leaves
1 teaspoon fresh rosemary *or*
  ¼ teaspoon dried rosemary
¼ teaspoon fresh ground black
  pepper
2 ounces uncooked "no-yolk"
  broad noodles
1 cup diced cooked chicken

1 Place celery, leek, carrot, turnip and ⅓ cup chicken broth in large saucepan. Cover and cook over medium heat until vegetables are tender, stirring occasionally.

2 Stir in remaining chicken broth, parsley, vinegar, thyme, rosemary and black pepper. Bring to a boil; add noodles. Cook until noodles are tender; stir in chicken. Reduce heat to medium. Simmer until heated through.

Makes 6 (1½-cup) servings

Nutrients per Serving:

Calories	98 (14% of calories from fat)				
Total Fat	2 g	Carbohydrate	12 g	Iron	1 mg
Saturated Fat	<1 g	Dietary Fiber	1 g	Vitamin A	267 RE
Cholesterol	18 mg	Protein	10 g	Vitamin C	7 mg
Sodium	73 mg	Calcium	38 mg		

DIETARY EXCHANGES: ½ Starch/Bread, 1 Lean Meat, ½ Vegetable

CHICKEN RAVIOLI SOUP

Wonton wrappers are paper-thin sheets of dough cut into squares that are available in the produce section of the supermarket. In this soup recipe, they are stuffed with a seasoned low fat ground chicken mixture for a hurry-up version of ravioli.

Chicken Ravioli (recipe
   follows)
8 cups ⅓-less-salt chicken broth
2 cups sliced spinach leaves

1 cup sliced carrots
¼ teaspoon salt
⅛ teaspoon ground black pepper

1 Prepare Chicken Ravioli.

2 Combine chicken broth, spinach, carrots, salt and pepper in large saucepan. Bring to a boil over high heat. Reduce heat to low; cover and simmer 10 minutes.

3 Return soup to a boil; add Chicken Ravioli. Reduce heat to low and simmer, uncovered, 2 to 3 minutes or until ravioli are tender and rise to surface of soup.

Makes 6 servings

CHICKEN RAVIOLI

⅓ cup ground chicken
1 tablespoon minced shallot or
   onion
1 clove garlic, minced

⅛ teaspoon salt
⅛ teaspoon ground nutmeg
⅛ teaspoon ground black pepper
24 wonton wrappers

1 Combine chicken, shallot, garlic, salt, nutmeg and pepper in small bowl. Place rounded teaspoonful of chicken mixture in center of each of 12 wonton wrappers. Moisten edges of wonton wrappers with water. Top with remaining wonton wrappers; press to seal edges. Cover and refrigerate until ready to cook.

Makes 12 ravioli

Nutrients per Serving:

Calories	130 (14% of calories from fat)				
Total Fat	2 g	Carbohydrate	21 g	Iron	2 mg
Saturated Fat	<1 g	Dietary Fiber	2 g	Vitamin A	667 RE
Cholesterol	26 mg	Protein	7 g	Vitamin C	7 mg
Sodium	205 mg	Calcium	45 mg		

DIETARY EXCHANGES: 1½ Starch/Bread, 1 Vegetable

GINGER WONTON SOUP

A Chinese specialty similar to Italian ravioli, these bite-size dumplings consist of paper-thin dough filled with pork, ricotta cheese, cilantro and Chinese 5-spice powder.

4 ounces lean ground pork
½ cup reduced fat ricotta cheese
½ tablespoon minced fresh cilantro
½ teaspoon ground black pepper
⅛ teaspoon Chinese 5-spice powder
20 fresh or frozen, thawed wonton skins
1 teaspoon vegetable oil

⅓ cup chopped red bell pepper
1 teaspoon grated fresh ginger
2 cans (14½ ounces each) ⅓-less-salt chicken broth
2 teaspoons reduced sodium soy sauce
4 ounces fresh pea pods
1 can (8¾ ounces) baby corn, rinsed and drained
2 green onions, thinly sliced

1 Cook pork in small nonstick skillet over medium-high heat 4 minutes or until no longer pink. Cool slightly; stir in ricotta cheese, cilantro, black pepper and 5-spice powder.

2 Place 1 teaspoon filling in center of each wonton skin. Fold top corner of wonton over filling. Lightly brush remaining corners with water. Fold left and right corners over filling. Tightly roll filled end toward remaining corner in jelly-roll fashion. Moisten edges with water to seal. Cover and set aside.

3 Heat oil in large saucepan. Add bell pepper and ginger; cook 1 minute. Add chicken broth and soy sauce; bring to a boil. Add pea pods, baby corn and wontons. Reduce heat to medium-low and simmer 4 to 5 minutes or until wontons are tender. Sprinkle with onions.   *Makes 4 (1½-cup) servings*

Nutrients per Serving:

Calories	259 (17% of calories from fat)				
Total Fat	5 g	Carbohydrate	39 g	Iron	3 mg
Saturated Fat	1 g	Dietary Fiber	3 g	Vitamin A	72 RE
Cholesterol	53 mg	Protein	16 g	Vitamin C	43 mg
Sodium	261 mg	Calcium	74 mg		

DIETARY EXCHANGES: 2½ Starch/Bread, 1 Lean Meat, ½ Vegetable, ½ Fat

MULLIGATAWNY SOUP

This lively chicken soup originated in southern India. Mulligatawny—literally "pepper water"—is an appropriate name because of its highly seasoned broth. Curry powder, one of the main seasonings, is actually a blend of up to twenty spices. Start by adding only a small amount to the soup if you are unfamiliar with its flavor.

Nonstick cooking spray
2 cups finely chopped carrots
1 cup chopped green bell pepper
2 ribs celery, thinly sliced
½ cup finely chopped onion
3 cloves garlic, minced
¼ cup all-purpose flour
1 to 2 teaspoons curry powder
¼ teaspoon ground nutmeg
3 cups ⅓-less-salt chicken broth

1 cup 2% low fat milk
1 pound boneless skinless
    chicken breasts, cooked and
    cut into ½-inch pieces
1 cup chopped seeded tomato
1 medium apple, cored, sliced,
    peeled
¼ cup uncooked converted rice
½ teaspoon salt
⅛ teaspoon ground black pepper

1 Spray large nonstick saucepan with cooking spray; heat over medium heat until hot. Add carrots, bell pepper, celery, onion and garlic; cook and stir 5 minutes. Sprinkle with flour, curry powder and nutmeg; cook and stir 1 to 2 minutes.

2 Add chicken broth, milk, chicken, tomato, apple, rice, salt and black pepper; heat to a boil. Reduce heat to low and simmer, covered, 20 minutes or until rice is tender.

Makes 8 servings

Nutrients per Serving:					
Calories	157 (14% of calories from fat)				
Total Fat	2 g	Carbohydrate	20 g	Iron	2 mg
Saturated Fat	1 g	Dietary Fiber	3 g	Vitamin A	834 RE
Cholesterol	31 mg	Protein	14 g	Vitamin C	37 mg
Sodium	225 mg	Calcium	80 mg		

DIETARY EXCHANGES: ½ Starch/Bread, 1½ Lean Meat, 1½ Vegetable

MEDITERRANEAN FISH SOUP

Each bustling Mediterranean seaport has a traditional seafood soup or stew. Within each city, recipes vary according to the day's catch. This energy-packed soup is just a sample of what is overseas.

4 ounces uncooked pastina or
  other small pasta
  Nonstick cooking spray
¾ cup chopped onion
2 cloves garlic, minced
1 teaspoon fennel seeds
1 can (14½ ounces) no-salt-
  added stewed tomatoes
1 can (14½ ounces) ⅓-less-salt
  chicken broth

1 tablespoon minced fresh
  parsley
½ teaspoon ground black pepper
¼ teaspoon ground turmeric
8 ounces firm, white-fleshed fish,
  cut into 1-inch pieces
3 ounces small shrimp, peeled
  and deveined

1 Cook pasta according to package directions, omitting salt. Drain and set aside.

2 Spray large nonstick saucepan with cooking spray. Add onion, garlic and fennel seeds; cook over medium heat 3 minutes or until onion is soft.

3 Stir in tomatoes, chicken broth, parsley, pepper and turmeric. Bring to a boil; reduce heat and simmer 10 minutes. Add fish and cook 1 minute. Add shrimp and cook until shrimp just begins to turn pink and opaque.

4 Divide pasta among bowls; ladle soup over pasta.

Makes 4 (1½-cup) servings

Nutrients per Serving:					
Calories	209 (10% of calories from fat)				
Total Fat	2 g	Carbohydrate	28 g	Iron	3 mg
Saturated Fat	<1 g	Dietary Fiber	3 g	Vitamin A	104 RE
Cholesterol	59 mg	Protein	19 g	Vitamin C	28 mg
Sodium	111 mg	Calcium	45 mg		

DIETARY EXCHANGES: 1½ Starch/Bread, 1½ Lean Meat, 1½ Vegetable

FOCACCIA

This focaccia is made into three small rounds rather than one large round so it may be cut into small pie-shaped wedges for spreading or dipping as an appetizer. This recipe calls for whole wheat flour to increase the fiber content. Recipe pictured on page 17.

¾ cup warm water (110° to 115°F)
1½ teaspoons sugar
1 teaspoon active dry yeast
1 tablespoon extra virgin olive oil

1 teaspoon salt
1 teaspoon dried rosemary
1 cup all-purpose flour
1 cup whole wheat flour
Nonstick cooking spray

1 Pour water into large bowl. Dissolve sugar and yeast in water; let stand 10 minutes or until bubbly. Stir in oil, salt and rosemary. Add flours, ½ cup at a time, stirring until dough begins to pull away from side of bowl and forms a ball.

2 Turn dough onto lightly floured surface. Knead 5 minutes or until dough is smooth and elastic, adding more flour if necessary. Place dough in bowl lightly sprayed with cooking spray and turn dough so all sides are coated; cover with towel. Let rise in warm place about 1 hour or until doubled in bulk.

3 Turn dough onto lightly floured surface and knead 1 minute. Divide into 3 balls; roll each into 6-inch circle. Using fingertips, dimple surfaces of dough. Place on baking sheet sprayed with cooking spray; cover and let rise 30 minutes more.

4 Preheat oven to 400°F. Spray tops of dough circles with cooking spray; bake about 13 minutes or until golden brown. Remove from oven and cut each loaf into 10 wedges.

Makes 10 servings

Nutrients per Serving:
3 wedges

Calories	102 (15% of calories from fat)					
Total Fat	2 g	Carbohydrate	19 g	Iron	1 mg
Saturated Fat	<1 g	Dietary Fiber	2 g	Vitamin A	<1 RE
Cholesterol	0 mg	Protein	3 g	Vitamin C	<1 mg
Sodium	214 mg	Calcium	9 mg		

DIETARY EXCHANGES: 1½ Starch/Bread

GARLIC BREAD

Both the taste and texture of good sourdough bread are perfect for this savory hot bread. Adding just a small amount of extra virgin olive oil to the roasted garlic prevents the bread from getting dry. Recipe pictured on page 221.

6 whole heads of garlic
1 teaspoon dried oregano leaves
4½ teaspoons extra virgin olive oil

1 loaf crusty sourdough or
   French bread, cut
   horizontally in half
   (1½ pounds)
Ground black pepper

1 Preheat oven to 350°F. Cut tops off heads of garlic and peel each head. Place heads, cut sides up, in small baking pan and sprinkle with oregano. Cover tightly with foil and bake 30 minutes. Uncover and bake 30 minutes more. Remove from oven; cool until easy to handle.

2 Carefully squeeze soft roasted garlic out of each clove to yield about ¾ cup. Place in food processor or blender; add oil and process until smooth.

3 Spread garlic mixture evenly on both halves of bread and sprinkle lightly with black pepper. Place halves together and cut loaf vertically into 8 equal pieces, being careful to keep loaf intact. Wrap tightly in foil. Bake 30 minutes.

4 To serve, unwrap loaf leaving foil crushed around outside to keep warm.

Makes 16 servings

Nutrients per Serving:					
1 piece					
Calories	149 (16% of calories from fat)				
Total Fat	3 g	Carbohydrate	27 g	Iron	1 mg
Saturated Fat	<1 g	Dietary Fiber	<1 g	Vitamin A	1 RE
Cholesterol	0 mg	Protein	5 g	Vitamin C	4 mg
Sodium	261 mg	Calcium	58 mg		

DIETARY EXCHANGES: 1½ Starch/Bread, 1 Vegetable, ½ Fat

SODA BREAD

Although it sounds as if buttermilk should be high in fat, it is usually made from low fat or skim milk.

1½ cups whole wheat flour
1 cup all-purpose flour
½ cup rolled oats
¼ cup sugar
1½ teaspoons baking powder
½ teaspoon baking soda

¼ teaspoon ground cinnamon
⅓ cup raisins (optional)
½ cup walnuts (optional)
1¼ cups buttermilk
1 tablespoon vegetable oil

1 Preheat oven to 375°F.

2 Combine whole wheat flour, all-purpose flour, oats, sugar, baking powder, baking soda and cinnamon in large bowl. Stir in raisins and walnuts. Gradually stir in buttermilk and oil until dough forms. Knead in bowl for 30 seconds.

3 Spray loaf pan with nonstick cooking spray; place dough in pan.

4 Bake 40 to 50 minutes until wooden toothpick inserted in center comes out clean.   *Makes 16 slices*

Nutrients per Serving:

Calories	103 (12% of calories from fat)				
Total Fat	1 g	Carbohydrate	20 g	Iron	1 mg
Saturated Fat	<1 g	Dietary Fiber	2 g	Vitamin A	3 RE
Cholesterol	1 mg	Protein	3 g	Vitamin C	1 mg
Sodium	77 mg	Calcium	34 mg		

DIETARY EXCHANGES: 1½ Starch/Bread

WHOLE WHEAT HERB BREAD

This flavorful bread is wonderful served right out of the oven. Why not try it toasted with a little jam?

⅔ cup water	3 tablespoons olive oil
⅔ cup skim milk	1 teaspoon salt
2 teaspoons sugar	½ teaspoon dried basil
2 envelopes active dry yeast	½ teaspoon dried oregano leaves
3 egg whites, lightly beaten	4 to 4½ cups whole wheat flour

1 Bring water to a boil in small saucepan. Remove from heat; stir in milk and sugar. Let mixture cool to 110° to 115°F; add yeast.* Mix well; let stand 10 minutes or until bubbly.

2 Combine egg whites, oil, salt, basil and oregano in large bowl until well blended. Add yeast mixture; mix well. Add 4 cups flour, ½ cup at a time, mixing well after each addition, until dough is no longer sticky. Knead about 5 minutes or until smooth and elastic, adding more flour if dough is sticky. Form into a ball. Place dough in medium bowl sprayed with nonstick cooking spray. Turn dough so all sides are coated; cover with towel. Let rise in warm place about 1 hour or until doubled in bulk.

3 Preheat oven to 350°F. Punch dough down and place on lightly floured surface. Divide into 4 pieces and roll each piece into a ball. Lightly spray baking sheet with nonstick cooking spray. Place dough balls on prepared baking sheet. Bake 30 to 35 minutes until golden brown and loaves sound hollow when tapped with finger.

Makes 24 slices

*Too much heat will kill the yeast.

Nutrients per Serving:
1 slice

Calories	99 (18% of calories from fat)					
Total Fat	2 g	Carbohydrate	17 g	Iron	1 mg	
Saturated Fat	<1 g	Dietary Fiber	3 g	Vitamin A	5 RE	
Cholesterol	<1 mg	Protein	4 g	Vitamin C	<1 mg	
Sodium	101 mg	Calcium	18 mg			

DIETARY EXCHANGES: 1 Starch/Bread, ½ Fat

BRAN AND HONEY RYE BREADSTICKS

There is more than one way to get your fiber and these breadsticks are a delightfully delicious way. The rye flour and whole bran cereal raise the fiber tally to 3.4 grams for each serving.

1 package (¼ ounce) active dry yeast
1 teaspoon sugar
1½ cups warm water (110° to 115°F)
3¾ cups all-purpose flour, divided

1 tablespoon honey
1 tablespoon vegetable oil
½ teaspoon salt
1 cup rye flour
½ cup whole bran cereal
Skim milk

1 Dissolve yeast and sugar in warm water in large bowl. Let stand 10 minutes. Add 1 cup all-purpose flour, honey, oil and salt. Beat with electric mixer at medium speed 3 minutes. Stir in rye flour, bran cereal and 2 cups all-purpose flour as needed to make moderately stiff dough.

2 Knead dough on lightly floured surface 10 minutes or until smooth and elastic, adding remaining ½ cup all-purpose flour as needed to prevent sticking. Place dough in medium bowl sprayed with nonstick cooking spray. Turn dough so all sides are coated; cover with towel. Let rise in warm place 40 to 45 minutes or until doubled in bulk.

3 Spray 2 baking sheets with nonstick cooking spray. Punch dough down. Divide into 24 equal pieces on lightly floured surface. Roll each piece into an 8-inch rope. Place on prepared baking sheets. Cover with towel; let rise in warm place 30 to 35 or until doubled in bulk.

4 Preheat oven to 375°F. Brush breadsticks with milk. Bake 18 to 20 minutes or until breadsticks are golden brown. Remove from baking sheets. Cool on wire racks.

Makes 24 breadsticks

Nutrients per Serving:
2 breadsticks

Calories	198 (8% of calories from fat)					
Total Fat	2 g	Carbohydrate	40 g	Iron	2 mg
Saturated Fat	<1 g	Dietary Fiber	3 g	Vitamin A	0 RE
Cholesterol	0 mg	Protein	5 g	Vitamin C	3 mg
Sodium	109 mg	Calcium	10 mg		

DIETARY EXCHANGES: 2½ Starch/Bread

ROSEMARY BREADSTICKS

These amusing looking and low fat breadsticks are real conversation pieces as well as being simply delicious. They are also so easy to make that you may find them a fun addition to many menus. Try other herb and spice variations, such as thyme or cumin, in place of the rosemary.

⅔ cup 2% low fat milk
¼ cup finely chopped fresh chives
2 teaspoons baking powder
1 teaspoon finely chopped fresh
    rosemary or dried rosemary

¾ teaspoon salt
½ teaspoon ground black pepper
¾ cup whole wheat flour
¾ cup all-purpose flour
    Nonstick cooking spray

1 Combine milk, chives, baking powder, rosemary, salt and pepper in large bowl; mix well. Stir in flours, ½ cup at a time, until blended. Turn onto floured surface and knead dough about 5 minutes or until smooth and elastic, adding a little more flour if dough is sticky. Let stand 30 minutes at room temperature.

2 Preheat oven to 375°F. Spray baking sheet with cooking spray. Divide dough into 12 equal balls, about 1¼ ounces each. Roll each ball into long thin rope and place on prepared baking sheet. Lightly spray breadsticks with cooking spray. Bake about 12 minutes or until bottoms are golden brown. Turn breadsticks over and bake about 10 minutes more or until other side is browned.

Makes 12 breadsticks

Nutrients per Serving:
1 breadstick

Calories	62 (7% of calories from fat)				
Total Fat	1 g	Carbohydrate	12 g	Iron	1 mg
Saturated Fat	<1 g	Dietary Fiber	1 g	Vitamin A	13 RE
Cholesterol	1 mg	Protein	2 g	Vitamin C	1 mg
Sodium	196 mg	Calcium	33 mg		

DIETARY EXCHANGES: 1 Starch/Bread

BUBBLING WISCONSIN CHEESE BREAD

Adding cheese to your diet provides calcium and protein but should be eaten sparingly because it is also high in fat.

½ cup (2 ounces) shredded
　　Wisconsin mozzarella cheese
⅓ cup mayonnaise or salad
　　dressing
⅛ teaspoon garlic powder

⅛ teaspoon onion powder
1 loaf (16 ounces) French bread,
　　halved lengthwise
⅓ cup (1 ounce) grated
　　Wisconsin Parmesan cheese

1 Preheat oven to 350°F.

2 Combine mozzarella cheese, mayonnaise, garlic powder and onion powder in mixing bowl; mix well (mixture will be very thick).

3 Spread half the mixture over each bread half. Sprinkle half the Parmesan cheese over each half.

4 Bake 20 to 25 minutes or until bubbly and lightly browned.* Cut each half into 8 slices.   *Makes 16 servings*

*To broil, position on rack 4 inches from heat for 3 to 5 minutes.

Nutrients per Serving:

Calories	110 (28% of calories from fat)				
Total Fat	3 g	Carbohydrate	15 g	Iron	1 mg
Saturated Fat	1 g	Dietary Fiber	0 g	Vitamin A	11 RE
Cholesterol	5 mg	Protein	4 g	Vitamin C	0 mg
Sodium	233 mg	Calcium	73 mg		

DIETARY EXCHANGES: 1 Starch/Bread, ½ Fat

CHIVE WHOLE WHEAT DROP BISCUITS

Wheat germ is the embryo of the wheat plant. It contains most of the nutrient content of the wheat kernel and is especially high in vitamin E.

1¼ cups whole wheat flour
¾ cup all-purpose flour
3 tablespoons toasted wheat germ, divided
1 tablespoon baking powder
1 tablespoon chopped fresh chives *or* 1 teaspoon dried chives

2 teaspoons sugar
3 tablespoons margarine
1 cup skim milk
½ cup (2 ounces) shredded low fat process American cheese

1 Preheat oven to 450°F.

2 Spray baking sheet with nonstick cooking spray.

3 Combine whole wheat flour, all-purpose flour, 2 tablespoons wheat germ, baking powder, chives and sugar in medium bowl. Cut in margarine with pastry blender until mixture resembles coarse meal. Add milk and American cheese; stir until just combined.

4 Drop dough by rounded teaspoonfuls onto prepared baking sheet about 1 inch apart. Sprinkle with remaining 1 tablespoon wheat germ. Bake 10 to 12 minutes or until golden brown. Remove immediately from baking sheet. Serve warm.

Makes 12 servings

Nutrients per Serving:

Calories	125 (28% of calories from fat)				
Total Fat	4 g	Carbohydrate	18 g	Iron	1 mg
Saturated Fat	1 g	Dietary Fiber	2 g	Vitamin A	59 RE
Cholesterol	2 mg	Protein	5 g	Vitamin C	<1 mg
Sodium	152 mg	Calcium	88 mg		

DIETARY EXCHANGES: 1 Starch/Bread, 1 Fat

BANANA NUT BREAD

Green bananas can be ripened uncovered or in a brown paper bag at room temperature. After they're ripe, further ripening can be delayed by placing them in the refrigerator. The skin may turn dark, but the fruit will be fine.

½ cup granulated sugar
2 tablespoons packed brown
  sugar
5 tablespoons margarine
1 whole egg
2 egg whites

1⅓ cups mashed ripe bananas
2½ cups all-purpose flour
1 teaspoon baking soda
½ teaspoon salt
⅓ cup walnuts

1 Preheat oven to 375°F.

2 Spray large loaf pan with nonstick cooking spray.

3 Cream sugars and margarine with electric mixer at medium speed in large bowl. Add whole egg, egg whites and bananas. Sift together flour, baking soda and salt in separate bowl; add to banana mixture. Stir in walnuts. Pour into prepared pan. Bake 1 hour or until wooden toothpick inserted in center comes out clean. Cool. *Makes 16 servings*

Nutrients per Serving:

Calories	174 (28% of calories from fat)				
Total Fat	6 g	Carbohydrate	28 g	Iron	1 mg
Saturated Fat	1 g	Dietary Fiber	1 g	Vitamin A	52 RE
Cholesterol	13 mg	Protein	4 g	Vitamin C	2 mg
Sodium	171 mg	Calcium	11 mg		

DIETARY EXCHANGES: 1½ Starch/Bread, ½ Fruit, 1 Fat

SESAME CRUNCH BANANA MUFFINS

Sesame Crunch Topping
(recipe follows)
2 ripe medium bananas, mashed
1 cup 2% low fat milk
2 egg whites
2 tablespoons vegetable oil
1 teaspoon vanilla

1½ cups quick-cooking rolled oats
½ cup all-purpose flour
½ cup whole wheat flour
2 tablespoons granulated sugar
1 tablespoon baking powder
½ teaspoon salt

1 Prepare Sesame Crunch Topping; set aside.

2 Spray nonstick cooking spray in muffin cups or use paper liners.

3 Preheat oven to 400°F.

4 Combine bananas, milk, egg whites, oil and vanilla in large bowl; set aside.

5 Combine oats, all-purpose flour, whole wheat flour, sugar, baking powder and salt in medium bowl. Stir in banana mixture until just moistened (batter will be lumpy). Fill prepared muffin cups about half full. Sprinkle 2 teaspoons Sesame Crunch over batter in each muffin cup and bake 20 to 25 minutes or until golden on top and wooden toothpick inserted in center comes out clean. Cool slightly in pan before transferring to wire rack. Serve warm.

Makes 17 muffins

SESAME CRUNCH TOPPING

4 tablespoons packed brown
   sugar
2 tablespoons chopped walnuts
2 tablespoons whole wheat flour

1 tablespoon sesame seeds
1 tablespoon margarine
¼ tablespoon ground nutmeg
¼ teaspoon ground cinnamon

1 Combine all ingredients in small bowl; mix well.

Makes about ¾ cup

Nutrients per Serving:					
Calories	124 (28% of calories from fat)				
Total Fat	4 g	Carbohydrate	20 g	Iron	1 mg
Saturated Fat	1 g	Dietary Fiber	1 g	Vitamin A	20 RE
Cholesterol	1 mg	Protein	4 g	Vitamin C	1 mg
Sodium	105 mg	Calcium	33 mg		

DIETARY EXCHANGES: 1 Starch/Bread, ½ Fruit, ½ Fat

MINIATURE FRUIT MUFFINS

These high fiber, nearly fat free muffins are just as delicious as they are appealing in appearance. Dividing the basic batter into thirds allows you to offer your guests three choices.

1 cup whole wheat flour	1 cup buttermilk, divided
¾ cup all-purpose flour	¾ cup frozen blueberries
½ cup firmly packed dark brown sugar	1 small ripe banana, mashed
2 teaspoons baking powder	¼ teaspoon vanilla
½ teaspoon baking soda	⅓ cup unsweetened applesauce
¼ teaspoon salt	2 tablespoons raisins
	½ teaspoon ground cinnamon

1 Preheat oven to 400°F. Spray 36 miniature muffin cups with nonstick cooking spray.

2 Combine flours, brown sugar, baking powder, baking soda and salt in medium bowl. Place ⅔ cup dry ingredients in each of 2 small bowls.

3 To one portion of flour mixture, add ⅓ cup buttermilk and blueberries. Stir just until blended; spoon into 12 prepared muffin cups. To second portion, add ⅓ cup buttermilk, banana and vanilla. Stir just until blended; spoon into 12 muffin cups. To final portion, add remaining ⅓ cup buttermilk, applesauce, raisins and cinnamon. Stir just until blended; spoon into 12 muffin cups.

4 Bake 18 minutes or until lightly browned and wooden pick inserted into centers comes out clean. Cool slightly before serving. *Makes 12 servings*

Nutrients per Serving:

3 miniature muffins (1 blueberry, 1 banana, 1 applesauce-raisin)

Calories	130 (4% of calories from fat)				
Total Fat	1 g	Carbohydrate	29 g	Iron	1 mg
Saturated Fat	<1 g	Dietary Fiber	2 g	Vitamin A	4 RE
Cholesterol	1 mg	Protein	3 g	Vitamin C	2 mg
Sodium	178 mg	Calcium	49 mg		

DIETARY EXCHANGES: 1 Starch/Bread, 1 Fruit

MEATS

FRAGRANT BEEF WITH GARLIC SAUCE

Good-for-you garlic is the star here. Ten cloves are cooked until tender, then puréed into an aromatic sauce that perfectly complements beef.

⅓ cup teriyaki sauce
1 boneless beef top sirloin steak, cut 1 inch thick (about 1¼ pounds)

10 large cloves garlic, peeled
½ cup ⅓-less-salt beef broth
4 cups hot, cooked white rice

1 Place teriyaki sauce in large resealable plastic food storage bag; add beef. Seal bag; turn to coat. Marinate in refrigerator 30 minutes or up to 4 hours, turning occasionally.

2 Preheat broiler. Combine garlic and beef broth in small saucepan; bring to a boil over high heat. Reduce heat to medium; simmer, uncovered, 5 minutes. Cover; simmer 8 to 9 minutes until garlic is softened. Transfer to blender or food processor; process until smooth.

3 Meanwhile, drain beef; reserve marinade. Spray rack of broiler pan with nonstick cooking spray. Place beef on rack; brush with half of reserved marinade. Broil 4 inches from heat, 10 minutes or until desired doneness, turning occasionally and basting with remaining marinade.

4 Thinly slice beef. Spoon garlic sauce over beef and rice.

Makes 4 servings

Nutrients per Serving:

Calories	411 (29% of calories from fat)					
Total Fat	13 g	Carbohydrate	48 g	Iron	4 mg
Saturated Fat	5 g	Dietary Fiber	1 g	Vitamin A	6 RE
Cholesterol	95 mg	Protein	37 g	Vitamin C	3 mg
Sodium	480 mg	Calcium	36 mg		

DIETARY EXCHANGES: 2½ Starch/Bread, 3½ Lean Meat

BEEF AND BROCCOLI

Fresh broccoli is loaded with vitamins and minerals, and beef tenderloin is one of the leanest cuts around. Together they make this classic Chinese dish an excellent choice for lighter eating.

1 pound lean beef tenderloin
2 teaspoons minced fresh ginger
2 cloves garlic, minced
½ teaspoon vegetable oil

3 cups broccoli flowerets
¼ cup water
2 tablespoons teriyaki sauce
2 cups hot, cooked white rice

1 Cut beef across grain into ⅛-inch slices; cut each slice into 1½-inch pieces. Combine beef, ginger and garlic in medium bowl; blend well.

2 Heat oil in wok or large nonstick skillet over medium heat until hot. Add beef mixture; stir-fry 3 to 4 minutes until beef is barely pink in center. Remove beef from wok; reserve.

3 Add broccoli and water to wok. Cover; steam 3 to 5 minutes or until broccoli is crisp-tender.

4 Return beef and any accumulated juices to wok. Add teriyaki sauce. Cook until heated through. Spoon beef and broccoli over rice. Garnish with red pepper strips, if desired.

Makes 4 servings

Nutrients per Serving:

Calories	392 (26% of calories from fat)				
Total Fat	11 g	Carbohydrate	34 g	Iron	6 mg
Saturated Fat	4 g	Dietary Fiber	3 g	Vitamin A	102 RE
Cholesterol	95 mg	Protein	37 g	Vitamin C	62 mg
Sodium	393 mg	Calcium	56 mg		

DIETARY EXCHANGES: 2 Starch/Bread, 4 Lean Meat, 1 Vegetable

BEEF BURGERS WITH CORN SALSA

Corn, an excellent source of vitamins and minerals, adds a colorful twist to this delicious homemade salsa. Its sweet, delicate flavor adds a cool contrast to the heat of the chilies.

½ cup frozen whole kernel corn
½ cup peeled, seeded and
    chopped tomato
1 can (4 ounces) diced green
    chilies, divided
1 tablespoon chopped fresh
    cilantro *or* 1 teaspoon dried
    cilantro leaves

1 tablespoon vinegar
1 teaspoon olive oil
¼ cup fine dry bread crumbs
3 tablespoons skim milk
¼ teaspoon garlic powder
¾ pound 95% lean ground beef

1 Prepare corn according to package directions, omitting salt; drain. To make Corn Salsa, combine corn, tomato, 2 tablespoons green chilies, cilantro, vinegar and oil in small bowl. Cover; refrigerate.

2 Preheat broiler.

3 Combine remaining green chilies, bread crumbs, skim milk and garlic powder in medium bowl. Add beef; blend well. Shape to form four ¾-inch-thick patties.

4 Spray rack of broiler pan with nonstick cooking spray. Place patties on rack. Broil 4 inches from heat, 12 to 14 minutes or until desired doneness, turning occasionally. Spoon salsa over patties.

Makes 4 servings

Nutrients per Serving:

Calories	180 (30% of calories from fat)				
Total Fat	6 g	Carbohydrate	13 g	Iron	2 mg
Saturated Fat	2 g	Dietary Fiber	2 g	Vitamin A	43 RE
Cholesterol	33 mg	Protein	19 g	Vitamin C	52 mg
Sodium	101 mg	Calcium	35 mg		

DIETARY EXCHANGES: ½ Starch/Bread, 2½ Lean Meat, 1 Vegetable

FAJITAS

There are as many versions of fajitas as there are restaurants preparing them. A low fat, generally chewy piece of meat is made tender by quick cooking, then slicing thinly across the prominent lengthwise grain. Lots of roasted bell peppers, rich in vitamin C, are standard.

Fajita Marinade (page 184)
1 pound beef flank steak
Salsa Cruda (page 38)
6 (10-inch) flour tortillas *or*
    12 (7-inch) flour tortillas
4 bell peppers, any color, halved
1 large bunch green onions

1 cup coarsely chopped fresh
    cilantro
1 ripe avocado, peeled, pitted,
    thinly sliced (optional)
6 tablespoons low fat sour cream
    (optional)

1 Prepare Fajita Marinade. Pour marinade in large resealable plastic food storage bag; add steak. Seal bag; turn to coat. Marinate in refrigerator 30 minutes or up to 24 hours, turning occasionally.

2 Prepare Salsa Cruda; set aside. Place tortillas in stacks of 3. Wrap each stack in aluminum foil; set aside.

3 To prevent sticking, spray grill with nonstick cooking spray. Prepare coals for grilling.

4 Drain marinade from meat into small saucepan; bring to a boil over high heat. Remove saucepan from heat.

5 Place meat on grill, 4 inches from medium-hot coals. Place peppers, skin side down, around meat; cover. Grill peppers 12 minutes or until tender and skin is browned in spots. Move peppers to sides of grill. Grill meat 16 minutes or until desired doneness, turning occasionally and basting with marinade. During last 4 minutes of grilling, brush onions with remaining marinade. Grill onions 4 minutes or until tender and skin is browned in spots, turning occasionally.

6 Place packets of tortillas on grill; heat about 5 minutes. Slice peppers and onions into thin 2-inch-long pieces. Thinly slice meat across the grain.

7 Place tortilla on plate. Place meat, peppers, onions, Salsa Cruda and cilantro in center of each tortilla. Fold sides completely over filling to enclose. Serve with avocado and sour cream, if desired.

Makes 6 servings

(continued on page 184)

Fajitas, continued

FAJITA MARINADE

½ cup lime juice *or* ¼ cup lime
   juice and ¼ cup tequila or
   beer
1 tablespoon dried oregano
   leaves

1 tablespoon minced garlic
2 teaspoons ground cumin
2 teaspoons ground black pepper

 Combine lime juice, oregano, garlic, cumin and pepper in 1-cup glass measure; blend well.

Nutrients per Serving:				
1 large fajita				
Calories	304 (28% of calories from fat)			
Total Fat	9 g	Carbohydrate	25 g	Iron	4 mg
Saturated Fat	4 g	Dietary Fiber	3 g	Vitamin A	129 RE
Cholesterol	44 mg	Protein	30 g	Vitamin C	63 mg
Sodium	198 mg	Calcium	78 mg		

DIETARY EXCHANGES: 1 Starch/Bread, 3 Lean Meat, 2 Vegetable, ½ Fat

Cook's Tip
Bell peppers are naturally delicious and grilling them
at medium-high heat gives them a wonderful new flavor
complexity without adding any fat.

PEPPER-SPICED BEEF SKEWERS AND BEANS

Pepper-Spice Seasoning
(page 186)
1½ pounds lean beef such as
tenderloin
1 large red bell pepper
1 large green bell pepper
1 large onion, halved, divided
2 tablespoons lemon juice
2 teaspoons olive oil

3 cups cooked, drained Great
Northern, navy or pinto
beans *or* 2 cans (16 ounces
each) beans, rinsed and
drained
1 can (28 ounces) no-salt-added
stewed tomatoes, drained
2 tablespoons brown sugar
2 tablespoons chopped fresh
parsley

1 To prevent sticking, spray grill with nonstick cooking spray. Prepare coals
for grilling.

2 Prepare Pepper-Spice Seasoning.

3 Cut beef into ¾- to 1-inch cubes. Cut peppers and half of onion into ¾- to
1-inch squares (about 24 to 30 squares of each). Alternately thread meat,
peppers and vegetables onto 6 (10- to 12-inch) metal skewers. (If using
bamboo skewers, soak in water 20 minutes before using to prevent them from
burning.) Combine 2 tablespoons Pepper-Spice Seasoning with lemon juice
in small bowl; blend well. Brush mixture over beef cubes.

4 Place skewers on grill, 4 inches from medium-hot coals. Grill 8 to 10
minutes or until desired doneness, turning occasionally.

5 Meanwhile, finely chop remaining onion half. Heat oil in medium
saucepan over medium-high heat until hot. Add onion and remaining 2
tablespoons spice mixture. Cook and stir 3 minutes or until onion is tender
(do not let spices burn). Stir in beans, tomatoes and brown sugar; cook and
stir until heated through. Stir in parsley.   *Makes 6 servings*

(continued on page 186)

Pepper-Spiced Beef Skewers and Beans, continued

PEPPER-SPICE SEASONING

2 tablespoons lemon juice

2 tablespoons pressed or minced
   garlic

2 teaspoons dried oregano leaves

2 teaspoons ground black pepper

1 teaspoon ground cumin

1 teaspoon ground allspice

1 Combine all ingredients in small bowl; blend well.   *Makes 6 servings*

Nutrients per Serving:

1 skewer with ½ cup beans

Calories	263 (19% of calories from fat)				
Total Fat	6 g	Carbohydrate	37 g	Iron	5 mg
Saturated Fat	2 g	Dietary Fiber	7 g	Vitamin A	125 RE
Cholesterol	27 mg	Protein	19 g	Vitamin C	62 mg
Sodium	41 mg	Calcium	103 mg		

DIETARY EXCHANGES: 1½ Starch/Bread, 2 Lean Meat, 2 Vegetable

Health Note

As a good source of protein and fiber, beans are hard to beat. There are about 5 grams of protein and almost 6 grams of fiber in a ⅓-cup portion of beans. What is more, they have no cholesterol and only a trace of fat.

PEPPERCORN BEEF KABOBS

Sirloin steaks are cut from the beef loin, which is where the most tender cuts of meat are found.

1 pound boneless beef sirloin steak, cut 1 inch thick
1½ teaspoons black peppercorns, crushed
½ teaspoon salt

½ teaspoon paprika
1 clove garlic, minced
1 medium onion, cut into 12 wedges

1 Preheat broiler.

2 Cut beef steak into 1-inch pieces. Combine peppercorns, salt, paprika and garlic in shallow dish. Add beef; turn to coat.

3 Thread an equal number of beef pieces and 3 onion wedges onto each of 4 (12-inch) metal skewers. (If using bamboo skewers, soak in water 20 minutes before using to prevent them from burning.)

4 Spray rack of broiler pan with nonstick cooking spray. Place kabobs on rack. Broil 4 inches from heat, 9 to 12 minutes or until desired doneness, turning occasionally. Garnish with tomatoes, if desired.   *Makes 4 servings*

Nutrients per Serving:

Calories	158 (26% of calories from fat)				
Total Fat	4 g	Carbohydrate	3 g	Iron	3 mg
Saturated Fat	2 g	Dietary Fiber	1 g	Vitamin A	16 RE
Cholesterol	54 mg	Protein	25 g	Vitamin C	3 mg
Sodium	339 mg	Calcium	33 mg		

DIETARY EXCHANGES: 3 Lean Meat

HONEY-CITRUS GLAZED VEAL CHOPS

This blend of honey, ginger and lime adds a subtle zip to the delicate flavor of veal.

3 tablespoons fresh lime juice
2 tablespoons honey
2 teaspoons grated fresh ginger

½ teaspoon grated lime peel
4 veal rib chops, cut 1 inch thick
　　(about 8 ounces each)

1 Combine lime juice, honey, ginger and lime peel in small bowl. Place chops in large dish. Brush lime mixture liberally over both sides of chops. Cover; marinate in refrigerator 30 minutes.

2 To prevent sticking, spray grill with nonstick cooking spray. Prepare coals for grilling.

3 Remove chops from dish; brush with remaining lime mixture. Place chops on grill, 4 inches from coals. Grill 12 to 14 minutes or until desired doneness, turning occasionally. Or, place chops on rack of broiler pan coated with nonstick cooking spray. Broil 4 inches from heat, 10 to 12 minutes or until desired doneness, turning occasionally.　　　　　*Makes 4 servings*

Nutrients per Serving:

Calories	479 (29% of calories from fat)				
Total Fat	15 g	Carbohydrate	10 g	Iron	3 mg
Saturated Fat	4 g	Dietary Fiber	<1 g	Vitamin A	<1 RE
Cholesterol	267 mg	Protein	72 g	Vitamin C	4 mg
Sodium	204 mg	Calcium	55 mg		

DIETARY EXCHANGES: 4 Lean Meat

MARGARITA PORK KABOBS

This margarita marinade sets the tone for a festive menu, making it a perfect dish for outdoor entertaining.

1 cup margarita drink mix *or* 1 cup lime juice, 4 teaspoons sugar and ½ teaspoon salt
1 teaspoon ground coriander
1 clove garlic, minced
1 pound pork tenderloin, cut into 1-inch cubes
2 tablespoons margarine, softened

1 tablespoon minced fresh parsley
2 teaspoons lime juice
⅛ teaspoon sugar
1 large green or red bell pepper, cut into 1-inch cubes
2 ears corn, cut into 8 pieces

1 Combine margarita mix, coriander and garlic in large resealable plastic food storage bag; add pork. Seal bag; turn to coat. Marinate in refrigerator at least 30 minutes, turning occasionally.

2 To prevent sticking, spray grill with nonstick cooking spray. Prepare coals for grilling.

3 Combine margarine, parsley, lime juice and sugar in small bowl; set aside.

4 Alternately thread pork, bell pepper and corn onto skewers. (If using bamboo skewers, soak in water 20 minutes before using to prevent them from burning.) Place kabobs on grill, 4 inches from hot coals. Grill 15 to 20 minutes or until pork is barely pink in center, turning occasionally and basting with margarine mixture.   *Makes 4 servings*

Nutrients per Serving:

Calories	298 (27% of calories from fat)				
Total Fat	9 g	Carbohydrate	28 g	Iron	2 mg
Saturated Fat	2 g	Dietary Fiber	2 g	Vitamin A	102 RE
Cholesterol	64 mg	Protein	26 g	Vitamin C	23 mg
Sodium	309 mg	Calcium	18 mg		

DIETARY EXCHANGES: 1 Starch/Bread, 3 Lean Meat, 1 Fruit

PORK CHOPS WITH RED PEPPER AND SWEET POTATO

Pork is an excellent source of niacin which works in the body, along with other B vitamins, to release energy from food.

4 pork loin chops (about 1 pound), cut ½ inch thick
1 teaspoon lemon pepper
Nonstick cooking spray
½ cup water
1 tablespoon lemon juice
1 teaspoon dried fines herbes
½ teaspoon beef bouillon granules

1¼ cups red or yellow bell pepper strips
1 cup sliced sweet potato, cut into 1-inch pieces
¾ cup sliced onion
4 cups hot, cooked white rice

1 Trim fat from chops; rub both sides with lemon pepper. Spray large skillet with cooking spray; heat skillet over medium-high heat until hot. Add chops; cook until browned, turning occasionally.

2 Combine water, lemon juice, fines herbes and bouillon granules in small bowl; pour over chops. Reduce heat to medium-low. Cover; simmer 5 minutes.

3 Add bell pepper, sweet potato and onion; bring to a boil over high heat. Reduce heat to medium-low. Cover; simmer 10 to 15 minutes or until chops are barely pink in center and vegetables are crisp-tender. Remove chops and vegetables from skillet; keep warm.

4 Bring sauce remaining in skillet to a boil over high heat. Reduce heat to medium. Cook and stir until mixture slightly thickens. Arrange chops and vegetables over rice. Spoon sauce over chops and vegetables.

Makes 4 servings

Nutrients per Serving:

Calories	443 (21% of calories from fat)				
Total Fat	10 g	Carbohydrate	63 g	Iron	3 mg
Saturated Fat	3 g	Dietary Fiber	2 g	Vitamin A	772 RE
Cholesterol	59 mg	Protein	23 g	Vitamin C	72 mg
Sodium	286 mg	Calcium	59 mg		

DIETARY EXCHANGES: 3½ Starch/Bread, 2 Lean Meat, 2 Vegetable

ROASTED PORK

Pork is a real nutritional bargain. Lean cuts, such as the tenderloin, are low in fat and an excellent source of the B vitamins, such as thiamine, B_6 and B_{12}, as well as iron and zinc.

3 tablespoons barbecue sauce
1 tablespoon reduced sodium soy sauce
1 tablespoon dry sherry
2 cloves garlic, minced
½ teaspoon crushed Szechuan peppercorns or crushed red pepper

2 whole pork tenderloins (about 1¼ to 1½ pounds total)
Hot, cooked white rice (optional)

1 Preheat oven to 350°F. Combine barbecue sauce, soy sauce, sherry, garlic and peppercorns in small bowl.

2 Brush ¼ of mixture evenly over each roast. Place roasts on rack in shallow foil-lined roasting pan. Cook roasts 15 minutes; turn and brush with remaining barbecue sauce mixture. Continue to cook until thermometer inserted into center of pork registers 155°F. (Timing will depend on thickness of pork; test at 30 minutes.)

3 Let pork stand, tented with foil, on cutting board 5 minutes. (Temperature of pork will rise to 160°F.) Slice diagonally and serve warm with rice, if desired. Or, for use in other recipes, cut into portions and refrigerate up to 3 days or freeze up to 3 months.   *Makes 4 servings*

Variation: For Chinese Barbecued Pork, add 1 teaspoon red food coloring to barbecue sauce mixture. Prepare roasts as recipe directs. Roasts may be grilled over medium coals until an internal temperature of 155°F is reached. (Turn pork after 8 minutes; check temperature at 16 minutes.)

Nutrients per Serving:

Calories	199 (26% of calories from fat)				
Total Fat	5 g	Carbohydrate	3 g	Iron	2 mg
Saturated Fat	2 g	Dietary Fiber	<1 g	Vitamin A	22 RE
Cholesterol	101 mg	Protein	32 g	Vitamin C	2 mg
Sodium	301 mg	Calcium	15 mg		

DIETARY EXCHANGES: 3½ Lean Meat

PORK LOIN ROASTED IN CHILI-SPICE SAUCE

1 cup chopped onion
¼ cup orange juice
2 cloves garlic
1 tablespoon cider vinegar
1½ teaspoons chili powder
¼ teaspoon dried thyme leaves
¼ teaspoon ground cumin
¼ teaspoon ground cinnamon

⅛ teaspoon ground allspice
⅛ teaspoon ground cloves
1½ pounds pork loin, fat trimmed
3 firm large bananas
2 limes, divided
1 ripe large papaya, peeled, seeded, cubed
1 green onion, minced

1 Preheat oven to 350°F. In food processor or blender combine onion, orange juice and garlic; process until finely chopped. Pour into medium saucepan; stir in vinegar, chili powder, thyme, cumin, cinnamon, allspice and cloves. Simmer over medium-high heat about 5 minutes or until thickened.

2 Cut ¼-inch-deep lengthwise slits down top and bottom of roast at 1½-inch intervals. Spread about 1 tablespoon spice paste over bottom; place roast in baking pan. Spread remaining 2 tablespoons spice mixture over sides and top, working mixture into slits. Cover. Bake 45 minutes or until meat thermometer registers 140°F.

3 Remove roast from oven; *increase oven temperature to 450°F.* Pour off liquid; discard. Return roast to oven; bake, uncovered, 15 minutes or until spice mixture browns lightly and thermometer inserted into center of pork registers 155°F. Remove roast from oven. Let stand, tented with foil, 5 minutes before slicing. (Temperature will rise to 160°F.)

4 Meanwhile, spray 9-inch pie plate or cake pan with nonstick cooking spray. Peel bananas and slice diagonally into ½-inch-thick pieces. Place in pan. Squeeze juice from 1 lime over bananas; toss to coat evenly. Cover; bake in oven while roast stands or until hot. Stir in papaya, juice of remaining lime and green onion.

Makes 6 servings

Nutrients per Serving:

Calories	255 (27% of calories from fat)					
Total Fat	8 g	Carbohydrate	30 g	Iron	1 mg
Saturated Fat	3 g	Dietary Fiber	3 g	Vitamin A	58 RE
Cholesterol	51 mg	Protein	18 g	Vitamin C	71 mg
Sodium	53 mg	Calcium	48 mg		

DIETARY EXCHANGES: 2½ Lean Meat, 2 Fruit

PORK TENDERLOIN WITH SHERRY-MUSHROOM SAUCE

The leanest cuts of pork are tenderloin, loin roast and loin chops.
A 3-ounce portion of pork tenderloin has approximately 140 calories
and 4 grams of fat.

1 pork tenderloin (1 to 1½ pounds)
1 tablespoon reduced calorie margarine
1½ cups chopped mushrooms or shiitake mushroom caps
2 tablespoons sliced green onion
1 clove garlic, minced
1 tablespoon cornstarch

1 tablespoon chopped fresh parsley
½ teaspoon dried thyme leaves
 Dash ground black pepper
⅓ cup water
1 tablespoon dry sherry
½ teaspoon beef bouillon granules

1 Preheat oven to 375°F.

2 Place pork on rack in shallow baking pan. Insert meat thermometer into thickest part of tenderloin. Roast, uncovered, 25 to 35 minutes or until thermometer inserted into center of pork registers 155°F. Let pork stand, tented with foil, 5 to 10 minutes. (Temperature of pork will rise to 160°F.) Slice pork.

3 Melt margarine in small saucepan over medium heat. Add mushrooms, green onion and garlic; cook and stir until vegetables are tender. Stir in cornstarch, parsley, thyme and pepper. Stir in water, sherry and bouillon granules. Cook and stir until sauce thickens and boils; boil 2 minutes. Spoon sauce over pork.

Makes 4 servings

Nutrients per Serving:

Calories	179 (30% of calories from fat)					
Total Fat	6 g	Carbohydrate	4 g	Iron		2 mg
Saturated Fat	2 g	Dietary Fiber	<1 g	Vitamin A		53 RE
Cholesterol	81 mg	Protein	26 g	Vitamin C		3 mg
Sodium	205 mg	Calcium	16 mg			

DIETARY EXCHANGES: 3 Lean Meat, 1 Vegetable

HONEY GLAZED PORK

Quick-cooking pork tenderloin is an ideal choice for easy entertaining. Here, it's infused with flavor from a simple marinade and roasted to juicy succulence.

¼ cup reduced sodium soy sauce
2 cloves garlic, minced
1 large or 2 small pork tenderloins (about 1¼ pounds total)
3 tablespoons honey

2 tablespoons brown sugar
1 teaspoon minced fresh ginger
1 tablespoon toasted sesame seeds*
Washed and torn lettuce leaves (optional)

1 Combine soy sauce and garlic in large resealable plastic food storage bag; add pork. Seal bag; turn to coat. Marinate in refrigerator up to 2 hours, turning occasionally.

2 Preheat oven to 400°F. Drain pork; reserve 1 tablespoon marinade. Combine honey, brown sugar, ginger and reserved marinade in small bowl.

3 Place pork in shallow foil-lined roasting pan. Brush with half of honey mixture. Roast 10 minutes. Turn pork over; brush with remaining honey mixture; sprinkle with sesame seeds. Roast 10 minutes for small or 15 minutes for large tenderloin or until internal temperature reaches 155°F when tested with a meat thermometer inserted in thickest part of pork.

4 Let pork stand, tented with foil, on cutting board 5 minutes. (Temperature of pork will rise to 160°F.) Cut into ½-inch slices. Serve on lettuce and garnish with mushrooms, if desired. *Makes 4 servings*

*To toast sesame seeds, spread seeds in small skillet. Shake skillet over medium heat 2 minutes or until seeds begin to pop and turn golden.

Nutrients per Serving:

Calories	279 (20% of calories from fat)				
Total Fat	6 g	Carbohydrate	21 g	Iron	3 mg
Saturated Fat	2 g	Dietary Fiber	<1 g	Vitamin A	2 RE
Cholesterol	101 mg	Protein	33 g	Vitamin C	1 mg
Sodium	605 mg	Calcium	24 mg		

DIETARY EXCHANGES: 4 Lean Meat, 1 Fruit

TANDOORI PORK SAUTE

The sweetness of the plums offsets the earthy flavors of this traditional Indian dish.

Nutty Rice (recipe follows)
½ pound lean pork, cut into
    2 × ½-inch strips
½ cup sliced onion
1 clove garlic, minced
4 fresh California plums, halved,
    pitted and cut into thick
    wedges

1 cup plain low fat yogurt
1 tablespoon all-purpose flour
1½ teaspoons grated fresh ginger
½ teaspoon ground turmeric
⅛ teaspoon ground black pepper
Additional plum wedges,
    orange sections and sliced
    green onions

1 Prepare Nutty Rice.

2 Cook pork in nonstick skillet over medium-high heat, 2 minutes or until browned, turning occasionally. Remove pork from skillet; set aside.

3 Add onion and garlic to skillet; cook 1 minute. Add plums; cook and stir 1 minute. Remove from heat.

4 Return pork to skillet. Combine yogurt and flour; add to skillet. Stir in ginger, turmeric and pepper; bring to a boil over high heat. Reduce heat. Simmer 10 minutes, stirring occasionally.

5 Spoon pork and fruit over Nutty Rice; surround with plum wedges, orange sections and green onions.   *Makes 4 servings*

Nutty Rice: Heat 2 cups water in medium saucepan to a boil. Add ¾ cup brown rice and ¼ cup wheat berries. (Or, omit wheat berries and use 1 cup brown rice.) Return to a boil. Cover; reduce heat to low. Simmer 40 to 45 minutes or until rice is tender and liquid is absorbed. Makes about 2 cups.

Nutrients per Serving:
includes ½ cup rice

Calories	287 (13% of calories from fat)				
Total Fat	4 g	Carbohydrate	43 g	Iron	2 mg
Saturated Fat	2 g	Dietary Fiber	3 g	Vitamin A	20 RE
Cholesterol	44 mg	Protein	19 g	Vitamin C	3 mg
Sodium	73 mg	Calcium	127 mg		

DIETARY EXCHANGES: 2 Starch/Bread, 2 Lean Meat, ½ Fruit

CHILE VERDE

"Sweating"—cooking meat and onion in a little water to extract the meat's juices—is a handy technique that replaces cooking in oil. After 30 minutes the lid is removed and the liquid is boiled down and browned to provide that rich color and flavor usually associated with sautéing.

½ to ¾ pound boneless lean pork
1 large onion, halved, thinly
    sliced
4 cloves garlic, chopped or sliced
½ cup water
1 pound fresh tomatillos
1 can (about 14 ounces) ⅓-less-
    salt chicken broth
1 can (4 ounces) diced mild
    green chilies

1 teaspoon ground cumin
1½ cups cooked navy or Great
    Northern beans *or* 1 can
    (15 ounces) Great Northern
    beans, rinsed and drained
½ cup lightly packed fresh
    cilantro, chopped
Plain nonfat yogurt (optional)

1 Trim fat from pork; discard. Cut meat into ¾- to 1-inch cubes. Place pork, onion, garlic and ½ cup water in large saucepan. Cover; simmer over medium-low heat 30 minutes, stirring occasionally (add more water if necessary). Uncover; boil over medium-high heat until liquid evaporates and meat browns.

2 Add tomatillos and chicken broth; stir. Cover; simmer over medium heat 20 minutes or until tomatillos are tender. Tear tomatillos apart with 2 forks. Add chilies and cumin. Cover; simmer over medium-low heat 45 minutes or until meat is tender and tears apart easily (add more water or broth to keep liquid level the same). Add beans; simmer 10 minutes or until heated through. Stir in cilantro. Serve with yogurt, if desired.   *Makes 4 servings*

Nutrients per Serving:

Calories	311 (14% of calories from fat)				
Total Fat	5 g	Carbohydrate	42 g	Iron	4 mg
Saturated Fat	1 g	Dietary Fiber	6 g	Vitamin A	51 RE
Cholesterol	40 mg	Protein	26 g	Vitamin C	56 mg
Sodium	51 mg	Calcium	89 mg		

DIETARY EXCHANGES: 1 Starch/Bread, 2 Lean Meat, ½ Vegetable

TACOS WITH CARNITAS

2 pounds pork leg, shoulder or
   butt roast, fat trimmed
1 medium onion, peeled,
   quartered
2 tablespoons chili powder
1 tablespoon dried oregano
   leaves
3 bay leaves
1 teaspoon ground cumin

Salsa Cruda (page 38)
16 (6-inch) corn tortillas
4 cups washed and torn lettuce
   leaves
1 cup crumbled feta cheese
   (optional)
1 can (4 ounces) diced mild
   green chilies

1 Preheat oven to 450°F. Place pork, onion, chili powder, oregano, bay leaves and cumin in large saucepan or Dutch oven. Add enough water to cover pork. Cover; bring to a boil over high heat. Reduce heat to medium-low; simmer 3 hours or until meat pulls apart easily when tested with fork.

2 Meanwhile, prepare Salsa Cruda; set aside.

3 Transfer meat to baking pan. Bake 20 minutes or until surface is browned and crisp. Meanwhile, skim fat from cooking liquid. Bring to a boil over high heat; boil 20 minutes or until mixture reduces to about 1 cup. Remove bay leaves; discard.

4 Shred meat by pulling apart with 2 forks. Add meat to reduced cooking liquid; stir to coat completely. Cover; simmer 10 minutes or until meat absorbs most of liquid.

5 Heat large nonstick skillet over medium-high heat until hot. Place 2 inches water in medium bowl. Dip 1 tortilla in water; shake off excess. Place in skillet. Cook 30 seconds on each side or until tortilla is hot, pliable and slightly firm. Transfer to plate; cover to keep warm. Repeat with remaining tortillas.

6 Top each tortilla with ¼ cup lettuce, ¼ cup meat, 1 tablespoon cheese, if desired, 1 teaspoon chilies and 1 tablespoon Salsa Cruda.   *Makes 8 servings*

Nutrients per Serving:

Calories	292 (24% of calories from fat)				
Total Fat	8 g	Carbohydrate	28 g	Iron	3 mg
Saturated Fat	2 g	Dietary Fiber	2 g	Vitamin A	153 RE
Cholesterol	55 mg	Protein	28 g	Vitamin C	32 mg
Sodium	163 mg	Calcium	130 mg		

DIETARY EXCHANGES: 2 Starch/Bread, 3 Lean Meat

RACK OF LAMB WITH DIJON-MUSTARD CRUST

If you prefer really rare lamb turn the oven off after 5 minutes. If you like your lamb well done leave the oven on for 10 to 12 minutes. You may leave the lamb in the oven for more than 30 minutes; what is crucial is that you turn off the oven at the correct time.

1 rack of lamb (3 pounds), all
    visible fat removed
1 cup finely chopped fresh
    parsley
½ cup Dijon mustard
½ cup soft whole wheat bread
    crumbs

1 tablespoon chopped fresh
    rosemary *or* 2 teaspoons
    dried rosemary
1 teaspoon minced garlic
    Rosemary Bread Sticks
    (page 166)

1 Preheat oven to 500°F. Place lamb in large baking pan.

2 Combine parsley, mustard, bread crumbs, rosemary and garlic in small bowl; blend well. Brush evenly over top of lamb. Place in center of oven; cook 7 minutes for medium-rare. *Turn off oven but do not open door for at least 30 minutes.*

3 Serve 2 to 3 chops on each plate, depending on size and total number of chops. Serve with Rosemary Bread Sticks. Garnish with additional fresh rosemary, lemon slices and lemon peel strips, if desired.

Makes 6 servings

Nutrients per Serving:

4 ounces lamb with 2 bread sticks

Calories	437 (37% of calories from fat)				
Total Fat	18 g	Carbohydrate	28 g	Iron	5 mg
Saturated Fat	6 g	Dietary Fiber	3 g	Vitamin A	71 RE
Cholesterol	111 mg	Protein	40 g	Vitamin C	14 mg
Sodium	790 mg	Calcium	131 mg		

DIETARY EXCHANGES: 2 Starch/Bread, 4 Medium-Fat Meat

LAMB & GREEN CHILE STEW

Stew, in one form or another, is a basic dish worldwide. The combination of meats, fruits, vegetables and often grains offers a nearly perfect balance of nutrients—all from only one pot.

1 pound boneless lean lamb, cubed
½ cup water
1 large onion, halved, sliced
6 cloves garlic, chopped or sliced
2 cans (15 ounces each) no-salt-added whole tomatoes, undrained
1 pound potatoes

3 cans (4 ounces each) diced mild green chilies
2 teaspoons dried rosemary
1 teaspoon dried oregano leaves
1 pound zucchini
1 cup frozen whole kernel corn, thawed, drained
Ground black pepper to taste

1 Combine lamb, water, onion and garlic in large saucepan; bring to a simmer over medium-high heat. Cover; simmer 30 minutes or until onion is tender. Uncover; bring to a boil over high heat until liquid evaporates, stirring occasionally. Add tomatoes with liquid; stir. Reduce heat to medium-low. Cover; simmer 30 minutes.

2 Meanwhile, cut potatoes into 1½-inch pieces. Add potatoes, chilies, rosemary and oregano to saucepan. Cover; simmer 20 to 30 minutes or until potatoes and lamb are tender.

3 Halve zucchini lengthwise and cut crosswise into ½- to ¾-inch pieces. Add zucchini and corn to saucepan. Cover; simmer 10 minutes or until zucchini is crisp-tender. Season with pepper. Garnish with jalapeños, if desired.

Makes 6 servings

Nutrients per Serving:

Calories	246 (15% of calories from fat)					
Total Fat	4 g	Carbohydrate	37 g	Iron	4 mg
Saturated Fat	1 g	Dietary Fiber	6 g	Vitamin A	126 RE
Cholesterol	38 mg	Protein	18 g	Vitamin C	123 mg
Sodium	58 mg	Calcium	85 mg		

DIETARY EXCHANGES: 1½ Starch/Bread, 1½ Lean Meat, 2½ Vegetable

APPLE-ICIOUS LAMB KABOBS

1 cup apple juice or cider
2 tablespoons Worcestershire sauce
½ teaspoon lemon pepper
2 cloves garlic, peeled and sliced
1½ pounds fresh American lamb, cut into 1¼-inch cubes

Apple Barbecue Sauce (recipe follows)
1 large apple, cut into 12 wedges
Assorted vegetables, cut into wedges

1 Combine apple juice, Worcestershire sauce, lemon pepper and garlic in large resealable plastic food storage bag; add lamb. Seal bag; turn to coat. Marinate in refrigerator 2 to 24 hours, turning occasionally.

2 To prevent sticking, spray grill with nonstick cooking spray. Prepare coals for grilling. Prepare Apple Barbecue Sauce; set aside.

3 Remove meat from marinade. Alternately thread meat, apple and vegetables onto skewers. (If using bamboo skewers, soak in water 20 minutes before using to prevent them from burning.) Place kabobs on grill, 4 inches from medium coals. Grill 10 to 12 minutes or until desired doneness, turning occasionally and brushing with Apple Barbecue Sauce.   *Makes 6 servings*

APPLE BARBECUE SAUCE

½ cup finely chopped onion
½ cup apple juice or cider
1 cup chili sauce
½ cup unsweetened applesauce
2 tablespoons brown sugar

1 tablespoon Worcestershire sauce
1 teaspoon dry mustard
5 drops hot pepper sauce

1 Combine onion and apple juice in 1-quart saucepan; simmer 2 minutes. Stir in remaining ingredients. Simmer 10 minutes. Makes about 2 cups.

Nutrients per Serving:

includes 2 tablespoons Apple Barbecue Sauce

Calories	180 (29% of calories from fat)					
Total Fat	5 g	Carbohydrate	11 g	Iron		2 mg
Saturated Fat	2 g	Dietary Fiber	2 g	Vitamin A		21 RE
Cholesterol	57 mg	Protein	19 g	Vitamin C		26 mg
Sodium	64 mg	Calcium	26 mg			

DIETARY EXCHANGES: 2 Lean Meat, 1 Vegetable, 1 Fruit

PRONTO PIZZA

6 ounces lean fresh ground
   American lamb
½ teaspoon onion salt
½ teaspoon fennel seeds
¼ teaspoon dried oregano leaves
¼ teaspoon dried basil leaves
⅛ teaspoon crushed red pepper
   Nonstick cooking spray
½ cup chopped green or red bell
   pepper
½ cup chopped Italian plum
   tomatoes

1 (10- to 12-inch) prebaked pizza
   shell
½ cup pizza sauce
1 tablespoon grated Parmesan
   cheese
¼ cup thinly sliced fresh basil
   leaves (optional)
½ cup (2 ounces) shredded part-
   skim mozzarella cheese

1 Preheat oven to 450°F. Combine lamb, onion salt, fennel, oregano, dried basil and red pepper in small bowl; blend well.

2 Spray large nonstick skillet with cooking spray; add lamb. Cook over medium-high heat until lightly browned, stirring occasionally to crumble. Drain on paper towel. In same skillet, cook and stir bell pepper 3 to 4 minutes. Add tomatoes; cook and stir 1 minute.

3 Place pizza shell on cookie sheet or pizza pan; top with pizza sauce and vegetables. Sprinkle with Parmesan cheese, fresh basil, cooked lamb and mozzarella cheese. Bake 8 to 10 minutes. Cool 5 minutes; slice into wedges.

Makes 6 servings

Microwave Directions: Cook lamb mixture in 2-quart microwavable dish at HIGH 3 minutes, stirring occasionally to crumble. Add bell pepper and tomatoes; microwave at HIGH 2 minutes, stirring once. Drain well. Assemble and bake pizza as directed.

Nutrients per Serving:

Calories	218 (22% of calories from fat)				
Total Fat	5 g	Carbohydrate	31 g	Iron	2 mg
Saturated Fat	2 g	Dietary Fiber	1 g	Vitamin A	83 RE
Cholesterol	20 mg	Protein	12 g	Vitamin C	26 mg
Sodium	360 mg	Calcium	96 mg		

DIETARY EXCHANGES: 1½ Starch/Bread, 1 Lean Meat, 1 Vegetable

ZESTY LAMB TACO SKILLET

Substituting lamb for beef or chicken creates a tasty new version of this traditional Mexican dish.

1 tablespoon vegetable or olive oil
1 pound boneless lamb, cut into ⅛-inch strips (leg or shoulder)
1 clove garlic, minced
1½ cans (21 ounces) ⅓-less-salt beef broth
1½ cans (12 ounces) tomato sauce
1 package taco seasoning mix (about 1.25 ounces)

2 cups green or red bell pepper strips
1½ cups whole kernel corn, fresh or frozen
2 cups quick-cooking rice, white or brown
Shredded Cheddar cheese (optional)
Sliced ripe olives (optional)
Tortilla chips (optional)

1 Heat oil in large skillet over medium-high heat until hot. Add lamb strips and garlic. Cook and stir lamb until desired doneness.

2 Add beef broth, tomato sauce and seasoning mix; bring to a boil over high heat. Reduce heat. Cover; simmer 5 minutes.

3 Add bell peppers and corn; bring to a boil over high heat. Stir in rice; remove from heat. Cover; let stand 5 minutes or until liquid is absorbed. Fluff with fork. Top with cheese, sliced ripe olives and crushed tortilla chips, if desired.

Makes 6 servings

Nutrients per Serving:

Calories	341 (20% of calories from fat)				
Total Fat	8 g	Carbohydrate	48 g	Iron	3 mg
Saturated Fat	2 g	Dietary Fiber	3 g	Vitamin A	113 RE
Cholesterol	46 mg	Protein	21 g	Vitamin C	72 mg
Sodium	960 mg	Calcium	33 mg		

DIETARY EXCHANGES: 2½ Starch/Bread, 2 Lean Meat, 2 Vegetable, ½ Fat

POULTRY

GRILLED MARINATED CHICKEN

Although dark meat has more fat than white meat, removing the skin before grilling eliminates a lot of the fat. By marinating the chicken overnight in this tasty fat free marinade, the chicken stays moist even without the skin.

8 chicken hind quarters (thigh and drumsticks attached, about 3½ lbs)
6 ounces frozen lemonade concentrate, thawed
2 tablespoons white wine vinegar
1 tablespoon grated lemon peel
2 cloves garlic, minced
Garlic Bread (page 160)

1 Remove skin and all visible fat from chicken. Place chicken in 13×9-inch glass baking dish. Combine remaining ingredients except Garlic Bread in small bowl; blend well. Pour over chicken; turn to coat. Cover; refrigerate 3 hours or overnight, turning occasionally.

2 To prevent sticking, spray grill with nonstick cooking spray. Prepare coals for grilling.

3 Place chicken on grill 4 inches from medium-hot coals. Grill 20 to 30 minutes or until chicken is no longer pink near bone, turning occasionally. (Do not overcook or chicken will be dry.) Serve with Garlic Bread. Garnish with curly endive and lemon peel strips, if desired.   *Makes 8 servings*

Nutrients per Serving:
1 chicken quarter with 2 pieces Garlic Bread

Calories	518 (28% of calories from fat)				
Total Fat	16 g	Carbohydrate	57 g	Iron	4 mg
Saturated Fat	4 g	Dietary Fiber	1 g	Vitamin A	21 RE
Cholesterol	93 mg	Protein	35 g	Vitamin C	11 mg
Sodium	609 mg	Calcium	129 mg		

DIETARY EXCHANGES: 4 Starch/Bread, 3½ Lean Meat, ½ Vegetable, ½ Fat

GRILLED CHICKEN WITH SOUTHERN BARBECUE SAUCE

Nonstick cooking spray
½ cup chopped onion
4 cloves garlic, minced
1 can (16 ounces) no-salt-added tomato sauce
¾ cup water
3 tablespoons firmly packed light brown sugar
3 tablespoons chili sauce
2 teaspoons chili powder

2 teaspoons dried thyme leaves
2 teaspoons white wine Worcestershire sauce
¾ teaspoon ground red pepper
½ teaspoon ground cinnamon
½ teaspoon ground black pepper
6 skinless chicken breast halves (2¼ pounds)
6 medium Idaho potatoes, baked, hot

1 To prevent sticking, spray grill with nonstick cooking spray. Prepare coals for grilling.

2 Spray medium nonstick skillet with cooking spray; heat over medium heat until hot. Add onion and garlic; cook and stir about 5 minutes or until tender. Stir in tomato sauce, water, sugar, chili sauce, chili powder, thyme, Worcestershire sauce, red pepper, cinnamon and black pepper; bring to a boil over high heat. Reduce heat to low; simmer, uncovered, 30 minutes or until mixture is reduced to 1½ cups. Pour ¾ cup sauce into small bowl for basting; reserve.

3 Place chicken on grill 4 inches from medium-hot coals. Grill, covered, 40 to 45 minutes or until chicken is no longer pink in center, turning occasionally and basting with reserved sauce.

4 Heat reserved sauce in skillet over medium heat until hot; spoon over chicken. Serve with potatoes. Serve with additional vegetables, if desired.

Makes 6 servings

Nutrients per Serving:

Calories	357 (8% of calories from fat)				
Total Fat	3 g	Carbohydrate	51 g	Iron	3 mg
Saturated Fat	1 g	Dietary Fiber	5 g	Vitamin A	132 RE
Cholesterol	69 mg	Protein	30 g	Vitamin C	11 mg
Sodium	218 mg	Calcium	61 mg		

DIETARY EXCHANGES: 2 Starch/Bread, 3 Lean Meat, 1 Fruit

CHICKEN AND CURRIED FRUIT

The intense, sweet flavor and chewy texture of dried fruit is highlighted by curry and other flavorings in this simple entrée. Leftover dried fruit may be sprinkled over cereal or tossed in pilafs or stuffings. Remember, a little goes a long way—although low in fat, dried fruit is higher in calories than fresh fruit.

6 skinless chicken breast halves
   (2¼ pounds)
1 cup mixed diced dried fruit
½ cup chopped onion
¼ cup chopped chutney
3 cloves garlic, minced
1 to 1½ teaspoons curry powder

1 teaspoon ground cumin
¼ teaspoon ground red pepper
¼ teaspoon ground allspice
2½ cups ⅓-less-salt chicken broth
½ cup dry sherry or apple juice
3 cups hot, cooked white rice or
   couscous

1 Preheat oven to 350°F. Arrange chicken, breast side up, in single layer in 13×9-inch baking pan. Place dried fruit around chicken. Combine onion, chutney, garlic, curry powder, cumin, red pepper and allspice in medium bowl; stir in chicken broth and sherry. Pour mixture over chicken and fruit.

2 Cover; bake 30 minutes. Uncover; bake about 15 minutes or until chicken is no longer pink in center.

3 Remove chicken from pan; arrange over rice on serving platter. In food processor or blender combine half the fruit and half the liquid mixture from pan; process until smooth. Spoon over chicken. Discard remaining liquid mixture. Arrange remaining fruit over chicken.   *Makes 6 servings*

Nutrients per Serving:

Calories	383 (7% of calories from fat)				
Total Fat	4 g	Carbohydrate	52 g	Iron	3 mg
Saturated Fat	1 g	Dietary Fiber	3 g	Vitamin A	70 RE
Cholesterol	69 mg	Protein	29 g	Vitamin C	11 mg
Sodium	81 mg	Calcium	51 mg		

DIETARY EXCHANGES: 2 Starch/Bread, 3 Lean Meat, 1 Fruit

MANDARIN ORANGE CHICKEN

1 pound boneless skinless
   chicken breasts
⅛ teaspoon salt
⅛ teaspoon ground black pepper
   Nonstick cooking spray
½ cup finely chopped onion
½ cup orange juice
2 teaspoons minced fresh ginger

1 teaspoon sugar
¼ cup cold water
2 teaspoons cornstarch
1 can (11 ounces) mandarin
   orange segments, drained
2 to 3 tablespoons finely chopped
   fresh cilantro
2 cups hot, cooked white rice

1 Preheat broiler.

2 Place chicken between 2 pieces of waxed paper; pound to ¼-inch thickness using flat side of meat mallet or rolling pin.

3 Spray rack of broiler pan with cooking spray. Place chicken on rack. Broil, 4 inches from heat, 14 to 16 minutes or until chicken is no longer pink in center, turning occasionally. Or, place chicken 4 inches from medium-hot coals. Grill, covered, 20 minutes or until chicken is no longer pink in center, turning occasionally. Sprinkle with salt and pepper.

4 Spray medium nonstick saucepan with cooking spray; heat over medium heat until hot. Add onion; cook and stir about 5 minutes or until tender. Add orange juice, ginger and sugar; bring to a boil over high heat.

5 Combine water and cornstarch in small bowl; add to juice mixture, stirring until thickened. Boil 1 minute, stirring constantly. Stir in orange segments and cilantro.

6 Serve chicken over rice; top with sauce. Garnish with additional cilantro.

Makes 4 servings

Nutrients per Serving:

Calories	310 (9% of calories from fat)				
Total Fat	3 g	Carbohydrate	43 g	Iron	2 mg
Saturated Fat	1 g	Dietary Fiber	2 g	Vitamin A	36 RE
Cholesterol	58 mg	Protein	25 g	Vitamin C	39 mg
Sodium	122 mg	Calcium	44 mg		

DIETARY EXCHANGES: 2 Starch/Bread, 2½ Lean Meat, ½ Fruit

CHICKEN WITH MANDARIN ORANGE AND WATER CHESTNUT SAUCE

Water chestnuts, which are often mistaken for the chestnut, are the edible tubers of the water chestnut plant. They are cultivated in the southeastern regions of Asia and the United States and their mildly sweet flavor is a refreshing addition to this sauce.

¼ cup water
2 teaspoons cornstarch
1 can (11 ounces) mandarin oranges, drained
1 can (8 ounces) sliced water chestnuts, drained
2 tablespoons white vinegar

4 teaspoons brown sugar
1 tablespoon reduced sodium soy sauce
1½ cups chicken broth or stock
4 boneless skinless chicken breasts (about 1 pound)

1 Combine water and cornstarch in cup. Combine cornstarch mixture, mandarin oranges, water chestnuts, vinegar, brown sugar and soy sauce in small saucepan; cook over medium-high heat 4 to 5 minutes or until sauce is clear, and thickens, stirring occasionally. Remove from heat.

2 Meanwhile, place chicken broth in large skillet; bring to a simmer over medium heat.

3 Place chicken breasts between 2 pieces of waxed paper; pound to ½-inch thickness using flat side of meat mallet or rolling pin. Place chicken in skillet; cover. Simmer over medium-low heat 8 to 10 minutes or until chicken is no longer pink in center. Remove chicken from skillet; place on serving platter. Heat sauce if needed; spoon sauce over chicken.

Makes 4 servings

Nutrients per Serving:

Calories	253 (18% of calories from fat)				
Total Fat	5 g	Carbohydrate	22 g	Iron	2 mg
Saturated Fat	1 g	Dietary Fiber	<1 g	Vitamin A	31 RE
Cholesterol	73 mg	Protein	20 g	Vitamin C	23 mg
Sodium	755 mg	Calcium	35 mg		

DIETARY EXCHANGES: 3 Lean Meat, 1 Fruit, 1 Vegetable

HONEY LIME GLAZED CHICKEN

A cinch to prepare, this is truly a honey of a dish. The sweet-sour sauce glazes the chicken beautifully.

1 broiler-fryer chicken,
    quartered (about 3 pounds)
    or 3 pounds chicken pieces
⅓ cup honey
2 tablespoons fresh lime juice

1½ tablespoons reduced sodium
    soy sauce
3 cups hot, cooked noodles
    (3½ ounces uncooked)

1 Preheat oven to 375°F. Arrange chicken, skin side up, in single layer in shallow casserole dish or 11×7-inch baking dish.

2 Combine remaining ingredients except noodles in small bowl; blend well. Brush one-third of honey mixture over chicken; bake 15 minutes.

3 Brush remaining honey mixture over chicken; bake 10 to 15 minutes more or until juices run clear. Transfer to serving platter. Serve with noodles.

Makes 4 servings

Nutrients per Serving:

Calories	683 (30% of calories from fat)				
Total Fat	23 g	Carbohydrate	56 g	Iron	3 mg
Saturated Fat	6 g	Dietary Fiber	1 g	Vitamin A	39 RE
Cholesterol	163 mg	Protein	60 g	Vitamin C	2 mg
Sodium	295 mg	Calcium	30 mg		

DIETARY EXCHANGES: 1 Starch/Bread, 4½ Lean Meat, 1½ Fruit

CHICKEN SCALOPPINE WITH LEMON-CAPER SAUCE

Healthy eating requires healthy cooking techniques. To minimize the oil normally used to pan-fry scaloppine, use a well seasoned or heavy-bottomed pan and spray it with nonstick cooking spray before heating.

1 pound boneless skinless
    chicken breasts
3 tablespoons all-purpose flour,
    divided
¼ teaspoon ground black pepper
¼ teaspoon chili powder

½ cup ⅓-less-salt chicken broth
1 tablespoon lemon juice
1 tablespoon drained capers
    Nonstick cooking spray
½ teaspoon olive oil, divided

1 Place chicken between 2 pieces of waxed paper; pound to ¼-inch thickness using flat side of meat mallet or rolling pin. Combine 2 tablespoons flour, pepper and chili powder in shallow plate. Dip chicken in flour mixture; lightly coat both sides.

2 Combine remaining flour, chicken broth, lemon juice and capers in small bowl.

3 Spray large skillet with cooking spray; heat over medium-high heat until hot. Place chicken in skillet in single layer; cook 1½ minutes. Turn over; cook 1 to 1½ minutes or until chicken is no longer pink in center. Repeat with remaining chicken (brush pan with ¼ teaspoon oil each time you add pieces to prevent sticking). If cooking more than 2 batches, reduce heat to medium to prevent chicken from burning.

4 Pour broth mixture into skillet. Boil, uncovered, until thickened and reduced to about ¼ cup. Spoon sauce over chicken; serve immediately.

Makes 4 servings

Nutrients per Serving:					
Calories	144 (26% of calories from fat)				
Total Fat	4 g	Carbohydrate	4 g	Iron	1 mg
Saturated Fat	1 g	Dietary Fiber	<1 g	Vitamin A	22 RE
Cholesterol	58 mg	Protein	22 g	Vitamin C	2 mg
Sodium	67 mg	Calcium	13 mg		

DIETARY EXCHANGES: 2½ Lean Meat

LIGHT-STYLE LEMON CHICKEN

Cabbage is an excellent source of indoles—a family of compounds that enhance the activity of our body's cancer-fighting enzymes.

2 egg whites, slightly beaten
¾ cup fresh bread crumbs
2 tablespoons sesame seeds
   (optional)
¾ teaspoon salt
¼ teaspoon ground black pepper
4 boneless skinless chicken
   breast halves (about
   1¼ pounds)

2 tablespoons all-purpose flour
¾ cup ⅓-less-salt chicken broth
4 teaspoons cornstarch
¼ cup fresh lemon juice
2 tablespoons brown sugar
1 tablespoon honey
2 tablespoons vegetable oil
4 cups thinly sliced napa
   cabbage or romaine lettuce

1 Place egg whites in shallow dish. Combine bread crumbs, sesame seeds, salt and pepper in another shallow dish.

2 Dust chicken with flour; dip into egg whites. Roll in crumb mixture to coat.

3 Combine chicken broth and cornstarch in small bowl; blend until smooth. Stir in lemon juice, brown sugar and honey.

4 Heat oil in large nonstick skillet over medium heat until hot. Add chicken; cook 5 minutes. Turn chicken over; cook 5 to 6 minutes or until no longer pink in center. Transfer to cutting board; keep warm.

5 Wipe skillet clean with paper towel. Stir broth mixture; add to skillet. Cook and stir 3 to 4 minutes until sauce boils and thickens.

6 Place cabbage on serving dish. Cut chicken crosswise into ½-inch slices; place over cabbage. Spoon sauce over chicken. Garnish with lemon slices and fresh herbs, if desired.

Makes 4 servings

Nutrients per Serving:

Calories	397 (31% of calories from fat)				
Total Fat	14 g	Carbohydrate	37 g	Iron	3 mg
Saturated Fat	2 g	Dietary Fiber	4 g	Vitamin A	32 RE
Cholesterol	73 mg	Protein	33 g	Vitamin C	103 mg
Sodium	607 mg	Calcium	131 mg		

DIETARY EXCHANGES: 2 Starch/Bread, 3 Lean Meat, 2 Vegetable, ½ Fat

SWEET AND SOUR CHICKEN

To lighten this dish, the chicken is stir-fried instead of deep-fat fried. The result is a very flavorful, low fat entrée sure to delight sweet and sour lovers.

6 ounces boneless skinless
    chicken breasts
2 tablespoons rice vinegar
2 tablespoons reduced sodium
    soy sauce
3 cloves garlic, minced
½ teaspoon minced fresh ginger
¼ teaspoon crushed red pepper
    (optional)
1 teaspoon vegetable oil
3 green onions, cut into 1-inch
    pieces

1 large green bell pepper, cut
    into 1-inch squares
1 tablespoon cornstarch
½ cup ⅓-less-salt chicken broth
2 tablespoons apricot fruit
    spread
1 can (11 ounces) mandarin
    orange segments
2 cups hot, cooked white rice or
    Chinese egg noodles

1 Cut chicken crosswise into ½-inch strips. Combine vinegar, soy sauce, garlic, ginger and red pepper in large resealable plastic food storage bag; add chicken. Seal bag; turn to coat. Marinate at room temperature for no more than 20 minutes, turning occasionally.

2 Heat oil in wok or large nonstick skillet over medium heat until hot. Drain chicken; reserve marinade. Add chicken to wok; stir-fry 3 minutes or until no longer pink in center. Stir in onions and bell pepper.

3 Stir cornstarch into reserved marinade.

4 Stir marinade mixture, chicken broth and fruit spread into wok. Cook and stir 1 minute or until sauce boils and thickens. Add orange segments; heat through. Serve over rice. Garnish with orange slices and fresh herbs, if desired.

Makes 4 servings

Nutrients per Serving:

Calories	256 (8% of calories from fat)					
Total Fat	2 g	Carbohydrate	48 g	Iron	2 mg
Saturated Fat	<1 g	Dietary Fiber	2 g	Vitamin A	98 RE
Cholesterol	17 mg	Protein	11 g	Vitamin C	46 mg
Sodium	291 mg	Calcium	36 mg		

DIETARY EXCHANGES: 2 Starch/Bread, 1 Lean Meat, 1 Vegetable, ½ Fruit

SESAME CHICKEN AND VEGETABLE STIR-FRY

Start on your way toward eating five servings of fruits and vegetables a day with this delicious stir-fry, flavored with traditional Chinese spices and a touch of sesame oil.

1 tablespoon Oriental sesame oil
1 pound chicken tenders, cut
    into 1-inch pieces
2 cups broccoli flowerets
1 small red bell pepper, sliced
½ cup onion slices
½ cup snow peas
1 can (8 ounces) water
    chestnuts, sliced and
    drained

2 cloves garlic, minced
1 teaspoon five-spice powder
1 cup ⅓-less-salt chicken broth
2 teaspoons cornstarch
2 tablespoons cold water
2 cups hot, cooked white rice

1 Heat sesame oil in wok or large nonstick skillet over medium heat until hot. Add chicken; stir-fry about 8 minutes or until chicken is no longer pink in center. Remove chicken from wok; set aside.

2 Add broccoli, bell pepper, onion, peas, water chestnuts and garlic to wok; stir-fry 5 to 8 minutes or until vegetables are crisp-tender. Sprinkle with five-spice powder; stir-fry 1 minute.

3 Return chicken to wok. Add chicken broth; bring to a boil. Combine cornstarch and water in small bowl; stir into broth mixture. Boil 1 to 2 minutes, stirring constantly. Serve over rice. *Makes 4 servings*

Nutrients per Serving:						
Calories	354 (19% of calories from fat)					
Total Fat	7 g	Carbohydrate	44 g	Iron	3 mg
Saturated Fat	1 g	Dietary Fiber	3 g	Vitamin A	89 RE
Cholesterol	59 mg	Protein	27 g	Vitamin C	71 mg
Sodium	83 mg	Calcium	64 mg		

DIETARY EXCHANGES: 2 Starch/Bread, 2½ Lean Meat, 2 Vegetable, ½ Fat

SHANGHAI CHICKEN WITH ASPARAGUS AND HAM

At only 40 calories per cup, asparagus is loaded with nutrition. Not only is it low in fat and calories, it is also rich in potassium, niacin, and vitamins A and C.

2 cups diagonally cut 1-inch
   asparagus pieces*
1 pound boneless skinless
   chicken breasts
2 teaspoons vegetable oil

¾ cup coarsely chopped onion
2 cloves garlic, minced
2 tablespoons teriyaki sauce
¼ cup diced deli ham
2 cups hot, cooked white rice

1 To blanch asparagus pieces, cook 3 minutes in enough boiling water to cover. Plunge asparagus into cold water. Drain well.

2 Cut chicken into 1-inch pieces.

3 Heat oil in large nonstick skillet over medium heat until hot. Add onion and garlic; stir-fry 2 minutes. Add chicken; stir-fry 2 minutes. Add asparagus; stir-fry 2 minutes or until chicken is no longer pink in center.

4 Stir in teriyaki sauce; mix well. Add ham; stir-fry until heated through. Serve over rice. Garnish with carrot strips and fresh herbs, if desired.

Makes 4 servings

*Or substitute thawed frozen asparagus; omit step 1.

Nutrients per Serving:

Calories	289 (16% of calories from fat)				
Total Fat	5 g	Carbohydrate	37 g	Iron	2 mg
Saturated Fat	1 g	Dietary Fiber	3 g	Vitamin A	78 RE
Cholesterol	46 mg	Protein	24 g	Vitamin C	27 mg
Sodium	263 mg	Calcium	53 mg		

DIETARY EXCHANGES: 2 Starch/Bread, 2½ Lean Meat

CHICKEN CHOP SUEY

Chop suey was first concocted by Chinese cooks in the mid-nineteenth century to feed the workers on the Pacific railroad lines. It literally means "chopped up" leftovers.

1 package (1 ounce) dried black Chinese mushrooms
3 tablespoons reduced sodium soy sauce
1 tablespoon cornstarch
1 pound boneless skinless chicken breasts or thighs
2 cloves garlic, minced

1 tablespoon peanut or vegetable oil
½ cup thinly sliced celery
½ cup sliced water chestnuts
½ cup bamboo shoots
1 cup chicken broth
Hot, cooked white rice or chow mein noodles

1 Place mushrooms in small bowl; cover with warm water. Soak 20 minutes to soften. Drain; squeeze out excess water. Discard stems; chop caps.

2 Combine soy sauce and cornstarch in cup.

3 Cut chicken into 1-inch pieces; toss with garlic in small bowl.

4 Heat oil in wok or large skillet over medium-high heat until hot. Add chicken mixture and celery; stir-fry 2 minutes. Add water chestnuts and bamboo shoots; stir-fry 1 minute. Add mushrooms and chicken broth; stir-fry 3 minutes or until chicken is no longer pink in center.

5 Stir soy sauce mixture; add to wok. Stir-fry 1 to 2 minutes or until sauce boils and thickens. Serve chicken and vegetables over rice. Garnish with onions, if desired.

Makes 4 servings

Nutrients per Serving:

Calories	208 (28% of calories from fat)				
Total Fat	6 g	Carbohydrate	11 g	Iron	2 mg
Saturated Fat	1 g	Dietary Fiber	1 g	Vitamin A	7 RE
Cholesterol	58 mg	Protein	25 g	Vitamin C	3 mg
Sodium	657 mg	Calcium	27 mg		

DIETARY EXCHANGES: 3 Lean Meat, 2 Vegetable, ½ Fat

CHICKEN CHOW MEIN

Chow mein is a Chinese-American dish of bits of meat and vegetables served over crisp, fried noodles. This lighter version omits the extra fat and calories by serving over boiled noodles.

1 pound boneless skinless
   chicken breasts
2 cloves garlic, minced
6 ounces (2 cups) fresh snow
   peas *or* 1 package
   (6 ounces) frozen snow peas,
   thawed
1 teaspoon vegetable oil, divided

2 tablespoons reduced sodium
   soy sauce
2 tablespoons dry sherry
3 large green onions, cut
   diagonally into 1-inch pieces
4 ounces uncooked Chinese egg
   noodles or vermicelli,
   cooked, drained and rinsed
1 teaspoon Oriental sesame oil

1 Cut chicken into ¼-inch slices; cut each slice into 1-inch strips. Toss chicken with garlic in small bowl. Cut snow peas into halves.

2 Heat ½ teaspoon vegetable oil in wok or large nonstick skillet over medium heat until hot. Add chicken mixture; stir-fry 3 minutes or until chicken is no longer pink in center. Transfer to medium bowl; toss with soy sauce and sherry.

3 Heat remaining ½ teaspoon vegetable oil in wok. Add snow peas; stir-fry 2 minutes for fresh or 1 minute for frozen snow peas. Add onions; stir-fry 30 seconds. Add chicken mixture; stir-fry 1 minute.

4 Add noodles to wok; stir-fry 2 minutes or until heated through. Stir in sesame oil. Garnish with cherry tomatoes and fresh herbs, if desired.

Makes 4 servings

Nutrients per Serving:

Calories	185 (21% of calories from fat)				
Total Fat	4 g	Carbohydrate	14 g	Iron	3 mg
Saturated Fat	1 g	Dietary Fiber	1 g	Vitamin A	28 RE
Cholesterol	46 mg	Protein	20 g	Vitamin C	28 mg
Sodium	308 mg	Calcium	34 mg		

DIETARY EXCHANGES: 1 Starch/Bread, 2 Lean Meat

CHINESE SKILLET CHICKEN AND RICE

This Chinese version of chicken and rice is spicy. If you'd like to tone down the heat, reduce the amount of crushed red pepper according to your own taste.

½ teaspoon crushed red pepper
½ teaspoon Chinese five-spice powder
¼ teaspoon ground white pepper
1 pound boneless skinless chicken breasts
2 teaspoons vegetable oil
1 large onion, chopped
2 cloves garlic, minced
1 cup uncooked white rice
1¼ cups ⅓-less-salt chicken broth

½ cup water
1 tablespoon reduced sodium soy sauce
2 red bell peppers, sliced
1 cup fresh bean sprouts
1 cup sliced mushrooms
1 cup frozen peas, thawed
¾ cup canned water chestnuts, drained
1 teaspoon minced fresh ginger

1 Combine crushed red pepper, five-spice powder and white pepper in small bowl. Rub onto all surfaces of chicken. Heat oil in large nonstick skillet over medium heat until hot. Add chicken; cook 5 minutes. Turn chicken; cook 5 minutes. Remove from skillet; reserve.

2 Pour off all but 1 tablespoon drippings. Cook onion and garlic in drippings 3 minutes, stirring occasionally. Add rice; stir to coat. Stir in chicken broth, water and soy sauce. Bring to a boil over high heat; reduce heat to medium.

3 Arrange chicken and bell peppers over rice in skillet. Cover; simmer 15 minutes or until most of the liquid is absorbed and chicken is no longer pink in center. Remove from heat; stir bean sprouts, mushrooms, peas, water chestnuts and ginger into rice and chicken. Cover; let stand 10 minutes. Garnish with mushrooms and fresh herbs, if desired. *Makes 4 servings*

Nutrients per Serving:

Calories	369 (12% of calories from fat)				
Total Fat	5 g	Carbohydrate	55 g	Iron	4 mg
Saturated Fat	1 g	Dietary Fiber	4 g	Vitamin A	63 RE
Cholesterol	46 mg	Protein	25 g	Vitamin C	45 mg
Sodium	225 mg	Calcium	54 mg		

DIETARY EXCHANGES: 3 Starch/Bread, 2 Lean Meat, 2 Vegetable

ORIENTAL CHICKEN KABOBS

Chunks of chicken and vegetables are marinated in a mixture of soy, sherry and garlic, then broiled to succulent perfection. Serve the kabobs over seasoned rice or couscous.

1 pound boneless skinless
   chicken breasts
2 small zucchini or yellow
   squash, cut into 1-inch slices
8 large mushrooms
1 cup red, yellow or green bell
   pepper pieces

2 tablespoons reduced sodium
   soy sauce
2 tablespoons dry sherry
1 teaspoon Oriental sesame oil
2 cloves garlic, minced
2 large green onions, cut into
   1-inch pieces

1 Cut chicken into 1½-inch pieces; place in large resealable plastic food storage bag. Add zucchini, mushrooms and bell pepper to bag. Combine soy sauce, sherry, oil and garlic in cup; pour over chicken and vegetables. Seal bag; turn to coat. Marinate in refrigerator 30 minutes or up to 4 hours, turning occasionally.

2 Soak 4 (12-inch) bamboo skewers in water 20 minutes.

3 Preheat broiler.

4 Drain chicken and vegetables; reserve marinade. Alternately thread chicken, vegetables and onions onto skewers.

5 Spray rack of broiler pan with nonstick cooking spray. Place kabobs on rack. Brush with half of reserved marinade. Broil 4 inches from heat, 10 minutes or until chicken is no longer pink in center, turning occasionally and basting with marinade. Garnish with green onion brushes, if desired.

Makes 4 servings

Nutrients per Serving:

Calories	135 (21% of calories from fat)				
Total Fat	3 g	Carbohydrate	6 g	Iron	1 mg
Saturated Fat	1 g	Dietary Fiber	2 g	Vitamin A	50 RE
Cholesterol	46 mg	Protein	19 g	Vitamin C	25 mg
Sodium	307 mg	Calcium	27 mg		

DIETARY EXCHANGES: 2 Lean Meat, 1 Vegetable

MEDITERRANEAN CHICKEN KABOBS

Although eggplant is commonly thought of as a vegetable, it is actually a fruit—specifically a berry. Eggplant is a good source of folic acid and potassium. One cup of uncooked eggplant pieces contains only 22 calories.

2 pounds boneless skinless chicken breasts or chicken tenders, cut into 1-inch pieces

1 small eggplant, peeled, cut into 1-inch pieces

1 medium zucchini, cut crosswise into ½-inch slices

2 medium onions, each cut into 8 wedges

16 medium mushrooms, stems removed

16 cherry tomatoes

1 cup ⅓-less-salt chicken broth

⅔ cup balsamic vinegar

3 tablespoons olive oil or vegetable oil

2 tablespoons dried mint leaves

4 teaspoons dried basil leaves

1 tablespoon dried oregano leaves

2 teaspoons grated lemon peel
Chopped fresh parsley (optional)

4 cups hot, cooked couscous

1 Alternately thread chicken, eggplant, zucchini, onions, mushrooms and tomatoes onto 16 metal skewers; place in large glass baking dish.

2 Combine chicken broth, vinegar, oil, mint, basil and oregano in small bowl. Pour over kabobs; turn to coat. Cover; marinate in refrigerator 2 hours, turning occasionally.

3 Preheat broiler.

4 Spray rack of broiler pan with nonstick cooking spray. Place kabobs on rack. Broil, 6 inches from heat, 10 to 15 minutes or until chicken is no longer pink in center, turning occasionally. Or, grill kabobs, covered, over medium-hot coals, 10 to 15 minutes or until chicken is no longer pink in center, turning occasionally. Stir lemon peel and parsley into couscous; serve with kabobs.

Makes 8 servings

Nutrients per Serving:						
Calories	293 (23% of calories from fat)					
Total Fat	8 g	Carbohydrate	34 g	Iron		3 mg
Saturated Fat	1 g	Dietary Fiber	7 g	Vitamin A		49 RE
Cholesterol	46 mg	Protein	22 g	Vitamin C		16 mg
Sodium	60 mg	Calcium	56 mg			

DIETARY EXCHANGES: 1½ Starch/Bread, 2 Lean Meat, 2 Vegetable, ½ Fat

GREEK-STYLE CHICKEN STEW

This stew is ideal for today's health-conscious way of eating. It boasts plenty of authentic Greek flavor with eggplant, artichokes and oregano, yet it has just over 350 calories per serving.

3 pounds skinless chicken
    breasts
Flour
Nonstick cooking spray
2 cups cubed peeled eggplant
2 cups sliced mushrooms
¾ cup coarsely chopped onion
2 cloves garlic, minced
1 teaspoon dried oregano leaves
½ teaspoon dried basil leaves

½ teaspoon dried thyme leaves
2 cups ⅓-less-salt chicken broth
¼ cup dry sherry or ⅓-less-salt
    chicken broth
¼ teaspoon salt
¼ teaspoon ground black pepper
1 can (14 ounces) artichoke
    hearts, drained
3 cups hot, cooked wide egg
    noodles

1 Coat chicken very lightly with flour. Generously spray nonstick Dutch oven or large nonstick skillet with cooking spray; heat over medium heat until hot. Cook chicken 10 to 15 minutes or until browned on all sides. Remove chicken; drain fat from Dutch oven.

2 Add eggplant, mushrooms, onion, garlic, oregano, basil and thyme to Dutch oven; cook and stir over medium heat 5 minutes.

3 Return chicken to Dutch oven. Stir in chicken broth, sherry, salt and pepper; bring to a boil over high heat. Reduce heat to low; simmer, covered, about 1 hour or until chicken is no longer pink in center, adding artichoke hearts during last 20 minutes of cooking. Serve over noodles. Garnish as desired.

Makes 6 servings

Nutrients per Serving:

Calories	353 (14% of calories from fat)					
Total Fat	5 g	Carbohydrate	32 g	Iron	4 mg
Saturated Fat	1 g	Dietary Fiber	7 g	Vitamin A	29 RE
Cholesterol	117 mg	Protein	41 g	Vitamin C	10 mg
Sodium	246 mg	Calcium	76 mg		

DIETARY EXCHANGES: 1½ Starch/Bread, 3½ Lean Meat, 2 Vegetable

CHICKEN CACCIATORE

Cacciatore is an Italian word that refers to foods prepared "hunter-style"— a naturally healthy way of cooking with mushrooms, onions, tomatoes and various herbs. This classic chicken dish is served over spaghetti, a good source of complex carbohydrates.

Nonstick cooking spray
4 pounds chicken pieces
   (breasts, legs, thighs)
2 cups sliced mushrooms
2 cups chopped green bell
   peppers
¾ cup coarsely chopped onion
3 cloves garlic, minced
1 can (16 ounces) whole
   tomatoes, undrained and
   coarsely chopped

¾ cup tomato juice
½ cup water
¼ cup tomato paste
1 tablespoon sugar
2 teaspoons dried rosemary
1 teaspoon dried basil leaves
1 teaspoon dried oregano leaves
½ teaspoon salt
¼ teaspoon ground black pepper
6 cups hot, cooked spaghetti

1 Generously spray nonstick Dutch oven or large nonstick skillet with cooking spray; heat over medium heat until hot. Cook chicken 10 to 15 minutes or until browned on all sides. Drain fat from Dutch oven.

2 Add mushrooms, bell peppers, onion and garlic to Dutch oven; cook and stir 3 to 4 minutes.

3 Stir in canned tomatoes with juice, ¾ cup tomato juice, water, tomato paste, sugar, rosemary, basil, oregano, salt and pepper; bring to a boil over high heat. Reduce heat to low; simmer, covered, 45 minutes. Uncover; simmer about 30 minutes or until chicken is no longer pink in center. Serve over spaghetti. Garnish as desired.

Makes 8 servings

Nutrients per Serving:					
Calories	472 (30% of calories from fat)				
Total Fat	16 g	Carbohydrate	42 g	Iron	4 mg
Saturated Fat	4 g	Dietary Fiber	4 g	Vitamin A	153 RE
Cholesterol	107 mg	Protein	40 g	Vitamin C	69 mg
Sodium	470 mg	Calcium	68 mg		

DIETARY EXCHANGES: 2½ Starch/Bread, 4½ Lean Meat, 1½ Vegetable

CHICKEN FRICASSEE

3 pounds chicken pieces
  (breasts, legs, thighs)
Flour
Nonstick cooking spray
3 cups ⅓-less-salt chicken broth
1 bay leaf
1 pound whole baby carrots
¾ cup onion wedges
1 tablespoon margarine

3 tablespoons flour
¾ cup skim milk
1 tablespoon lemon juice
3 tablespoons minced fresh dill
  or 2 teaspoons dried dill
  weed
1 teaspoon sugar
½ teaspoon salt
6 cups hot, cooked noodles

1 Coat chicken pieces very lightly with flour. Spray large nonstick skillet with cooking spray; heat over medium heat until hot. Cook chicken 10 to 15 minutes or until browned on all sides. Drain fat from skillet.

2 Add chicken broth and bay leaf to skillet; bring to a boil over high heat. Reduce heat to low; simmer, covered, about 1 hour or until chicken is no longer pink in center, adding carrots and onion during last 20 minutes of cooking.

3 Transfer chicken and vegetables with slotted spoon to platter; keep warm. Bring broth to a boil over high heat; boil until broth is reduced to 1 cup. Discard bay leaf.

4 Melt margarine in small saucepan over low heat; stir in 3 tablespoons flour. Cook and stir 1 to 2 minutes. Stir in broth, milk and lemon juice; bring to a boil over high heat. Boil until thickened, stirring constantly. Stir in dill, sugar and salt. Arrange chicken over noodles on serving plates; top with sauce. Garnish as desired.

Makes 6 servings

Nutrients per Serving:

Calories	565 (30% of calories from fat)				
Total Fat	19 g	Carbohydrate	52 g	Iron	4 mg
Saturated Fat	5 g	Dietary Fiber	6 g	Vitamin A	2,226 RE
Cholesterol	158 mg	Protein	43 g	Vitamin C	10 mg
Sodium	357 mg	Calcium	110 mg		

DIETARY EXCHANGES: 3 Starch/Bread, 4½ Lean Meat, 2 Vegetable, ½ Fat

RICOTTA STUFFED CHICKEN WITH
SUN DRIED TOMATO LINGUINE

Sun-dried tomatoes are a new addition to many supermarket produce departments. These chewy tomatoes have a sweet taste and add a rich tomato flavor to soups, stews and sauces.

1 broiler-fryer chicken
    (3 pounds)
1 cup reduced fat ricotta cheese
1 cup washed and torn fresh
    spinach leaves
4 cloves garlic, minced
2 teaspoons dried basil leaves

2 teaspoons minced fresh parsley
1 teaspoon dried oregano leaves
¼ teaspoon salt
    Nonstick olive oil cooking spray
    Paprika
    Sun Dried Tomato Linguine
    (page 260)

1 Preheat oven to 375°F. Split chicken in half with sharp knife or poultry shears, cutting through breast bone. Place chicken, skin side up, on counter and press with palm of hand to crack bone so that chicken will lie flat.

2 Loosen skin over top of chicken using fingers and sharp paring knife; do not loosen skin over wings and drumsticks.

3 Combine ricotta cheese, spinach, garlic, basil, parsley, oregano and salt in small bowl. Stuff mixture under skin of chicken using small rubber spatula or spoon.

4 Place chicken in roasting pan. Spray top of chicken lightly with cooking spray; sprinkle with paprika. Bake about 1 hour 15 minutes or until chicken is no longer pink in center.

5 Meanwhile, prepare Sun Dried Tomato Linguine. Serve chicken with Sun Dried Tomato Linguine. Garnish as desired. *Makes 6 servings*

(continued on page 260)

Ricotta Stuffed Chicken with Sun Dried Tomato Linguine, continued

SUN DRIED TOMATO LINGUINE

6 sun-dried tomato halves, *not* packed in oil
Nonstick olive oil cooking spray
1 cup sliced mushrooms
3 cloves garlic, minced
1 tablespoon minced fresh parsley
¾ teaspoon dried rosemary

1 can (15 ounces) ⅓-less-salt chicken broth
2 tablespoons cornstarch
¼ cup cold water
1 package (9 ounces) linguine, cooked in salted water, drained, hot

1 Place sun-dried tomatoes in small bowl; pour hot water over to cover. Let stand 10 to 15 minutes or until tomatoes are soft. Drain well; cut tomatoes into quarters.

2 Spray medium nonstick skillet with cooking spray; heat over medium heat until hot. Add mushrooms and garlic; cook and stir about 5 minutes or until tender. Add sun-dried tomatoes, parsley and rosemary; cook and stir 1 minute.

3 Stir chicken broth into vegetable mixture; bring to a boil over high heat. Combine cornstarch and cold water in small bowl; stir into chicken broth mixture. Boil 1 to 2 minutes, stirring constantly. Pour mixture over linguine; toss to coat.

Makes 6 servings

Nutrients per Serving:

includes Sun Dried Tomato Linguine

Calories	529 (26% of calories from fat)				
Total Fat	15 g	Carbohydrate	54 g	Iron	5 mg
Saturated Fat	4 g	Dietary Fiber	4 g	Vitamin A	1,590 RE
Cholesterol	135 mg	Protein	45 g	Vitamin C	35 mg
Sodium	232 mg	Calcium	150 mg		

DIETARY EXCHANGES: 3 Starch/Bread, 4½ Lean Meat, 2 Vegetable

TUSCAN CHICKEN BREASTS WITH POLENTA

Cornmeal is ground from dried white or yellow corn and is a versatile grain high in fiber and many essential nutrients. Polenta, a staple of northern Italy, is a mush made from cornmeal. Here, it is cooled until firm, then sliced, lightly browned and topped with an herbed tomato sauce.

4 cups ⅓-less-salt chicken broth
1 cup yellow cornmeal
½ teaspoon garlic powder
½ teaspoon dried Italian
    seasoning
¼ teaspoon salt
¼ teaspoon ground black pepper

8 skinless chicken breast halves
    (3 pounds)
Tuscan Tomato Sauce
    (page 262)
Nonstick cooking spray
Fresh spinach leaves, steamed
    (optional)

1 Place chicken broth in large nonstick saucepan; bring to a boil over high heat. Slowly stir in cornmeal. Reduce heat to low; cook, stirring frequently, 15 to 20 minutes or until mixture is very thick and pulls away from side of pan. (Mixture may be lumpy.) Pour polenta into greased 9×5-inch loaf pan. Cool; refrigerate 2 to 3 hours or until firm.

2 Preheat oven to 350°F. Combine garlic powder, Italian seasoning, salt and pepper in small bowl; rub on all surfaces of chicken. Arrange chicken, breast side up, in single layer in 13×9-inch baking pan. Bake, uncovered, about 45 minutes or until chicken is no longer pink in center.

3 Meanwhile, prepare Tuscan Tomato Sauce.

4 Remove polenta from pan; transfer to cutting board. Cut polenta crosswise into 16 slices. Cut slices into triangles, if desired. Spray large nonstick skillet with cooking spray; heat over medium heat until hot. Cook polenta about 4 minutes per side or until lightly browned.

5 Place spinach leaves, if desired, on serving plates. Arrange polenta slices and chicken over spinach; top with Tuscan Tomato Sauce.

Makes 8 servings

(continued on page 262)

Tuscan Chicken Breasts with Polenta, continued

TUSCAN TOMATO SAUCE

Nonstick cooking spray
½ cup chopped onion
2 cloves garlic, minced
8 plum tomatoes, coarsely
   chopped

1 can (8 ounces) tomato sauce
2 teaspoons dried basil leaves
2 teaspoons dried oregano leaves
2 teaspoons dried rosemary
½ teaspoon ground pepper

 Spray medium nonstick saucepan with cooking spray; heat over medium heat until hot. Add onion and garlic; cook and stir about 5 minutes or until tender.

 Stir in tomatoes, tomato sauce, basil, oregano, rosemary and pepper; bring to a boil over high heat. Reduce heat to low; simmer, uncovered, about 6 minutes or until desired consistency, stirring occasionally.

Makes about 3 cups

Nutrients per Serving:
includes Tuscan Tomato Sauce

Calories	240 (16% of calories from fat)				
Total Fat	4 g	Carbohydrate	22 g	Iron	3 mg
Saturated Fat	1 g	Dietary Fiber	5 g	Vitamin A	126 RE
Cholesterol	69 mg	Protein	29 g	Vitamin C	27 mg
Sodium	345 mg	Calcium	51 mg		

DIETARY EXCHANGES: 1 Starch/Bread, 2½ Lean Meat, 1½ Vegetable

❖

Cook's Tip
To easily peel garlic, place a clove on a cutting board. Cover the clove with the flat side of a chef's knife blade, then firmly press down on the blade with your fist. This loosens the skin so that it comes right off.

❖

SHERRY BRAISED CHICKEN

Chicken is an excellent source of high-quality protein and B vitamins, yet is low in saturated fat.

1 teaspoon vegetable oil
6 ounces boneless skinless
  chicken breasts, cubed
1 large onion, coarsely chopped
2 cloves garlic, minced
1 cup ⅓-less-salt chicken broth
¼ cup dry sherry
¼ cup reduced sodium soy sauce

1½ tablespoons cornstarch
2 jars (7 ounces each) *or* 1 can
  (15 ounces) straw
  mushrooms, drained
6 ounces uncooked Chinese egg
  noodles or vermicelli, cooked
  and drained
¼ cup thinly sliced green onions

1 Heat oil in large nonstick skillet over medium heat until hot. Add chicken; cook 5 minutes. Turn chicken; cook 5 minutes. Remove chicken from skillet; reserve.

2 Pour off all but 1 tablespoon drippings. Cook chopped onion and garlic in drippings 6 minutes or until browned and tender, stirring occasionally. Add broth and sherry; bring to a boil over high heat. Blend soy sauce into cornstarch in cup until smooth. Stir into broth mixture. Return chicken to skillet; add mushrooms.

3 Reduce heat to medium-low. Cover; simmer 20 minutes or until chicken is no longer pink in center.

4 Serve chicken and sauce over noodles. Sprinkle with green onions. Garnish with pepper strips and green onions, if desired.

Makes 4 servings

Nutrients per Serving:

Calories	184 (11% of calories from fat)					
Total Fat	2 g	Carbohydrate	27 g	Iron	3 mg
Saturated Fat	1 g	Dietary Fiber	3 g	Vitamin A	26 RE
Cholesterol	17 mg	Protein	11 g	Vitamin C	5 mg
Sodium	712 mg	Calcium	33 mg		

DIETARY EXCHANGES: 1 Starch/Bread, 1 Lean Meat, 2 Vegetable

CHICKEN BOURGUIGNONNE

Wild rice is actually the seed of a marsh grass rather than a type of rice. Its nutty flavor and chewy texture make it a perfect accompaniment to all kinds of poultry. A half cup of cooked wild rice has about ten times the amount of folic acid as white rice. Folic acid is a nutrient important for the formation and growth of red blood cells.

4 pounds skinless chicken thighs and breasts
Flour
Nonstick cooking spray
2 cups ⅓-less-salt chicken broth
2 cups dry white wine or ⅓-less-salt chicken broth
1 pound whole baby carrots
¼ cup tomato paste
4 cloves garlic, minced
½ teaspoon dried thyme leaves

2 bay leaves
¼ teaspoon salt
¼ teaspoon ground black pepper
8 ounces fresh or thawed frozen pearl onions
8 ounces whole medium mushrooms
2 cups hot, cooked white rice
2 cups hot, cooked wild rice
¼ cup minced fresh parsley

1 Preheat oven to 325°F. Coat chicken very lightly with flour. Generously spray nonstick ovenproof Dutch oven or large nonstick ovenproof skillet with cooking spray; heat over medium heat until hot. Cook chicken 10 to 15 minutes or until browned on all sides. Drain fat from Dutch oven.

2 Add chicken broth, wine, carrots, tomato paste, garlic, thyme, bay leaves, salt and pepper to Dutch oven; bring to a boil over high heat. Cover; transfer to oven. Bake 1 hour. Add onions and mushrooms. Uncover; bake about 35 minutes or until vegetables are tender and chicken is no longer pink in center. Remove bay leaves. Combine white and wild rice; serve with chicken. Sprinkle rice with parsley.

Makes 8 servings

Nutrients per Serving:

Calories	396 (18% of calories from fat)				
Total Fat	8 g	Carbohydrate	36 g	Iron	4 mg
Saturated Fat	2 g	Dietary Fiber	4 g	Vitamin A	1,639 RE
Cholesterol	92 mg	Protein	35 g	Vitamin C	14 mg
Sodium	251 mg	Calcium	62 mg		

DIETARY EXCHANGES: 2 Starch/Bread, 3½ Lean Meat, 2½ Vegetable

CRISPY BAKED CHICKEN

Buy the freshest broccoli by choosing bunches that range in color from dark green to purple-green. Bud clusters should be compact, showing no yellow color. Avoid bunches with yellow, wilted leaves. Fresh or frozen, broccoli is a good source of vitamins A and C.

4 skinless chicken breast halves (1½ pounds)
2½ tablespoons Dijon-style mustard, divided
1 cup fresh whole wheat bread crumbs (2 slices bread)
½ teaspoon dried marjoram leaves
½ teaspoon dried thyme leaves
¼ teaspoon salt
¼ teaspoon dried sage leaves
¼ teaspoon ground black pepper
Nonstick cooking spray
1 small red bell pepper, sliced
2 cloves garlic, minced
2 cups broccoli flowerets, cooked crisp-tender
1 to 2 tablespoons lemon juice

1 Preheat oven to 375°F. Brush tops of chicken breasts with 2 tablespoons mustard. Combine remaining mustard, bread crumbs, marjoram, thyme, salt, sage and pepper in small bowl. Pat mixture evenly over mustard. Arrange chicken, breast side up, in single layer in 13×9-inch baking pan.

2 Bake, uncovered, about 40 minutes or until chicken is no longer pink in center.

3 Spray medium nonstick skillet with cooking spray; heat over medium heat until hot. Add bell pepper and garlic; cook and stir about 5 minutes or until tender. Add broccoli and lemon juice; cook and stir 2 to 3 minutes or until heated through.

4 Arrange chicken and broccoli mixture on serving plates.

Makes 4 servings

Nutrients per Serving:					
Calories	196 (18% of calories from fat)				
Total Fat	4 g	Carbohydrate	11 g	Iron	2 mg
Saturated Fat	1 g	Dietary Fiber	3 g	Vitamin A	86 RE
Cholesterol	69 mg	Protein	29 g	Vitamin C	62 mg
Sodium	412 mg	Calcium	66 mg		

DIETARY EXCHANGES: ½ Starch/Bread, 2½ Lean Meat, 1 Vegetable

CHICKEN CORDON BLEU

Pounding boneless chicken breasts to a uniform thickness flattens them so that a savory ham and cheese filling can be easily rolled up inside.

6 boneless skinless chicken
    breast halves (1¼ pounds)
1 tablespoon Dijon-style mustard
3 slices (1 ounce each) lean
    ham, cut into halves
3 slices (1 ounce each) reduced
    fat Swiss cheese, cut into
    halves

Nonstick cooking spray
¼ cup unseasoned dry bread
    crumbs
2 tablespoons minced fresh
    parsley
3 cups hot, cooked white rice

1 Preheat oven to 350°F. Place chicken between 2 pieces of waxed paper; pound to ¼-inch thickness using flat side of meat mallet or rolling pin. Brush mustard on 1 side of each chicken breast; layer 1 slice each of ham and cheese over mustard. Roll up each chicken breast from short end; secure with wooden picks. Spray tops of chicken rolls with cooking spray; sprinkle with bread crumbs.

2 Arrange chicken rolls in 11×7-inch baking pan. Cover; bake 10 minutes. Uncover; bake about 20 minutes or until chicken is no longer pink in center.

3 Stir parsley into rice; serve with chicken. Serve with vegetables, if desired.

Makes 6 servings

Nutrients per Serving:

Calories	297 (18% of calories from fat)				
Total Fat	6 g	Carbohydrate	32 g	Iron	2 mg
Saturated Fat	2 g	Dietary Fiber	1 g	Vitamin A	46 RE
Cholesterol	55 mg	Protein	27 g	Vitamin C	5 mg
Sodium	294 mg	Calcium	166 mg		

DIETARY EXCHANGES: 2 Starch/Bread, 2 Lean Meat

CHICKEN BAKED IN PARCHMENT

Parchment paper
4 boneless skinless chicken
   breast halves (4 ounces
   each)
1 cup matchstick size carrot
   strips
1 cup matchstick size zucchini
   strips
½ cup snow peas
½ cup thinly sliced red bell
   pepper
2¼ cups ⅓-less-salt chicken broth,
   divided
2 tablespoons all-purpose flour
2 cloves garlic, minced
½ teaspoon dried thyme leaves
¼ teaspoon salt
¼ teaspoon ground nutmeg
¼ teaspoon ground black pepper
1 package (6 ounces) wheat pilaf
   mix

1 Preheat oven to 375°F. Cut parchment paper into four 10-inch squares. Place 1 chicken breast in center of each piece of parchment; arrange carrots, zucchini, peas and bell pepper around chicken.

2 Combine ½ cup chicken broth and flour in small saucepan; stir in garlic, thyme, salt, nutmeg and black pepper. Bring to a boil over high heat, stirring constantly until thickened. Reduce heat to low; simmer 1 minute. Spoon broth mixture evenly over chicken and vegetables.

3 Fold each parchment square in half diagonally, enclosing chicken and vegetables to form a triangle. Fold edges over twice to seal. Place parchment packets into 15×10-inch jelly-roll pan. Bake 25 to 30 minutes or until parchment is browned and puffed.

4 Place remaining 1¾ cups chicken broth in medium saucepan. Bring to a boil over high heat. Stir in pilaf mix (discard spice packet). Reduce heat to low; simmer, covered, 15 minutes or until broth is absorbed.

5 Arrange parchment packets on serving plates; open carefully. Serve with pilaf.

Makes 4 servings

Nutrients per Serving:

Calories	321 (9% of calories from fat)				
Total Fat	3 g	Carbohydrate	41 g	Iron	2 mg
Saturated Fat	1 g	Dietary Fiber	3 g	Vitamin A	810 RE
Cholesterol	58 mg	Protein	28 g	Vitamin C	42 mg
Sodium	214 mg	Calcium	45 mg		

DIETARY EXCHANGES: 2 Starch/Bread, 2½ Lean Meat, 1½ Vegetable

CHICKEN AND VEGETABLES WITH MUSTARD SAUCE

Dry mustard and rice vinegar add a zesty twist to this satisfying entrée.

1 tablespoon sugar
2 teaspoons cornstarch
1½ teaspoons dry mustard
2 tablespoons reduced sodium soy sauce
2 tablespoons water
2 tablespoons rice vinegar
1 pound boneless skinless chicken breasts

4 teaspoons vegetable oil, divided
2 cloves garlic, minced
1 small red bell pepper, thinly sliced
½ cup thinly sliced celery
1 small onion, thinly sliced
3 cups hot, cooked Chinese egg noodles (3 ounces uncooked)

1 Combine sugar, cornstarch and mustard in small bowl. Blend soy sauce, water and vinegar into cornstarch mixture until smooth. Cut chicken into 1-inch pieces.

2 Heat 2 teaspoons oil in wok or large nonstick skillet over medium heat until hot. Add chicken and garlic; stir-fry 3 minutes or until chicken is no longer pink in center. Remove chicken from wok; reserve.

3 Add remaining 2 teaspoons oil to wok. Add bell pepper, celery and onion; stir-fry 3 minutes or until vegetables are crisp-tender.

4 Stir soy sauce mixture; add to wok. Stir-fry 30 seconds or until sauce boils and thickens.

5 Return chicken with any accumulated juices to wok; heat through. Serve over Chinese noodles. Garnish with celery leaves, if desired.

Makes 4 servings

Nutrients per Serving:					
Calories	350 (17% of calories from fat)				
Total Fat	7 g	Carbohydrate	50 g	Iron	5 mg
Saturated Fat	4 g	Dietary Fiber	1 g	Vitamin A	17 RE
Cholesterol	46 mg	Protein	22 g	Vitamin C	19 mg
Sodium	326 mg	Calcium	32 mg		

DIETARY EXCHANGES: 2½ Starch/Bread, 2 Lean Meat, 1½ Vegetable, 1 Fat

CHICKEN AND VEGETABLE COUSCOUS

Couscous, a staple of North African cuisine, is a quick-cooking food with many uses. Enjoy it as a cereal with milk, as a filler in casseroles or as a savory side-dish substitute for rice.

1 tablespoon vegetable oil
3 (3-ounce) boneless skinless
   chicken breast halves, cut
   into 3-inch cubes
½ cup chopped green onions
3 cloves garlic, minced
1¼ cups tomato sauce
¼ cup water
1¼ cups chopped carrots
1 cup canned Great Northern
   beans, rinsed and drained
1 large potato, cubed

1 yellow squash, chopped
1 medium tomato, chopped
¼ cup chopped red bell pepper
¼ cup raisins
2 tablespoons packed brown
   sugar
2 teaspoons ground cumin
¾ teaspoon ground cinnamon
3 to 4 drops hot pepper sauce
1½ cups water
1 cup uncooked couscous

1 Heat oil in medium skillet over medium heat until hot. Add chicken; cook and stir until browned. Add onions and garlic; cook and stir 1 minute. Stir in tomato sauce and ¼ cup water. Add remaining ingredients except 1½ cups water and couscous; bring to a simmer. Cook 15 minutes.

2 Meanwhile, heat water in medium saucepan; bring to a boil over high heat. Add couscous. Cover; remove from heat. Let stand 5 minutes.

3 Serve chicken and vegetables over couscous.
Makes 6 servings

Nutrients per Serving:					
Calories	322 (11% of calories from fat)				
Total Fat	4 g	Carbohydrate	56 g	Iron	3 mg
Saturated Fat	1 g	Dietary Fiber	9 g	Vitamin A	759 RE
Cholesterol	22 mg	Protein	17 g	Vitamin C	26 mg
Sodium	348 mg	Calcium	80 mg		

DIETARY EXCHANGES: 2½ Starch/Bread, 1 Lean Meat, ½ Fruit, 2 Vegetable

CHICKEN AND VEGETABLE RISOTTO

Arborio rice is a type of short-grain rice grown in Italy. It can be purchased in large supermarkets and Italian groceries. If you prepare the risotto with regular converted rice, you may not need to use all of the broth.

Nonstick olive oil cooking spray
2 cups sliced mushrooms
½ cup chopped onion
4 cloves garlic, minced
¼ cup finely chopped fresh parsley *or* 1 tablespoon dried parsley leaves
3 to 4 tablespoons finely chopped fresh basil *or* 1 tablespoon dried basil leaves
6 cups ⅓-less-salt chicken broth
1½ cups uncooked arborio rice or converted white rice

1 pound chicken tenders, cut into ½-inch pieces, cooked
2 cups broccoli flowerets, cooked crisp-tender
4 plum tomatoes, seeded, chopped
½ teaspoon salt
½ teaspoon ground black pepper
2 tablespoons grated Parmesan or Romano cheese

1 Spray large nonstick saucepan with cooking spray; heat over medium heat until hot. Add mushrooms, onion and garlic; cook and stir about 5 minutes or until tender. Add parsley and basil; cook and stir 1 minute.

2 Place chicken broth in medium saucepan; bring to a boil over high heat.

3 Add rice to mushroom mixture; cook and stir over medium heat 1 to 2 minutes. Add chicken broth to mushroom mixture, ½ cup at a time, stirring constantly until broth is absorbed before adding next ½ cup. Continue adding broth and stirring until rice is tender and mixture is creamy, 20 to 25 minutes.

4 Add chicken, broccoli, tomatoes, salt and pepper. Cook and stir 2 to 3 minutes or until heated through. Sprinkle with cheese.   *Makes 4 servings*

Nutrients per Serving:					
Calories	457 (9% of calories from fat)				
Total Fat	5 g	Carbohydrate	74 g	Iron	7 mg
Saturated Fat	1 g	Dietary Fiber	5 g	Vitamin A	225 RE
Cholesterol	48 mg	Protein	29 g	Vitamin C	90 mg
Sodium	449 mg	Calcium	153 mg		

DIETARY EXCHANGES: 4 Starch/Bread, 2 Lean Meat, 2½ Vegetable

CHICKEN POT PIE

Nonstick cooking spray
¾ pound boneless skinless
    chicken thighs, cut into
    1-inch pieces
¾ pound boneless skinless
    chicken breasts, cut into
    1-inch pieces
2 cups sliced carrots
1½ cups cubed potatoes
1 cup cubed turnip
1 cup fresh peas or thawed
    frozen peas
½ cup chopped onion

3 cloves garlic, sliced
1 teaspoon dried basil leaves
½ teaspoon dried marjoram
    leaves
½ teaspoon dried oregano leaves
½ teaspoon dried tarragon leaves
¼ teaspoon salt
¼ teaspoon ground black pepper
1 cup ⅓-less-salt chicken broth
3 tablespoons all-purpose flour
⅓ cup cold water
3 sheets thawed frozen phyllo
    pastry

1 Preheat oven to 425°F. Spray large nonstick skillet with cooking spray; heat over medium heat until hot. Add chicken; cook and stir about 10 minutes or until no longer pink in center. Remove chicken from skillet; reserve.

2 Add carrots, potatoes, turnip, peas, onion and garlic to skillet; cook and stir 5 minutes. Sprinkle with basil, marjoram, oregano, tarragon, salt and pepper; cook and stir 1 to 2 minutes. Stir in chicken broth; bring to a boil over high heat. Reduce heat to low; simmer, covered, about 10 minutes or until vegetables are tender.

3 Return chicken to skillet; return mixture to a boil over high heat. Combine flour and water in small bowl; stir into chicken mixture. Boil 1 minute, stirring constantly. Pour mixture into 1-quart casserole or 10-inch pie plate.

4 Spray 1 sheet phyllo with cooking spray; top with remaining 2 sheets phyllo, spraying each lightly. Place stack of phyllo on top of casserole; cut edges 1 inch larger than casserole. Fold under edges of phyllo. Bake about 15 minutes or until phyllo is brown and crisp. *Makes 6 servings*

Nutrients per Serving:

Calories	266 (17% of calories from fat)				
Total Fat	5 g	Carbohydrate	32 g	Iron	2 mg
Saturated Fat	2 g	Dietary Fiber	5 g	Vitamin A	1,061 RE
Cholesterol	59 mg	Protein	23 g	Vitamin C	19 mg
Sodium	300 mg	Calcium	50 mg		

DIETARY EXCHANGES: 1½ Starch/Bread, 2½ Lean Meat, 1 Vegetable

TEX-MEX CHICKEN

Boneless skinless chicken breasts are a favorite choice for today's cook because of their quick-cooking appeal and their low fat, high protein content. If you skin and debone your own chicken breasts, save the bones and skin in a plastic bag in your freezer to make flavorful homemade chicken stock.

1 teaspoon ground red pepper
¾ teaspoon onion powder
¾ teaspoon garlic powder
½ teaspoon dried basil leaves
½ teaspoon salt, divided
⅛ teaspoon dried oregano leaves
⅛ teaspoon dried thyme leaves

⅛ teaspoon gumbo filé powder*
6 boneless skinless chicken
   breast halves (1½ pounds)
¾ pound potatoes, cut into 1-inch
   wedges
Nonstick cooking spray
¼ teaspoon ground black pepper

1 Combine red pepper, onion powder, garlic powder, basil, ¼ teaspoon salt, oregano, thyme and gumbo filé powder in small bowl. Rub mixture on all surfaces of chicken. Place chicken in single layer in 13×9-inch baking pan. Refrigerate, covered, 4 to 8 hours.

2 Preheat oven to 350°F. Place potatoes in medium bowl. Spray potatoes lightly with cooking spray; toss to coat. Sprinkle with remaining ¼ teaspoon salt and black pepper; toss to coat. Add to chicken in pan.

3 Bake, uncovered, 40 to 45 minutes or until potatoes are tender and chicken is no longer pink in center. Or, place chicken and potatoes in aluminum foil pan. Grill, covered, 4 inches from medium-hot coals, 20 to 30 minutes or until potatoes are tender and chicken is no longer pink in center. Serve with additional vegetables, if desired. *Makes 6 servings*

*Gumbo filé powder is a seasoning widely used in Creole cooking. It is available in the spice or gourmet section of most large supermarkets.

Nutrients per Serving:

Calories	262 (9% of calories from fat)				
Total Fat	3 g	Carbohydrate	36 g	Iron	2 mg
Saturated Fat	1 g	Dietary Fiber	0 g	Vitamin A	18 RE
Cholesterol	55 mg	Protein	24 g	Vitamin C	23 mg
Sodium	237 mg	Calcium	25 mg		

DIETARY EXCHANGES: 1 Starch/Bread, 2 Lean Meat

TEX-MEX BBQ PIZZA

Welcome to the days of the mean, lean pizza—only 18% of calories from fat compared to some traditional versions that surpass the 75% mark.

4 cups water
4 to 6 ounces boneless skinless
    chicken breasts
1 12-inch prepared pizza crust
⅓ cup barbecue sauce
⅓ cup finely chopped onion
1 tablespoon lemon juice
2 tablespoons diced mild green
    chilies

2 to 3 small tomatoes, seeded,
    sliced
1 cup (4 ounces) shredded
    reduced fat Monterey Jack
    cheese
¼ cup lightly packed fresh
    cilantro, chopped

1 Preheat oven to 450°F.

2 Place water in large saucepan; bring to a boil over high heat. Add chicken. Cover; remove from heat. Let stand 15 minutes or until chicken is no longer pink in center. Drain; cut into small cubes.

3 If recommended cooking time for crust is longer than 5 to 7 minutes, prebake crust until this amount of time remains.

4 Combine barbecue sauce, onion and lemon juice in small bowl; spread over crust leaving ½-inch border. Top with chicken; sprinkle with chilies and tomatoes. Sprinkle cheese evenly over top. Bake 5 to 7 minutes or until cheese begins to brown. Cut pizza into 8 wedges; top with cilantro.

Makes 4 servings

Nutrients per Serving:

Calories	413 (18% of calories from fat)				
Total Fat	8 g	Carbohydrate	61 g	Iron	3 mg
Saturated Fat	2 g	Dietary Fiber	2 g	Vitamin A	122 RE
Cholesterol	25 mg	Protein	25 g	Vitamin C	38 mg
Sodium	358 mg	Calcium	327 mg		

DIETARY EXCHANGES: 3½ Starch/Bread, 2 Lean Meat, 1 Vegetable, ½ Fat

THE CALIFORNIAN

Alfalfa sprouts add a delicate nutty flavor plus crunchy goodness to these open-faced sandwiches. Sprouts are low in calories and fat free. Purchase sprouts that are moist and crisp; refrigerate and use within a few days of purchase.

3 tablespoons reduced fat cream
    cheese, softened
1 tablespoon chutney
4 slices pumpernickel bread
4 washed lettuce leaves
¾ pound thinly sliced chicken
    breast (from deli)

1⅓ cups alfalfa sprouts
1 medium mango, peeled, sliced
1 pear, cored, sliced
4 strawberries

1 Combine cream cheese and chutney in small bowl; spread about 1 tablespoon on each bread slice. Place 1 lettuce leaf over cream cheese mixture. Divide chicken evenly; place over lettuce.

2 Arrange alfalfa sprouts over chicken; arrange mango and pear slices over sprouts. Garnish each open-faced sandwich with a strawberry.

Makes 4 servings

Nutrients per Serving:					
Calories	318 (17% of calories from fat)				
Total Fat	6 g	Carbohydrate	36 g	Iron	2 mg
Saturated Fat	2 g	Dietary Fiber	6 g	Vitamin A	239 RE
Cholesterol	72 mg	Protein	30 g	Vitamin C	45 mg
Sodium	304 mg	Calcium	69 mg		

DIETARY EXCHANGES: 1 Starch/Bread, 3 Lean Meat, 1½ Fruit

GRILLED CHICKEN BREAST AND PEPERONATA SANDWICHES

Peperonata is an Italian mixture of sweet peppers, onions and garlic cooked in olive oil. Look for peppers that are firm, thick-fleshed and bright in color. Peppers contain twice as much vitamin C as oranges and are high in vitamin A and fiber. One-half cup of raw pieces contains only 14 calories.

1 tablespoon olive oil or
   vegetable oil
1 medium red bell pepper, sliced
   into strips
1 medium green bell pepper,
   sliced into strips
¾ cup onion slices
2 cloves garlic, minced

¼ teaspoon salt
¼ teaspoon ground black pepper
4 boneless skinless chicken
   breast halves (about
   1 pound)
4 small French rolls, split and
   toasted

1 To prevent sticking, spray grill with nonstick cooking spray. Prepare coals for grilling.

2 Heat oil in large nonstick skillet over medium heat until hot. Add bell peppers, onion and garlic; cook and stir 5 minutes. Reduce heat to low; cook and stir about 20 minutes or until vegetables are tender. Sprinkle with salt and pepper.

3 Place chicken on grill, 4 inches from medium-hot coals. Grill, covered, 20 minutes or until chicken is no longer pink in center, turning occasionally. Or, place chicken on rack of broiler pan coated with nonstick cooking spray. Broil 4 inches from heat, 14 to 16 minutes or until chicken is no longer pink in center, turning occasionally.

4 Place chicken in rolls. Divide pepper mixture evenly; spoon over chicken.

Makes 4 servings

Nutrients per Serving:					
Calories	321 (22% of calories from fat)				
Total Fat	8 g	Carbohydrate	36 g	Iron	2 mg
Saturated Fat	2 g	Dietary Fiber	3 g	Vitamin A	28 RE
Cholesterol	58 mg	Protein	27 g	Vitamin C	36 mg
Sodium	497 mg	Calcium	48 mg		

DIETARY EXCHANGES: 2 Starch/Bread, 2½ Lean Meat, 1½ Vegetable

MEDITERRANEAN SANDWICHES

Oregano grows in abundance on the Mediterranean hillsides and fills the air with fragrance. Literally translated, oregano means "joy of the mountain." It is related to two other herbs, marjoram and thyme. These and other dried herbs should be stored in a cool, dark place for no more than six months.

Nonstick cooking spray
1¼ pounds chicken tenders, cut crosswise in half
1 large tomato, cut into bite-size pieces
½ small cucumber, seeded, sliced
½ cup sweet onion slices
2 tablespoons cider vinegar
1 tablespoon olive oil or vegetable oil

3 teaspoons minced fresh oregano *or* ½ teaspoon dried oregano leaves
2 teaspoons minced fresh mint *or* ½ teaspoon dried mint leaves
¼ teaspoon salt
12 washed lettuce leaves (optional)
6 whole wheat pita breads, cut crosswise in half

1 Spray large nonstick skillet with cooking spray; heat over medium heat until hot. Add chicken; cook and stir 7 to 10 minutes or until browned and no longer pink in center. Cool slightly.

2 Combine chicken, tomato, cucumber and onion in medium bowl. Drizzle with vinegar and oil; toss to coat. Sprinkle with oregano, mint and salt; toss to combine.

3 Place 1 lettuce leaf in each pita bread half, if desired. Divide chicken mixture evenly; spoon into pita bread halves.   *Makes 6 servings*

Nutrients per Serving:					
Calories	242 (21% of calories from fat)				
Total Fat	6 g	Carbohydrate	24 g	Iron	2 mg
Saturated Fat	1 g	Dietary Fiber	2 g	Vitamin A	30 RE
Cholesterol	50 mg	Protein	23 g	Vitamin C	7 mg
Sodium	353 mg	Calcium	57 mg		

DIETARY EXCHANGES: 1½ Starch/Bread, 2½ Lean Meat

TARRAGON CHICKEN SALAD SANDWICHES

Fresh grapes are added to this chicken salad for a burst of flavor and nutritional value. Besides supplying fiber and vitamin A, grapes are low in calories, which make them a great snack food. Green grapes that have a tinge of yellow and red grapes that are predominantly crimson will be the sweetest.

1¼ pounds boneless skinless
     chicken breasts, cooked
1 cup thinly sliced celery
1 cup seedless red or green
     grapes, cut into halves
½ cup raisins
½ cup plain nonfat yogurt
¼ cup reduced fat mayonnaise or
     salad dressing

2 tablespoons finely chopped
     shallots or onion
2 tablespoons minced fresh
     tarragon *or* 1 teaspoon dried
     tarragon leaves
½ teaspoon salt
⅛ teaspoon white pepper
6 washed lettuce leaves
6 whole wheat buns, split

1 Cut chicken into scant ½-inch pieces. Combine chicken, celery, grapes and raisins in large bowl. Combine yogurt, mayonnaise, shallots, tarragon, salt and pepper in small bowl. Spoon over chicken mixture; mix lightly.

2 Place 1 lettuce leaf in each bun. Divide chicken mixture evenly; spoon into buns.

Makes 6 servings

Nutrients per Serving:

Calories	353 (18% of calories from fat)				
Total Fat	7 g	Carbohydrate	41 g	Iron	2 mg
Saturated Fat	1 g	Dietary Fiber	4 g	Vitamin A	62 RE
Cholesterol	76 mg	Protein	34 g	Vitamin C	6 mg
Sodium	509 mg	Calcium	120 mg		

DIETARY EXCHANGES: 1½ Starch/Bread, 4 Lean Meat, ½ Fruit

CHICKEN AND MOZZARELLA MELTS

Mozzarella is a soft white cheese that melts easily. In southern Italy, where it originated, it is made from the milk of buffaloes. In other parts of Italy and North America, it is made from cow's milk.

2 cloves garlic, crushed
4 boneless skinless chicken
   breast halves (¾ pound)
   Nonstick cooking spray
⅛ teaspoon salt
⅛ teaspoon ground black pepper
1 tablespoon prepared pesto
   sauce

4 small hard rolls, split
12 washed spinach leaves
  8 fresh basil leaves* (optional)
  3 plum tomatoes, sliced
  ½ cup (2 ounces) shredded
     part-skim mozzarella cheese

1 Preheat oven to 350°F. Rub garlic on all surfaces of chicken. Spray medium nonstick skillet with cooking spray; heat over medium heat until hot. Add chicken; cook 5 to 6 minutes on each side or until no longer pink in center. Sprinkle with salt and pepper.

2 Brush pesto sauce on bottom halves of rolls; layer with spinach, basil, if desired, and tomatoes. Place chicken in rolls; sprinkle cheese evenly over chicken. (If desired, sandwiches may be prepared up to this point and wrapped in aluminum foil. Refrigerate until ready to bake. Bake in preheated 350°F oven until chicken is warm, about 20 minutes.)

3 Wrap sandwiches in aluminum foil; bake about 10 minutes or until cheese is melted. *Makes 4 servings*

*Omit basil leaves if fresh are unavailable. Do not substitute dried basil leaves.

Nutrients per Serving:

Calories	299 (16% of calories from fat)				
Total Fat	5 g	Carbohydrate	37 g	Iron	3 mg
Saturated Fat	3 g	Dietary Fiber	3 g	Vitamin A	198 RE
Cholesterol	47 mg	Protein	27 g	Vitamin C	24 mg
Sodium	498 mg	Calcium	188 mg		

DIETARY EXCHANGES: 2 Starch/Bread, 2½ Lean Meat, 1 Vegetable

MEATBALL GRINDERS

When purchasing ground chicken, be sure to check the label. Some brands are ground primarily from white meat. Others add dark meat and skin which dramatically increases the fat and cholesterol content. You can also ask your butcher to grind breast meat for you.

1 pound ground chicken
½ cup fresh whole wheat or white
 bread crumbs (1 slice bread)
1 egg white
3 tablespoons finely chopped
 fresh parsley
2 cloves garlic, minced
¼ teaspoon salt
⅛ teaspoon ground black pepper
 Nonstick cooking spray
¼ cup chopped onion

1 can (8 ounces) whole
 tomatoes, drained and
 coarsely chopped
1 can (4 ounces) no-salt-added
 tomato sauce
1 teaspoon dried Italian
 seasoning
4 small hard rolls, split
2 tablespoons grated Parmesan
 cheese

1 Combine chicken, bread crumbs, egg white, parsley, garlic, salt and pepper in medium bowl. Form mixture into 12 to 16 meatballs. Spray medium nonstick skillet with cooking spray; heat over medium heat until hot. Add meatballs; cook and stir about 5 minutes or until browned on all sides. Remove meatballs from skillet.

2 Add onion to skillet; cook and stir 2 to 3 minutes. Stir in tomatoes, tomato sauce and Italian seasoning; bring to a boil over high heat. Reduce heat to low; simmer, covered, 15 minutes. Return meatballs to skillet; simmer, covered, 15 minutes.

3 Place 3 to 4 meatballs in each roll. Divide sauce evenly; spoon over meatballs. Sprinkle with cheese.

Makes 4 servings

Nutrients per Serving:

Calories	340 (17% of calories from fat)				
Total Fat	7 g	Carbohydrate	40 g	Iron	3 mg
Saturated Fat	2 g	Dietary Fiber	3 g	Vitamin A	94 RE
Cholesterol	63 mg	Protein	31 g	Vitamin C	16 mg
Sodium	702 mg	Calcium	121 mg		

DIETARY EXCHANGES: 2 Starch/Bread, 3 Lean Meat, 1½ Vegetable

MINI BURGERS

High fat ground beef burgers get a major overhaul when well-seasoned ground chicken takes over the starring role in these easy appetizers. Fun finger food is no longer off limits with these mini burgers.

1 pound ground chicken
¼ cup Italian-style dry bread crumbs
¼ cup chili sauce
1 egg white
1 tablespoon white wine Worcestershire sauce
2 teaspoons Dijon mustard
½ teaspoon dried thyme leaves
¼ teaspoon garlic powder

32 thin slices plum tomatoes (about 3 medium)
½ cup sweet onion slices
16 slices cocktail rye or pumpernickel bread
Mustard (optional)
Pickle slices (optional)
Snipped chives or green onion tops (optional)

1 Preheat oven to 350°F. Combine chicken, bread crumbs, chili sauce, egg white, Worcestershire sauce, mustard, thyme and garlic powder in medium bowl. Form mixture into 16 patties.

2 Place patties in 15×10-inch jelly-roll pan. Bake, uncovered, 10 to 15 minutes or until no longer pink in centers.

3 Place 2 tomato slices and 1 onion slice on each bread slice. Top each with 1 patty; add dollops of mustard, pickle slices and chives, if desired.

Makes 8 servings

Nutrients per Serving:						
2 Mini Burgers						
Calories	148 (27% of calories from fat)					
Total Fat	4 g	Carbohydrate	14 g	Iron		2 mg
Saturated Fat	2 g	Dietary Fiber	2 g	Vitamin A		50 RE
Cholesterol	28 mg	Protein	12 g	Vitamin C		10 mg
Sodium	298 mg	Calcium	30 mg			
DIETARY EXCHANGES: 1 Starch/Bread, 1 Lean Meat						

BROILED CHICKEN BREAST WITH CILANTRO SALSA

Skinless white meat of poultry has one of the lowest fat content of all meats, with only 25% of calories coming from fat. To keep it light, use dry heat cooking methods like broiling or grilling.

2 tablespoons pine nuts (optional)
4 tablespoons lime juice, divided
½ cup lightly packed fresh cilantro, chopped
⅓ cup thinly sliced or minced green onions

¼ to ½ jalapeño pepper, seeded, minced*
4 small boneless skinless chicken breast halves (4 ounces each)
Ground black pepper

1 To make Cilantro Salsa, heat large nonstick skillet over medium heat until hot. Add pine nuts. Cook and stir 6 to 8 minutes or until golden. Combine pine nuts, 2 tablspoons lime juice, cilantro, onions and jalapeño in small bowl. Blend well. Set aside.

2 Preheat broiler.

3 Spray rack of broiler pan with nonstick cooking spray.

4 Brush chicken with remaining 2 tablespoons lime juice. Place chicken on rack of prepared pan. Sprinkle generously with pepper.

5 Broil 4 inches from heat, 8 to 10 minutes or until chicken is no longer pink in center, turning occasionally. Serve with Cilantro Salsa. Garnish with lime slices, if desired.

Makes 4 servings

*Jalapeño peppers can sting and irritate the skin; wear rubber gloves when handling peppers and do not touch eyes. Wash hands after handling.

Nutrients per Serving:

Calories	122 (19% of calories from fat)				
Total Fat	3 g	Carbohydrate	2 g	Iron	1 mg
Saturated Fat	1 g	Dietary Fiber	1 g	Vitamin A	79 RE
Cholesterol	58 mg	Protein	22 g	Vitamin C	15 mg
Sodium	80 mg	Calcium	26 mg		

DIETARY EXCHANGES: 3 Lean Meat, 1 Vegetable

CHICKEN & CHILE CHIMICHANGAS

Get that crisp texture the low fat way by brushing chimichangas lightly with water, then baking until tortillas are crisp and golden.

4 cups water
2 boneless skinless chicken
    breast halves (5 ounces
    each)
½ teaspoon ground cumin
1 cup (4 ounces) shredded
    reduced fat Monterey Jack
    cheese

1 can (4 ounces) diced mild
    green chilies
6 (8-inch) flour tortillas
    Green Onion-Cilantro Sauce
    (recipe follows)
    Washed and torn romaine
    lettuce leaves
    Tomato slices

1 Preheat oven to 400°F. Place water in large saucepan; bring to a boil over high heat. Add chicken. Cover; remove from heat. Let stand 15 minutes or until chicken is no longer pink in center. Drain; let cool slightly. Tear into small pieces. Place in medium bowl; sprinkle with cumin. Add cheese and chilies; stir to combine.

2 Spoon about ½ cup chicken mixture down center of each tortilla. Fold bottom of tortilla up over filling, then fold sides over filling. Brush each chimichanga lightly with water to coat. Place on baking sheet, about 1 inch apart. Bake 12 to 15 minutes or until tortillas are crisp and just barely golden.

3 Meanwhile, prepare Green Onion-Cilantro Sauce. Serve with romaine lettuce, tomato slices and Green Onion-Cilantro Sauce.   *Makes 6 servings*

GREEN ONION–CILANTRO SAUCE

¼ cup plain nonfat yogurt
¼ cup low fat sour cream
⅓ cup chopped green onions

⅓ cup lightly packed fresh
    cilantro

1 In food processor or blender combine all ingredients; process until smooth.   *Makes 6 servings*

Nutrients per Serving:					
Calories	248 (29% of calories from fat)				
Total Fat	8 g	Carbohydrate	23 g	Iron	2 mg
Saturated Fat	3 g	Dietary Fiber	<1 g	Vitamin A	159 RE
Cholesterol	43 mg	Protein	20 g	Vitamin C	17 mg
Sodium	578 mg	Calcium	277 mg		

DIETARY EXCHANGES: 1½ Starch/Bread, 2 Lean Meat, ½ Vegetable, ½ Fat

CHICKEN FAJITAS

The name of this popular Southwestern dish actually refers to the strips of marinated and grilled skirt steak that are wrapped inside warmed tortillas. This chicken version eliminates more than 80 calories and 10 grams of fat per serving.

¼ cup lime juice
4 cloves garlic, minced, divided
1 pound chicken tenders
  Nonstick cooking spray
1 cup sliced red bell peppers
1 cup sliced green bell peppers
1 cup sliced yellow bell peppers
¾ cup onion slices

½ teaspoon ground cumin
¼ teaspoon salt
¼ teaspoon ground red pepper
8 teaspoons low fat sour cream
8 (6-inch) flour tortillas, warm
  Green onion tops (optional)
  Salsa (optional)

1 Combine lime juice and 2 cloves minced garlic in large resealable plastic food storage bag; add chicken. Seal bag; turn to coat. Marinate in refrigerator 30 minutes, turning occasionally.

2 Spray large nonstick skillet with cooking spray; heat over medium heat until hot. Add chicken mixture; cook and stir 5 to 7 minutes or until chicken is browned and no longer pink in center. Remove chicken from skillet. Drain excess liquid from skillet, if necessary.

3 Add remaining 2 cloves minced garlic, bell peppers and onion to skillet; cook and stir about 5 minutes or until tender. Sprinkle with cumin, salt and red pepper. Return chicken to skillet. Cook and stir 1 to 2 minutes.

4 Spread 1 teaspoon sour cream on 1 side of each tortilla. Spoon chicken and pepper mixture over sour cream; roll up tortillas. Tie each tortilla with green onion top, if desired. Serve with salsa, if desired.   *Makes 4 servings*

Nutrients per Serving:

Calories	382 (17% of calories from fat)					
Total Fat	7 g	Carbohydrate	51 g	Iron		4 mg
Saturated Fat	2 g	Dietary Fiber	5 g	Vitamin A		119 RE
Cholesterol	60 mg	Protein	29 g	Vitamin C		159 mg
Sodium	421 mg	Calcium	134 mg			

DIETARY EXCHANGES: 2 Starch/Bread, 3 Lean Meat, 3 Vegetable

CHICKEN, SPINACH & RAISIN ENCHILADAS

With just one-fourth the calories from fat, more than 100% of daily vitamins A and C, 50% of daily calcium and plenty of B-complex vitamins and iron, this is one enchilada you can eat without guilt.

Roasted Tomato Enchilada
  Sauce (page 308)
2 boneless skinless chicken
  breasts (5 ounces each)
1 package (10 ounces) frozen
  chopped spinach, thawed,
  well drained

1½ cups (6 ounces) shredded
  reduced fat Monterey Jack
  cheese, divided
¾ cup part-skim ricotta cheese
½ cup raisins or currants
¼ teaspoon ground cloves
12 (6-inch) corn tortillas

1 Prepare Roasted Tomato Enchilada Sauce. Preheat oven to 350°F.

2 Place 4 cups water in large saucepan; bring to a boil over high heat. Add chicken. Cover; remove from heat. Let stand 15 minutes or until chicken is no longer pink in center. Drain; cool slightly. Tear into small pieces. Place spinach in large bowl with 1 cup Monterey Jack cheese, ricotta cheese, raisins and cloves; stir to combine. Stir in chicken.

3 Heat large nonstick skillet over medium-high heat until hot. Place 1 inch water in medium bowl. Dip 1 tortilla in water; shake off excess. Place in hot skillet. Cook 10 to 15 seconds on each side or until tortilla is hot and pliable. Repeat with remaining tortillas.

4 Spray 13×9-inch baking dish with nonstick cooking spray. Place 1 cup Roasted Tomato Enchilada Sauce in large bowl. Dip tortillas 1 at a time into sauce; shake off excess. Spread ⅓ cup chicken filling down center of each tortilla; fold sides over to enclose. Place seam side down in pan. Spread remaining Enchilada Sauce over enchiladas. Cover pan tightly with foil. (Recipe can be refrigerated up to 24 hours at this point.)

5 Bake 30 to 40 minutes or until heated through. Uncover; sprinkle with remaining ½ cup Monterey Jack cheese. Bake 3 minutes or until cheese melts.

Makes 6 servings

(continued on page 308)

Chicken, Spinach & Raisin Enchiladas, continued

ROASTED TOMATO ENCHILADA SAUCE

2 pounds small tomatoes
1 red bell pepper
4 cloves garlic, unpeeled
2 teaspoons olive oil

1 small onion, chopped
1 tablespoon chili powder
½ teaspoon ground cinnamon
¼ teaspoon ground cloves

1 Preheat broiler.

2 Place tomatoes, pepper and garlic in 13×9-inch baking dish. Broil 2 inches from heat 8 to 9 minutes or until vegetables are browned in spots. Turn vegetables; repeat 2 more times until vegetables are browned on all sides.

3 Place tomatoes in food processor or blender, discarding any liquid remaining in pan. Peel skin from pepper; remove stem and seeds. Add pepper to processor. Slice open garlic cloves; press into processor. Process until smooth; set aside.

4 Meanwhile, heat oil in large saucepan over medium-high heat until hot. Add onion; cook and stir 4 minutes or until tender. Add chili powder, cinnamon and cloves. Continue cooking 1 minute. Reduce heat to medium-low. Pour tomato mixture into pan; simmer, uncovered, 10 minutes or until heated through.

Makes 6 servings

Nutrients per Serving:

includes Roasted Tomato Enchilada Sauce

Calories	401 (23% of calories from fat)					
Total Fat	11 g	Carbohydrate	51 g	Iron	4 mg
Saturated Fat	4 g	Dietary Fiber	8 g	Vitamin A	624 RE
Cholesterol	43 mg	Protein	30 g	Vitamin C	49 mg
Sodium	283 mg	Calcium	561 mg		

DIETARY EXCHANGES: 2 Starch/Bread, 3 Lean Meat, ½ Fruit, 2 Vegetable, ½ Fat

TURKEY & ZUCCHINI ENCHILADAS WITH TOMATILLO AND GREEN CHILE SAUCE

1¼ pound turkey leg
    Tomatillo and Green Chile
    Sauce (page 310)
1 tablespoon olive oil
1 small onion, thinly sliced
1 tablespoon minced garlic
1 pound zucchini, quartered
    lengthwise, sliced thinly
    crosswise

1½ teaspoons ground cumin
½ teaspoon dried oregano leaves
¾ cup (3 ounces) shredded
    reduced fat Monterey Jack
    cheese
12 (6-inch) corn tortillas
    Nonstick cooking spray
½ cup crumbled feta cheese
6 sprigs fresh cilantro for garnish

1 Place turkey in large saucepan; cover with water. Bring to a boil over high heat. Reduce heat to medium-low. Cover; simmer 1½ to 2 hours or until meat pulls apart easily when tested with fork. Drain; discard skin and bone. Cut meat into small pieces. Place in large bowl; set aside.

2 Meanwhile, prepare Tomatillo and Green Chile Sauce.

3 Preheat oven to 350°F.

4 Heat oil in large skillet over medium-high heat until hot. Add onion; cook and stir 3 to 4 minutes or until tender. Reduce heat to medium. Add garlic; cook and stir 3 to 4 minutes or until onion is golden. Add zucchini, 2 tablespoons water, cumin and oregano. Cover; cook and stir over medium heat 10 minutes or until zucchini is tender. Add to turkey. Stir in Monterey Jack cheese.

5 Heat large nonstick skillet over medium-high heat until hot. Place 1 inch water in medium bowl. Dip 1 tortilla in water; shake off excess. Place in hot skillet; cook 10 to 15 seconds on each side or until tortilla is hot and pliable. Repeat with remaining tortillas.

6 Spray bottom of 13×9-inch baking pan with cooking spray. Spoon ¼ cup filling down center of each tortilla; fold sides over to enclose. Place seam side down in pan. Brush tops with ½ cup Tomatillo and Green Chile Sauce. Cover; bake 30 to 40 minutes or until heated through. Top enchiladas with remaining Tomatillo and Green Chile Sauce and feta cheese. Garnish with cilantro.

Makes 6 servings

(continued on page 310)

Turkey & Zucchini Enchiladas with Tomatillo and Green Chile Sauce, continued

TOMATILLO AND GREEN CHILE SAUCE

¾ pound fresh tomatillos *or* 2
     cans (18 ounces each) whole
     tomatillos, drained
1 can (4 ounces) diced mild
     green chilies, drained

½ cup ⅓-less-salt chicken broth
1 teaspoon dried oregano leaves
½ teaspoon ground cumin
2 tablespoons chopped fresh
     cilantro (optional)

 Place tomatillos in large saucepan; cover with water. Bring to a boil over high heat. Reduce heat to medium-high; simmer 20 to 30 minutes or until tomatillos are tender.

 In food processor or blender combine tomatillos, chilies, chicken broth (omit if using canned tomatillos), oregano and cumin; process until smooth. Return mixture to pan. Cover; heat over medium heat until bubbling. Stir in cilantro.

Makes about 3 cups

Nutrients per Serving:				
includes Tomatillo and Green Chile Sauce				

Calories	377 (28% of calories from fat)				
Total Fat	12 g	Carbohydrate	41 g	Iron	4 mg
Saturated Fat	3 g	Dietary Fiber	5 g	Vitamin A	76 RE
Cholesterol	48 mg	Protein	29 g	Vitamin C	34 mg
Sodium	284 mg	Calcium	320 mg		

DIETARY EXCHANGES: 1½ Starch/Bread, 1½ Lean Meat, 1 Fruit

❖

Cook's Tip

Herbs are a good way to add flavor to foods without adding calories, sodium or fat. This recipe combines oregano, cumin and fresh cilantro to pack it full of flavor.

❖

SEAFOOD

GARLIC SKEWERED SHRIMP

For a prettier presentation, leave the tails on the shrimp.

2 tablespoons reduced sodium
   soy sauce
1 tablespoon vegetable oil
3 cloves garlic, minced
¼ teaspoon crushed red pepper
   (optional)

1 pound large shrimp, peeled
   and deveined
3 green onions, cut into 1-inch
   pieces

1 Soak 4 (12-inch) bamboo skewers in water 20 minutes.

2 Combine soy sauce, oil, garlic and crushed red pepper in large resealable plastic food storage bag; add shrimp. Seal bag; turn to coat. Marinate at room temperature 10 to 15 minutes, turning occasionally.

3 Preheat broiler.

4 Drain shrimp; reserve marinade. Alternately thread shrimp and onions onto skewers. Spray rack of broiler pan with nonstick cooking spray. Place skewers on rack. Brush with reserved marinade; discard remaining marinade.

5 Broil 4 inches from heat, 10 minutes or until shrimp are opaque, turning occasionally. Serve on lettuce-lined plate. Garnish, if desired.

Makes 4 servings

Nutrients per Serving:

Calories	102 (19% of calories from fat)				
Total Fat	2 g	Carbohydrate	<1 g	Iron	3 mg
Saturated Fat	<1 g	Dietary Fiber	<1 g	Vitamin A	90 RE
Cholesterol	174 mg	Protein	19 g	Vitamin C	4 mg
Sodium	287 mg	Calcium	39 mg		

DIETARY EXCHANGES: 2 Lean Meat

HOT AND SOUR SHRIMP

The crushed red pepper creates the hot and the vinegar creates the sour in this scrumptious shrimp stir-fry.

½ package (½ ounce) dried black Chinese mushrooms*
½ small unpeeled cucumber
1 tablespoon brown sugar
2 teaspoons cornstarch
3 tablespoons rice vinegar
2 tablespoons reduced sodium soy sauce
1 tablespoon vegetable oil
1 pound medium shrimp, peeled and deveined
2 cloves garlic, minced
¼ teaspoon crushed red pepper
1 large red bell pepper, thinly sliced
Hot, cooked Chinese egg noodles (optional)

1 Place mushrooms in small bowl; cover with warm water. Soak 20 minutes to soften. Drain; squeeze out excess water. Discard stems; slice caps.

2 Cut cucumber in half lengthwise; scrape out seeds. Slice crosswise.

3 Combine brown sugar and cornstarch in small bowl. Add vinegar and soy sauce; blend until smooth.

4 Heat oil in wok or large nonstick skillet over medium heat until hot. Add shrimp, garlic and crushed red pepper; stir-fry 1 minute. Add mushrooms and bell pepper strips; stir-fry 2 minutes or until shrimp are opaque.

5 Stir vinegar mixture; add to wok. Stir-fry 30 seconds or until sauce boils and thickens. Add cucumber; stir-fry until heated through. Spoon shrimp and sauce over noodles, if desired.

Makes 4 servings

*Or substitute ¾ cup sliced mushrooms. Omit step 1.

Nutrients per Serving:

Calories	165 (24% of calories from fat)					
Total Fat	5 g	Carbohydrate	11 g	Iron	3 mg	
Saturated Fat	<1 g	Dietary Fiber	1 g	Vitamin A	91 RE	
Cholesterol	174 mg	Protein	20 g	Vitamin C	21 mg	
Sodium	466 mg	Calcium	49 mg			

DIETARY EXCHANGES: ½ Starch/Bread, 2 Lean Meat, ½ Vegetable

FLORIDA GRAPEFRUIT MARINATED SHRIMP

Shrimp, which are low in fat, are an excellent source of zinc. Zinc works in the body to help maintain the proper functioning of insulin and the immune system.

1 cup frozen Florida grapefruit juice concentrate, thawed
3 tablespoons chopped cilantro or parsley
1 tablespoon honey
2 cloves garlic, minced
2 teaspoons ketchup
½ teaspoon salt
¼ teaspoon crushed red pepper
1 pound medium shrimp, peeled and deveined

2 teaspoons cornstarch
1 cup long-grain white rice
1 tablespoon olive oil
1 large red bell pepper, thinly sliced
2 ribs celery, sliced diagonally into ¼-inch-thick slices
2 Florida grapefruit, peeled and sectioned

1 Combine grapefruit juice concentrate, cilantro, honey, garlic, ketchup, salt and crushed red pepper in large resealable plastic food storage bag; add shrimp. Seal bag; turn to coat. Marinate in refrigerator 20 minutes, turning occasionally.

2 Drain shrimp; reserve marinade. Place marinade with cornstarch in medium bowl; blend until smooth.

3 Meanwhile, prepare rice according to package directions, omitting salt.

4 Heat oil in large nonstick skillet over medium-high heat until hot; add shrimp. Cook and stir 2 to 3 minutes or until shrimp are opaque. Add reserved marinade, red bell pepper and celery; bring to a boil over high heat. Boil until mixture thickens slightly, stirring constantly. Add grapefruit; heat 30 seconds.

5 Garnish with fresh sprigs of cilantro. Spoon shrimp and vegetables over rice.

Makes 4 servings

Nutrients per Serving:					
Calories	422 (10% of calories from fat)				
Total Fat	5 g	Carbohydrate	75 g	Iron	6 mg
Saturated Fat	1 g	Dietary Fiber	3 g	Vitamin A	139 RE
Cholesterol	174 mg	Protein	24 g	Vitamin C	137 mg
Sodium	519 mg	Calcium	100 mg		

DIETARY EXCHANGES: 2½ Starch/Bread, 2 Lean Meat, 2 Fruit

ORANGE ALMOND SCALLOPS

Scallops are an excellent source of trace elements, including selenium. In the body, selenium teams up with vitamin E to prevent the oxidation of fatty acids. (Fatty acid oxidation has been linked to increased rates of certain cancers and heart disease.)

3 tablespoons orange juice
1 tablespoon reduced sodium soy sauce
1 clove garlic, minced
1 pound bay scallops or halved sea scallops
1 tablespoon cornstarch
1 teaspoon vegetable oil, divided
1 green bell pepper, thinly sliced

1 can (8 ounces) sliced water chestnuts, drained and rinsed
3 tablespoons toasted blanched almonds
3 cups hot, cooked white rice
½ teaspoon finely grated orange peel

1 Combine orange juice, soy sauce and garlic in medium bowl. Add scallops; toss to coat. Marinate at room temperature 15 minutes or cover and refrigerate up to 1 hour, tossing occasionally.

2 Drain scallops; reserve marinade. Combine marinade and cornstarch in small bowl; blend until smooth.

3 Heat ½ teaspoon oil in wok or large nonstick skillet over medium heat until hot. Add scallops; stir-fry 2 minutes or until scallops are opaque. Remove scallops from wok; reserve.

4 Add remaining ½ teaspoon oil to wok. Add bell pepper and water chestnuts. Stir-fry 3 minutes.

5 Return scallops along with any accumulated juices to wok. Stir marinade mixture; add to wok. Stir-fry 1 minute or until sauce boils and thickens. Stir in almonds. Spoon scallops and vegetables over rice. Sprinkle with orange peel. Garnish with orange peel and fresh herbs, if desired.

Makes 4 servings

Nutrients per Serving:

Calories	427 (15% of calories from fat)				
Total Fat	7 g	Carbohydrate	58 g	Iron	6 mg
Saturated Fat	<1 g	Dietary Fiber	3 g	Vitamin A	14 RE
Cholesterol	60 mg	Protein	33 g	Vitamin C	24 mg
Sodium	442 mg	Calcium	175 mg		

DIETARY EXCHANGES: 3 Starch/Bread, 4 Lean Meat

GARLIC CLAMS

Clams are high in protein and are an excellent source of calcium and iron.

2 pounds littleneck clams
2 teaspoons olive oil
2 tablespoons finely chopped
    onion
2 tablespoons chopped garlic

½ cup dry white wine
¼ cup chopped red bell pepper
2 tablespoons lemon juice
1 tablespoon chopped fresh
    parsley

1 Discard any clams that remain open when tapped with fingers. To clean clams, scrub with stiff brush under cold running water. Soak clams in mixture of ½ cup salt to 1 gallon water 20 minutes. Drain water; repeat 2 more times.

2 Heat oil in large saucepan over medium-high heat until hot. Add onion and garlic; cook and stir about 3 minutes or until garlic is tender but not brown. Add clams, wine, bell pepper and lemon juice. Cover; simmer 3 to 10 minutes or until clams open. Transfer clams as they open to large bowl; cover. Discard any clams that do not open. Increase heat to high. Add parsley; boil until liquid reduces to ¼ to ⅓ cup. Pour over clams; serve immediately. Garnish with parsley sprigs, if desired.   *Makes 4 servings*

Nutrients per Serving:

Calories	107 (25% of calories from fat)				
Total Fat	3 g	Carbohydrate	5 g	Iron	10 mg
Saturated Fat	<1 g	Dietary Fiber	<1 g	Vitamin A	77 RE
Cholesterol	25 mg	Protein	10 g	Vitamin C	24 mg
Sodium	44 mg	Calcium	48 mg		

DIETARY EXCHANGES: 1 Lean Meat, 1 Vegetable, ½ Fat

BAKED CRAB-STUFFED TROUT

Elegant stuffed trout are easier to make than you might imagine. Add a simple vegetable dish and you've got a terrific low fat, low cholesterol meal.

2 small whole trout (about
    6 ounces each), cleaned and
    boned
3 teaspoons reduced sodium soy
    sauce, divided
3 ounces frozen cooked
    crabmeat or imitation
    crabmeat, thawed, shredded
½ cup fresh bread crumbs

½ cup shredded carrot
¼ cup thinly sliced celery
¼ cup thinly sliced green onions
1 egg white, slightly beaten
2 tablespoons dry white wine
1 tablespoon grated lemon peel
1 teaspoon garlic powder
½ teaspoon ground black pepper
  Lemon wedges

1 Preheat oven to 375°F. Wash trout; pat dry with paper towels. Place on foil-lined baking sheet. Brush inside cavities lightly with 1½ teaspoons soy sauce.

2 Combine remaining 1½ teaspoons soy sauce, crabmeat, bread crumbs, carrot, celery, onions, egg white, wine, lemon peel, garlic powder and pepper in small bowl; blend well. Divide stuffing in half; place stuffing inside cavity of each trout.

3 Bake 30 minutes or until trout flakes easily when tested with fork. Serve with lemon wedges. Garnish, if desired.

Makes 4 servings

Nutrients per Serving:

Calories	108 (17% of calories from fat)				
Total Fat	2 g	Carbohydrate	6 g	Iron	2 mg
Saturated Fat	<1 g	Dietary Fiber	<1 g	Vitamin A	422 RE
Cholesterol	35 mg	Protein	15 g	Vitamin C	9 mg
Sodium	426 mg	Calcium	63 mg		

DIETARY EXCHANGES: 1½ Lean Meat, 1 Vegetable

CRAB AND CORN ENCHILADA CASSEROLE

This casserole shares an important trait with other one-dish meals; it provides substantial amounts of a wide array of key nutrients including vitamins A, C and B-complex, plus the minerals iron and calcium. What an easy way to get a balanced meal.

Spicy Tomato Sauce (page 326), divided

10 to 12 ounces fresh crabmeat *or* flaked or chopped surimi crab

1 package (10 ounces) frozen whole kernel corn, thawed, drained

1½ cups (6 ounces) shredded reduced fat Monterey Jack cheese, divided

1 can (4 ounces) diced mild green chilies

12 (6-inch) corn tortillas

1 lime, cut into 6 wedges

Low fat sour cream (optional)

1 Preheat oven to 350°F. Prepare Spicy Tomato Sauce.

2 Combine 2 cups Spicy Tomato Sauce, crab, corn, 1 cup cheese and chilies in medium bowl.

3 Cut each tortilla into 4 wedges. Place ⅓ of tortilla wedges in bottom of shallow 13 × 9-inch baking dish, overlapping to make solid layer. Spread half of crab mixture on top. Repeat with another layer tortilla wedges, remaining crab mixture and remaining tortillas. Spread remaining 1 cup Spicy Tomato Sauce over top; cover.

4 Bake 30 to 40 minutes or until heated through. Sprinkle with remaining ½ cup cheese; bake, uncovered, 5 minutes or until cheese melts. Squeeze lime over individual servings. Serve with low fat sour cream, if desired.

Makes 6 servings

(continued on page 326)

Crab and Corn Enchilada Casserole, continued

SPICY TOMATO SAUCE

2 cans (15 ounces each) no-salt-added stewed tomatoes, undrained *or* 6 medium tomatoes
2 teaspoons olive oil
1 medium onion, chopped
1 tablespoon minced garlic

2 tablespoons chili powder
2 teaspoons ground cumin
2 teaspoons dried oregano leaves
1 teaspoon ground cinnamon
¼ teaspoon crushed red pepper
¼ teaspoon ground cloves

1 In food processor or blender combine tomatoes with liquid; process until finely chopped. Set aside.

2 Heat oil in large saucepan or Dutch oven over medium-high heat until hot. Add onion and garlic. Cook and stir 5 minutes or until onion is tender. Add chili powder, cumin, oregano, cinnamon, red pepper and cloves. Cook and stir 1 minute.

3 Add tomatoes; reduce heat to medium-low. Simmer, uncovered, 20 minutes or until sauce is reduced to 3 to 3¼ cups.   *Makes about 3 cups*

Nutrients per Serving:

includes Spicy Tomato Sauce

Calories	366 (20% of calories from fat)				
Total Fat	9 g	Carbohydrate	51 g	Iron	4 mg
Saturated Fat	2 g	Dietary Fiber	7 g	Vitamin A	292 RE
Cholesterol	46 mg	Protein	27 g	Vitamin C	71 mg
Sodium	343 mg	Calcium	467 mg		

DIETARY EXCHANGES: 2½ Starch/Bread, 2½ Lean Meat, 2 Vegetable

SEAFOOD TACOS WITH FRUIT SALSA

Naturally low in fat, seafood adds a delicious touch to these tacos.

Fruit Salsa (page 328)
2 tablespoons lemon juice
1 teaspoon chili powder
1 teaspoon ground allspice
1 teaspoon olive oil
1 teaspoon minced garlic
1 to 2 teaspoons grated lemon
    peel
½ teaspoon ground cloves

1 pound halibut or snapper
    fillets
12 (6-inch) corn tortillas *or* 6
    (7- to 8-inch) flour tortillas
3 cups washed and torn romaine
    lettuce leaves
1 small red onion, halved, thinly
    sliced

1 To prevent sticking, spray grill with nonstick cooking spray. Prepare coals for grilling.

2 Prepare Fruit Salsa; set aside.

3 Combine lemon juice, chili powder, allspice, oil, garlic, lemon peel and cloves in small bowl. Rub fish with spice mixture. (Fish may be cut into smaller pieces for easier handling.)

4 Place fish on grill. Grill, covered, 5 minutes or until fish is opaque in center and flakes easily when tested with fork, turning occasionally. Remove from heat; cut into 12 pieces, removing bones if necessary. Cover to keep warm.

5 Place tortillas on grill in single layer; cook 20 seconds or until hot and pliable, turning occasionally. Stack; cover to keep warm.

6 Top each tortilla with ¼ cup lettuce and red onion. Add 1 piece of fish and about 2 tablespoons Fruit Salsa.   *Makes 6 servings*

(continued on page 328)

Seafood Tacos with Fruit Salsa, continued

FRUIT SALSA

1 small ripe papaya, peeled,
seeded, diced
1 firm small banana, diced
2 green onions, minced
3 tablespoons chopped fresh
cilantro or mint

3 tablespoons lime juice
2 jalapeño peppers, seeded,
minced*

 Combine all ingredients in small bowl. Serve at room temperature.

Makes 12 servings

*Jalapeño peppers can sting and irritate the skin; wear rubber gloves when handling peppers and do not touch eyes. Wash hands after handling.

Nutrients per Serving:

includes 2 tablespoons Fruit Salsa

Calories	294 (14% of calories from fat)				
Total Fat	5 g	Carbohydrate	43 g	Iron	3 mg
Saturated Fat	1 g	Dietary Fiber	6 g	Vitamin A	171 RE
Cholesterol	24 mg	Protein	21 g	Vitamin C	68 mg
Sodium	296 mg	Calcium	162 mg		

DIETARY EXCHANGES: 1½ Starch/Bread, 2 Lean Meat, 1 Fruit, ½ Vegetable

Health Note
Halibut is low in fat and also lower in cholesterol and sodium than many other kinds of fish.

SEAFOOD PAELLA

*Paella is the national dish of Spain, but varies from one region to another.
This version is most prevalent along the Spanish coast.*

1 tablespoon olive oil
4 cloves garlic, minced
4½ cups finely chopped onions
2 cups uncooked long-grain
    white rice
2 cups clam juice
2 cups dry white wine
3 tablespoons fresh lemon juice
½ teaspoon paprika
½ teaspoon saffron or ground
    turmeric
¼ cup boiling water

1½ cups peeled, diced plum
    tomatoes
½ cup chopped fresh parsley
1 jar (8 ounces) roasted red
    peppers, drained, thinly
    sliced, divided
1 pound bay scallops
1½ cups frozen peas, thawed
10 clams, scrubbed
10 mussels, scrubbed
20 large shrimp (1 pound), peeled
    and deveined

1 Preheat oven to 375°F. Heat oil in large ovenproof skillet or paella pan over medium-low heat until hot. Add garlic; cook just until garlic sizzles. Add onions and rice; cook and stir 10 minutes or until onions are soft. Stir in clam juice, wine, lemon juice and paprika; mix well.

2 Combine saffron and boiling water in small bowl; stir until saffron is dissolved. Stir into onion mixture. Stir in tomatoes, parsley and half the red peppers; bring to a boil over medium heat. Remove from heat; cover. Place on lowest shelf of oven. Bake 1 hour or until all liquid is absorbed. Remove from oven; stir in scallops and peas. *Turn oven off;* return paella to oven.

3 Place clams and mussels 1 inch above boiling water in large saucepan. Steam, covered 4 to 6 minutes, removing each as shells open. Discard any unopened clams or mussels. Steam shrimp 2 to 3 minutes or *just* until shrimp turn pink and opaque.

4 Remove paella from oven and arrange clams, mussels and shrimp on top. Garnish with remaining red peppers.   *Makes 10 servings*

Nutrients per Serving:

Calories	357 (9% of calories from fat)					
Total Fat	4 g	Carbohydrate	46 g	Iron		6 mg
Saturated Fat	1 g	Dietary Fiber	3 g	Vitamin A		90 RE
Cholesterol	98 mg	Protein	27 g	Vitamin C		43 mg
Sodium	281 mg	Calcium	99 mg			

DIETARY EXCHANGES: 2½ Starch/Bread, 2 Lean Meat, 2½ Vegetable

EASY SEAFOOD STIR-FRY

1 package (1 ounce) dried black Chinese mushrooms*
½ cup ⅓-less-salt chicken broth
2 tablespoons dry sherry
1 tablespoon reduced sodium soy sauce
4½ teaspoons cornstarch
1 teaspoon vegetable oil, divided
½ pound bay scallops or halved sea scallops

¼ pound medium shrimp, peeled and deveined
2 cloves garlic, minced
6 ounces (2 cups) fresh snow peas, cut diagonally into halves
2 cups hot, cooked white rice
¼ cup thinly sliced green onions

1 Place mushrooms in small bowl; cover with warm water. Soak 20 minutes to soften. Drain; squeeze out excess water. Discard stems; slice caps.

2 Place chicken broth, sherry, soy sauce and cornstarch in small bowl; blend until smooth.

3 Heat ½ teaspoon oil in wok or large nonstick skillet over medium heat until hot. Add scallops, shrimp and garlic; stir-fry 3 minutes or until seafood is opaque. Remove seafood from wok; reserve.

4 Add remaining ½ teaspoon oil to wok. Add mushrooms and snow peas; stir-fry 3 minutes or until snow peas are crisp-tender.

5 Stir chicken broth mixture; add to wok. Heat 2 minutes or until sauce boils and thickens.

6 Return seafood and any accumulated juices to wok; heat through. Spoon seafood over rice. Top with onions.

Makes 4 servings

*Or substitute 1½ cups sliced mushrooms. Omit step 1.

Nutrients per Serving:

Calories	304 (9% of calories from fat)				
Total Fat	3 g	Carbohydrate	42 g	Iron	5 mg
Saturated Fat	<1 g	Dietary Fiber	3 g	Vitamin A	34 RE
Cholesterol	74 mg	Protein	25 g	Vitamin C	29 mg
Sodium	335 mg	Calcium	119 mg		

DIETARY EXCHANGES: 2 Starch/Bread, 2 Lean Meat, 2 Vegetable

BROILED HUNAN FISH FILLETS

Dinner's on the table as easy as 1-2-3. A quick brush with Oriental seasonings and the fish is ready to broil. Vegetable Fried Rice (page 484) makes an ideal side dish.

3 tablespoons reduced sodium
    soy sauce
1 tablespoon finely chopped
    green onion
2 teaspoons Oriental sesame oil
1 clove garlic, minced

1 teaspoon minced fresh ginger
¼ teaspoon crushed red pepper
    Nonstick cooking spray
1 pound red snapper, scrod or
    cod fillets

1 Preheat broiler.

2 Place soy sauce, onion, oil, garlic, ginger and red pepper in small bowl; blend well.

3 Spray rack of broiler pan with nonstick cooking spray. Place fish on rack. Broil 4 inches from heat, 10 minutes or until fish flakes easily when tested with fork, turning occasionally and basting with marinade.

4 Serve on lettuce-lined plate, if desired.

Makes 4 servings

Nutrients per Serving:					
Calories	144 (24% of calories from fat)				
Total Fat	4 g	Carbohydrate	1 g	Iron	<1 mg
Saturated Fat	<1 g	Dietary Fiber	<1 g	Vitamin A	11 RE
Cholesterol	42 mg	Protein	25 g	Vitamin C	<1 mg
Sodium	446 mg	Calcium	40 mg		

DIETARY EXCHANGES: 2½ Lean Meat

BEIJING FILLET OF SOLE

These rolled, stuffed fillets are easy to make and they bake in just 30 minutes.

2 tablespoons reduced sodium soy sauce
2 teaspoons Oriental sesame oil
4 sole fillets (6 ounces each)
1¼ cups preshredded cabbage or coleslaw mix
½ cup crushed chow mein noodles

1 egg white, slightly beaten
2 teaspoons toasted sesame seeds*
1 package (10 ounces) frozen snow peas, cooked and drained

1 Preheat oven to 350°F. Combine soy sauce and oil in small bowl. Place sole in shallow dish. Lightly brush both sides of sole with soy mixture.

2 Combine remaining soy mixture, cabbage, crushed noodles and egg white in small bowl. Spoon evenly over sole. Roll up each fillet; place seam side down in shallow foil-lined roasting pan.

3 Sprinkle rolls with sesame seeds. Bake 25 to 30 minutes until fish flakes easily when tested with fork. Serve with snow peas.   *Makes 4 servings*

*To toast sesame seeds, spread seeds in small skillet. Shake skillet over medium heat 2 minutes or until seeds begin to pop and turn golden.

Nutrients per Serving:

Calories	252 (29% of calories from fat)				
Total Fat	8 g	Carbohydrate	6 g	Iron	2 mg
Saturated Fat	1 g	Dietary Fiber	<1 g	Vitamin A	237 RE
Cholesterol	80 mg	Protein	34 g	Vitamin C	32 mg
Sodium	435 mg	Calcium	86 mg		

DIETARY EXCHANGES: 4 Lean Meat, 1½ Vegetable

LEMON POACHED HALIBUT WITH CARROTS

3 medium carrots, cut into
    julienne strips
¾ cup water
¼ cup dry white wine
2 tablespoons lemon juice
1 teaspoon dried rosemary
1 teaspoon dried marjoram
    leaves

1 teaspoon chicken or fish
    bouillon granules
¼ teaspoon ground black pepper
4 fresh or frozen halibut steaks,
    cut 1 inch thick (about
    1½ pounds)
½ cup sliced green onions

1 Combine carrots, water, wine, lemon juice, rosemary, marjoram, bouillon granules and pepper in large skillet; bring to a boil over high heat.

2 Carefully place fish and onions in skillet. Return just to boiling. Reduce heat to medium-low. Cover; simmer 8 to 10 minutes or until fish flakes easily when tested with fork.

3 Carefully transfer fish to serving platter with slotted spatula. Spoon vegetables over fish. Garnish with lemon slices, if desired.

Makes 4 servings

Nutrients per Serving:

Calories	224 (17% of calories from fat)				
Total Fat	4 g	Carbohydrate	8 g	Iron	2 mg
Saturated Fat	1 g	Dietary Fiber	2 g	Vitamin A	1,670 RE
Cholesterol	55 mg	Protein	36 g	Vitamin C	14 mg
Sodium	338 mg	Calcium	110 mg		

DIETARY EXCHANGES: 4 Lean Meat, 1½ Vegetable

HALIBUT WITH CILANTRO AND LIME

Serve this low fat, speedy stir-fry with Chinese Vegetables (page 440) and brown rice for an extra fiber boost.

1 pound halibut, tuna or
    swordfish steaks
2 tablespoons fresh lime juice
¼ cup reduced sodium soy sauce
1 teaspoon cornstarch
½ teaspoon minced fresh ginger

½ teaspoon vegetable oil
½ cup slivered red or yellow
    onion
2 cloves garlic, minced
¼ cup coarsely chopped fresh
    cilantro

1 Cut halibut into 1-inch pieces; sprinkle with lime juice.

2 Place soy sauce and cornstarch in cup; blend until smooth. Stir in ginger.

3 Heat oil in wok or large nonstick skillet over medium heat until hot. Add onion and garlic; stir-fry 2 minutes. Add halibut; stir-fry 2 minutes or until fish flakes easily when tested with fork.

4 Stir soy sauce mixture; add to wok. Stir-fry 30 seconds or until sauce boils and thickens. Sprinkle with cilantro. Garnish with lime wedges, if desired.

Makes 4 servings

Nutrients per Serving:

Calories	154 (19% of calories from fat)				
Total Fat	3 g	Carbohydrate	5 g	Iron	2 mg
Saturated Fat	<1 g	Dietary Fiber	<1 g	Vitamin A	68 RE
Cholesterol	36 mg	Protein	25 g	Vitamin C	8 mg
Sodium	592 mg	Calcium	69 mg		

DIETARY EXCHANGES: 2½ Lean Meat, 1 Vegetable

CHILLED POACHED SALMON WITH CUCUMBER SAUCE

Salmon is an excellent source of omega-3 fatty acids. Research has shown that diets high in omega-3 fatty acids are associated with a reduced risk of developing heart disease.

1 cup water
½ teaspoon chicken or fish bouillon granules
⅛ teaspoon ground black pepper
4 fresh or frozen pink salmon fillets, thawed (about 6 ounces each)
½ cup chopped peeled seeded cucumber
⅓ cup plain nonfat yogurt

2 tablespoons sliced green onion
2 tablespoons commercial fat free salad dressing or mayonnaise
1 tablespoon chopped fresh cilantro *or* 1 teaspoon dried cilantro leaves
1 teaspoon Dijon mustard
2 cups washed and torn lettuce

1 Combine water, bouillon granules and pepper in large skillet; bring to a boil over high heat. Carefully place salmon in skillet. Return just to a boil. Reduce heat to medium-low. Cover; simmer 8 to 10 minutes or until fish flakes easily when tested with fork. Remove salmon from skillet. Cover; refrigerate.

2 Meanwhile, combine cucumber, yogurt, onion, salad dressing, cilantro and mustard in small bowl; blend well. Cover; refrigerate.

3 Place chilled salmon fillets on lettuce-lined plates. Spoon sauce over salmon.

Makes 4 servings

Nutrients per Serving:

Calories	223 (26% of calories from fat)				
Total Fat	6 g	Carbohydrate	4 g	Iron	2 mg
Saturated Fat	1 g	Dietary Fiber	1 g	Vitamin A	91 RE
Cholesterol	89 mg	Protein	36 g	Vitamin C	4 mg
Sodium	322 mg	Calcium	57 mg		

DIETARY EXCHANGES: 4 Lean Meat, 1 Vegetable

SALMON EN PAPILLOTE

To eliminate last minute clean up before your guest arrives, prepare this dish in advance and refrigerate until you are ready to cook. The Dilled Wine Sauce may either be spooned into the package when you open it or served on the side.

¾ cup water
1 teaspoon extra virgin olive oil
¼ teaspoon salt
⅛ teaspoon ground black pepper
½ cup couscous
  Parchment paper
1 small yellow squash, cut into julienned strips
½ pound fresh salmon fillet, bones removed, cut into 2 pieces
½ cup peeled, diced plum tomatoes

2 teaspoons chopped fresh dill *or* ¼ teaspoon dried dill weed
2 teaspoons chopped fresh tarragon *or* ¼ teaspoon dried tarragon leaves
2 teaspoons chopped fresh chives
2 teaspoons chopped fresh parsley
1 egg, beaten
  Dilled Wine Sauce (page 346)

1 Preheat oven to 350°F. Combine water, oil, salt and pepper in small saucepan with tight fitting lid; bring to a boil over high heat. Add couscous; blend well. Cover; remove from heat. Let stand 5 minutes or until all liquid is absorbed.

2 Make 2 large hearts with parchment paper by folding 2 pieces in half and cutting into half-heart shape. Unfold hearts and spoon ½ cup couscous on one side of each heart. Top each with ½ cup squash, 1 piece salmon, ¼ cup tomatoes and 1 teaspoon *each* dill, tarragon, chives and parsley. To seal, brush outer edges of hearts with beaten egg. Fold in half to make half-heart shapes; press edges together, crimping tightly with fingers. Place packages on ungreased baking sheet; bake 14 minutes. Meanwhile, prepare Dilled Wine Sauce.

3 To serve, place each package on large plate; cut an "X" in top. Fold corners back and drizzle sauce over each serving. Garnish with edible flowers, such as pansies, violets or nasturtiums, if desired.

Makes 2 servings

(continued on page 346)

Salmon en Papillote, continued

DILLED WINE SAUCE

1½ cups finely chopped onions
1 tablespoon dried dill weed *or*
   ½ cup chopped fresh dill
1½ teaspoons dried tarragon
   leaves *or* ¼ cup chopped
   fresh tarragon

1 clove garlic, peeled and
   quartered
½ cup dry white wine
2 teaspoons extra virgin olive oil

 In blender or food processor combine all ingredients except oil; process until smooth.

 Pour dill mixture into small saucepan; bring to a boil over high heat. Reduce heat to low; simmer until reduced by half. Strain sauce into small bowl, pressing all liquid through strainer with back of spoon. Slowly whisk in oil until smooth and well blended.   *Makes ½ cup*

Nutrients per Serving:					
includes ¼ cup Dilled Wine Sauce					
Calories	497 (26% of calories from fat)				
Total Fat	14 g	Carbohydrate	54 g	Iron	4 mg
Saturated Fat	3 g	Dietary Fiber	11 g	Vitamin A	146 RE
Cholesterol	127 mg	Protein	29 g	Vitamin C	24 mg
Sodium	387 mg	Calcium	131 mg		

DIETARY EXCHANGES: 3 Starch/Bread, 3 Lean Meat, 2 Vegetable, 1½ Fat

❖

Cook's Tip

To easily peel garlic, place a clove on a cutting board.
Cover the clove with the flat side of a chef's knife
blade, then firmly press down on the blade with your
fist. This loosens the skin so that it comes right off.

❖

RED SNAPPER WITH BROWN RICE AND TOMATO STUFFING

Red snapper is considered a lean fish—less than 5% of its weight and less than 9% of its calories come from fat.

Brown Rice and Tomato
    Stuffing (page 348)
3 to 4 lime slices
    Fresh savory sprigs (optional)
    Fresh oregano sprigs
    (optional)
2 to 2½ pounds fresh or frozen
    red or yellow tail snapper,
    scaled, head and tail
    removed

Diagonally sliced green onions
    or green onion fans for
    garnish

1 Prepare Brown Rice and Tomato Stuffing.

2 Preheat oven to 400°F.

3 Spray shallow baking pan with nonstick cooking spray. Arrange lime slices, savory and oregano sprigs in fish cavity. Place fish in pan. Bake fish and stuffing 25 to 30 minutes or until fish flakes easily when tested with fork and stuffing is heated through.

4 Spoon stuffing onto platter; arrange fish on top. Garnish fish with green onions, if desired.

Makes 4 servings

(continued on page 348)

Red Snapper with Brown Rice and Tomato Stuffing, continued

BROWN RICE AND TOMATO STUFFING

1 can (about 14 ounces) ⅓-less-salt chicken broth

⅓ cup water

1 cup brown rice

1½ tablespoons chopped fresh savory *or* 1½ teaspoons dried savory leaves

1 tablespoon chopped fresh oregano *or* ¾ teaspoon dried oregano leaves

⅛ teaspoon crushed red pepper

¾ cup coarsely chopped yellow summer squash

⅓ cup sliced green onions

¼ cup chopped fresh parsley

1 cup chopped tomatoes

 Combine chicken broth and water in medium saucepan; bring to a boil over high heat. Stir in rice, savory, oregano and red pepper. Return to a boil. Reduce heat to medium-low. Cover; simmer 20 minutes.

 Stir in squash, green onions and parsley. Cover; simmer 15 minutes more or until rice is almost tender and liquid is absorbed. Stir in tomatoes. Spoon into ungreased 1½-quart covered casserole.   *Makes 4 servings*

Nutrients per Serving:
includes Brown Rice and Tomato Stuffing

Calories	430 (11% of calories from fat)				
Total Fat	5 g	Carbohydrate	42 g	Iron	2 mg
Saturated Fat	1 g	Dietary Fiber	4 g	Vitamin A	101 RE
Cholesterol	83 mg	Protein	52 g	Vitamin C	21 mg
Sodium	130 mg	Calcium	130 mg		

DIETARY EXCHANGES: 2½ Starch/Bread, 4 Lean Meat, 1 Vegetable

❖

Cook's Tip

When buying summer squash, choose varieties that are brightly colored and spot-free. To reduce preparation times, precut squash and store in plastic bags up to 1 week in the refrigerator.

❖

GRILLED SWORDFISH WITH PINEAPPLE SALSA

One or more servings of seafood per week is linked with a lower risk of heart disease. All seafood is low in saturated fat and most is low in cholesterol.

Pineapple Salsa (recipe follows)
1 tablespoon lime juice
2 cloves garlic, minced

4 swordfish steaks (5 ounces each)
½ teaspoon chili powder or ground black pepper

1 Prepare Pineapple Salsa.

2 To prevent sticking, spray grill with nonstick cooking spray. Prepare coals for grilling.

3 Combine lime juice and garlic on plate. Dip swordfish in juice mixture; sprinkle with chili powder.

4 Place fish on grill, 4 inches from medium-hot coals. Grill 5 minutes or until just opaque in center and still very moist. Spoon about 3 tablespoons Pineapple Salsa over fish. *Makes 4 servings*

PINEAPPLE SALSA

½ cup finely chopped fresh pineapple
¼ cup finely chopped red bell pepper
1 green onion, thinly sliced

2 tablespoons lime juice
½ jalapeño pepper, seeded, minced*
1 tablespoon chopped fresh cilantro or fresh basil

1 Place all ingredients in small nonmetallic bowl; blend well. Serve at room temperature. *Makes 4 servings*

*Jalapeño peppers can sting and irritate the skin; wear rubber gloves when handling peppers and do not touch eyes. Wash hands after handling.

Nutrients per Serving:					
Calories	194 (28% of calories from fat)				
Total Fat	6 g	Carbohydrate	6 g	Iron	2 mg
Saturated Fat	2 g	Dietary Fiber	1 g	Vitamin A	76 RE
Cholesterol	56 mg	Protein	28 g	Vitamin C	20 mg
Sodium	183 mg	Calcium	16 mg		

DIETARY EXCHANGES: 3 Lean Meat, ½ Fruit

Pasta, Beans & More

PASTA PRIMAVERA

8 ounces uncooked linguine or
medium pasta shells
1 tablespoon reduced calorie
margarine
2 green onions, diagonally sliced
1 clove garlic, minced
1 cup fresh mushroom slices
1 cup broccoli flowerets
2½ cups fresh snow peas

4 to 8 asparagus spears, cut into
2-inch pieces
1 medium red bell pepper, cut
into thin strips
½ cup evaporated skimmed milk
½ teaspoon dried tarragon leaves
½ teaspoon ground black pepper
⅓ cup grated Parmesan cheese

1 Cook pasta according to package directions, omitting salt. Drain and set aside.

2 Melt margarine in large nonstick skillet. Add green onions and garlic; cook over medium heat until softened. Add mushrooms and broccoli. Cover. Cook 3 minutes or until mushrooms are tender. Add snow peas, asparagus, bell pepper, milk, tarragon and black pepper. Cook and stir until vegetables are crisp-tender and lightly coated.

3 Add cheese; pour over linguine and toss to coat evenly. Serve immediately.

Makes 4 (2-cup) servings

Nutrients per Serving:

Calories	329 (16% of calories from fat)				
Total Fat	6 g	Carbohydrate	51 g	Iron	4 mg
Saturated Fat	2 g	Dietary Fiber	6 g	Vitamin A	167 RE
Cholesterol	8 mg	Protein	18 g	Vitamin C	82 mg
Sodium	243 mg	Calcium	265 mg		

DIETARY EXCHANGES: 2½ Starch/Bread, ½ Lean Meat, ½ Fat, 1½ Vegetable

SAUCY BROCCOLI AND SPAGHETTI

Leeks, which look like giant green onions, have a milder and sweeter flavor than other members of the onion family. Along with oregano and hot pepper sauce, the leek adds enough flavor to the spaghetti and broccoli that there is no need to add salt.

3 ounces uncooked spaghetti
1 package (10 ounces) frozen chopped broccoli
½ cup thinly sliced leek, white part only
½ cup skim milk
2 teaspoons cornstarch
2 teaspoons chopped fresh oregano *or* ½ teaspoon dried oregano leaves

⅛ teaspoon hot pepper sauce
3 tablespoons reduced calorie soft cream cheese
1 tablespoon grated Romano or Parmesan cheese
1 tablespoon chopped fresh parsley

1 Prepare spaghetti according to package directions, omitting salt. Drain and keep warm.

2 Meanwhile, cook broccoli and leek together according to package directions for broccoli, omitting salt. Drain; reserve ¼ cup liquid. Add additional water if needed.

3 Stir milk into cornstarch, oregano and pepper sauce in medium saucepan until smooth. Stir in reserved liquid. Cook and stir over medium heat until mixture comes to a boil and thickens. Stir in cream cheese. Cook and stir until cheese melts. Stir in vegetables; heat through.

4 Serve vegetable mixture over pasta. Sprinkle with Romano cheese and parsley.

Makes 4 servings

Nutrients per Serving:

Calories	162 (16% of calories from fat)				
Total Fat	3 g	Carbohydrate	26 g	Iron	2 mg
Saturated Fat	2 g	Dietary Fiber	3 g	Vitamin A	176 RE
Cholesterol	9 mg	Protein	8 g	Vitamin C	32 mg
Sodium	133 mg	Calcium	120 mg		

DIETARY EXCHANGES: 1½ Starch/Bread, 1 Vegetable, ½ Fat

BROCCOLI, SCALLOP AND LINGUINE TOSS

Scallops are ideal for a healthy diet. They are low in calories (about 100 calories per 3-ounce serving), low in fat (about 1 g) and moderate in cholesterol (about 40 mg).

12 ounces fresh or thawed frozen scallops
2 medium onions, cut lengthwise into halves, then into slices
1 cup apple juice
2 tablespoons dry white wine
2 cloves garlic, minced
2 teaspoons dried marjoram leaves
1 teaspoon dried basil leaves
¼ teaspoon ground black pepper
3 cups broccoli flowerets
¼ cup water
4 teaspoons cornstarch
1½ cups chopped seeded tomatoes
¼ cup grated Parmesan cheese
4 cups cooked linguine

1 Cut large scallops into 1-inch pieces. Combine onions, apple juice, wine, garlic, marjoram, basil and pepper in large skillet. Bring to a boil over high heat. Add broccoli. Return to a boil. Reduce heat to medium-low. Cover; simmer 7 minutes. Add scallops. Return to a boil; reduce heat. Cover and simmer 1 to 2 minutes or until scallops are opaque. Remove scallops and vegetables.

2 Stir water into cornstarch in small bowl until smooth. Stir into mixture in skillet. Cook and stir over medium heat until mixture comes to a boil and thickens. Cook and stir 2 minutes more. Stir in tomatoes and cheese; heat through. Return scallops and vegetables to skillet; heat through. Toss mixture with linguine.

Makes 4 servings

Nutrients per Serving:

Calories	248 (13% of calories from fat)				
Total Fat	4 g	Carbohydrate	33 g	Iron	2 mg
Saturated Fat	1 g	Dietary Fiber	4 g	Vitamin A	185 RE
Cholesterol	33 mg	Protein	22 g	Vitamin C	109 mg
Sodium	309 mg	Calcium	174 mg		

DIETARY EXCHANGES: 1 Starch/Bread, 2 Meat, ½ Fruit, 1½ Vegetable

RIGATONI WITH FRESH TOMATOES

Roma tomatoes are small and plum shaped, and are also called Italian tomatoes. Romas are thick and meaty with less juice than regular tomatoes. They have about the same nutritional content as a regular tomato, which means they are high in vitamins A and C.

1 cup uncooked rigatoni or
    mostaccioli
Nonstick cooking spray
¼ cup sliced green onions
2 cloves garlic, minced
1 cup sliced zucchini
1 teaspoon chopped fresh basil
    or ¼ teaspoon dried basil
    leaves
1 teaspoon chopped fresh
    marjoram *or* ¼ teaspoon
    dried marjoram leaves

⅛ teaspoon salt
⅛ teaspoon ground black pepper
1 cup coarsely chopped seeded
    Roma tomatoes
¼ cup (1 ounce) crumbled feta
    cheese or shredded part-
    skim mozzarella cheese

1 Prepare rigatoni according to package directions, omitting salt. Drain and set aside.

2 Coat wok or large skillet with cooking spray; heat over medium-high heat until hot. Add onions and garlic. Stir-fry 1 minute. Add zucchini, basil, marjoram, salt and pepper. Stir-fry 2 to 3 minutes or until zucchini is tender. Stir in tomatoes and pasta; heat through.

3 Divide pasta mixture among four plates; sprinkle with cheese.

Makes 4 servings

Nutrients per Serving:

Calories	112 (17% of calories from fat)				
Total Fat	2 g	Carbohydrate	19 g	Iron	1 mg
Saturated Fat	1 g	Dietary Fiber	2 g	Vitamin A	84 RE
Cholesterol	6 mg	Protein	5 g	Vitamin C	16 mg
Sodium	154 mg	Calcium	55 mg		

DIETARY EXCHANGES: 1 Starch/Bread, 1 Vegetable, ½ Fat

VEGETABLE LASAGNA

Tomato Sauce (page 362)
8 ounces uncooked lasagna
    noodles (9 noodles)
2 teaspoons olive oil
⅓ cup finely chopped carrot
2 cloves garlic, minced
2 cups coarsely chopped fresh
    mushrooms
3 cups coarsely chopped
    broccoli, including stems
1 package (10 ounces) frozen
    chopped spinach, thawed
    and drained
⅛ teaspoon ground nutmeg

1 container (15 ounces) nonfat
    ricotta cheese
2 tablespoons minced fresh
    parsley
1 tablespoon minced fresh basil
1 tablespoon minced fresh
    oregano
2 teaspoons cornstarch
¼ teaspoon ground black pepper
1½ cups (6 ounces) shredded part-
    skim mozzarella cheese,
    divided
2 tablespoons grated Parmesan
    cheese

1 Prepare Tomato Sauce. Set aside. Cook noodles according to package directions, omitting salt. Drain and rinse well under cold water. Place noodles on sheet of aluminum foil.

2 Heat olive oil in large nonstick skillet over medium heat. Add carrot and garlic; cook until garlic is soft, about 3 minutes. Add mushrooms; cook and stir until moisture is evaporated. Reduce heat. Add broccoli; cover and simmer 3 to 5 minutes or until broccoli is crisp-tender. Remove from heat; stir in spinach and nutmeg.

3 Preheat oven to 350°F. Combine ricotta cheese, parsley, basil, oregano, cornstarch and pepper in small bowl. Stir in 1¼ cups mozzarella cheese.

4 Lightly spray 13×9-inch baking dish with nonstick cooking spray. Spread 2 tablespoons Tomato Sauce in bottom of dish. Arrange 3 noodles in dish. Spread with half of cheese mixture and half of vegetable mixture. Pour one third of tomato sauce over vegetable layer. Repeat layers, ending with noodles. Pour remaining one third of Tomato Sauce over noodles. Sprinkle with Parmesan cheese and remaining ¼ cup mozzarella. Cover; bake 30 minutes. Uncover; continue baking 10 to 15 minutes or until bubbly and heated through. Let stand 10 minutes before cutting.   *Makes 10 servings*

(continued on page 362)

Vegetable Lasagna, continued

TOMATO SAUCE

2 cans (16 ounces each) whole,
    peeled tomatoes, undrained
2 cans (6 ounces each) no-salt-
    added tomato paste

1 medium onion, finely chopped
¼ cup red wine
2 cloves garlic, minced
1 tablespoon Italian seasoning

 Combine tomatoes, tomato paste, onion, red wine, garlic and Italian seasoning in medium saucepan. Cover. Bring to a boil; reduce heat to low. Simmer 20 minutes.

Nutrients per Serving:
includes Tomato Sauce

Calories	273 (21% of calories from fat)				
Total Fat	7 g	Carbohydrate	37 g	Iron	4 mg
Saturated Fat	3 g	Dietary Fiber	6 g	Vitamin A	918 RE
Cholesterol	19 mg	Protein	21 g	Vitamin C	75 mg
Sodium	424 mg	Calcium	409 mg		

DIETARY EXCHANGES: 1 Starch/Bread, 2 Lean Meat, 4 Vegetable

Cook's Tip
Look for broccoli with a deep, strong green or green-purple color. The buds should be tightly closed and the leaves crisp.

KOREAN-STYLE BEEF AND PASTA

Rice noodles, also known as rice sticks, are made from rice flour and are as thin as string. They are usually coiled into nests and packaged in plastic bags.

¾ pound lean beef round steak
2 tablespoons reduced sodium
   soy sauce
1 tablespoon rice wine
2 teaspoons sugar
   Korean-Style Dressing (page 364)
1 package (6¾ ounces) rice
   noodles

2 cups thinly sliced napa
   cabbage
1¾ cups thinly sliced yellow bell
   peppers
½ cup thinly sliced radishes
1 medium carrot, shredded
2 green onions, thinly sliced

1 Freeze beef until partially firm; cut into very thin slices.

2 Combine soy sauce, rice wine and sugar in resealable plastic food storage bag; add beef slices. Seal bag; turn to coat. Marinate in refrigerator 8 hours or overnight, turning occasionally.

3 To prevent sticking, spray grill with nonstick cooking spray. Prepare coals for grilling.

4 Meanwhile, prepare Korean-Style Dressing; set aside.

5 Drain beef; discard marinade. Place beef on grill over medium-hot coals. Grill 2 to 3 minutes or until desired doneness, turning once. Or, place beef on rack of broiler pan coated with nonstick cooking spray. Broil 2 to 3 minutes or until desired doneness, turning once.

6 Cook noodles in boiling water 1 to 2 minutes or until tender; drain and rinse under cold water. Arrange noodles on platter.

7 Combine cabbage, bell peppers, radishes, carrot, green onions and beef in medium bowl. Add Korean-Style Dressing; toss to coat evenly. Serve over noodles. Garnish with green onion brush and carrot ribbons, if desired.

Makes 8 (1-cup) servings

(continued on page 364)

Korean-Style Beef and Pasta, continued

KOREAN–STYLE DRESSING

2 teaspoons sesame seeds	1 teaspoon Oriental sesame oil
⅓ cup orange juice	1 teaspoon grated fresh ginger
2 tablespoons rice wine	1 teaspoon sugar
2 teaspoons reduced sodium soy sauce	1 clove garlic, minced
	⅛ teaspoon crushed red pepper

1 Place sesame seeds in small nonstick skillet. Cook and stir over medium heat until golden brown and toasted, about 5 minutes. Cool completely.

2 Crush sesame seeds using mortar and pestle or with wooden spoon; transfer to small bowl.

3 Add orange juice, rice wine, soy sauce, sesame oil, ginger, sugar, garlic and crushed red pepper. Blend well. *Makes about ½ cup*

Nutrients per Serving:

includes 1 tablespoon dressing

Calories	194 (19% of calories from fat)				
Total Fat	4 g	Carbohydrate	24 g	Iron	3 mg
Saturated Fat	1 g	Dietary Fiber	1 g	Vitamin A	309 RE
Cholesterol	29 mg	Protein	13 g	Vitamin C	37 mg
Sodium	668 mg	Calcium	37 mg		

DIETARY EXCHANGES: 1½ Starch/Bread, 1½ Lean Meat, ½ Vegetable

Cook's Tip

Sesame oil is available in two types: dark and light. The Oriental sesame oil used to flavor this dish is the dark (amber-colored) variety. The oil is pressed from toasted sesame seeds, has a strong nutlike flavor and is best when used sparingly. The light sesame oil has a milder nutty taste and can be used in a manner similar to that of vegetable oil.

ORANGE BEEF AND BROCCOLI

Broccoli is said to be one of the healthiest foods you can eat! It is loaded with antioxidants and cancer-fighting agents, such as vitamin C.

1 pound lean boneless beef
　　steak, cut 1 inch thick
½ cup orange juice
2 teaspoons reduced sodium soy
　　sauce
1 teaspoon sugar
3 teaspoons vegetable oil,
　　divided
¾ pound broccoli, coarsely
　　chopped

1 cup diagonally sliced carrots
½ cup thinly sliced red bell
　　pepper
1 green onion, diagonally sliced
¾ cup cold water
2 teaspoons cornstarch
1 tablespoon grated orange peel
6 ounces uncooked "no-yolk"
　　broad noodles

1 Freeze beef until partially firm; slice beef across grain into ⅛-inch slices. Combine orange juice, soy sauce and sugar in resealable plastic food storage bag; add beef. Seal bag; turn to coat. Marinate at room temperature 30 minutes or in refrigerator overnight, turning occasionally.

2 Heat 2 teaspoons oil in large nonstick skillet or wok. Add broccoli, carrots, bell pepper and green onion. Cook 2 minutes, stirring frequently. Remove vegetables to large bowl.

3 Heat remaining 1 teaspoon oil in skillet. Drain beef strips; reserve marinade. Add beef to skillet; cook 1 to 2 minutes or until no longer pink. Add vegetables and reserved marinade to skillet. Bring to a boil. Stir water into cornstarch until smooth. Add to skillet and cook until thickened, stirring constantly. Sprinkle with grated orange peel.

4 Cook noodles according to package directions, omitting salt. Drain. Spoon beef mixture over noodles and serve immediately. Garnish with orange curls, if desired.

Makes 4 servings

Nutrients per Serving:

Calories	424 (27% of calories from fat)					
Total Fat	13 g	Carbohydrate	43 g	Iron	5 mg	
Saturated Fat	3 g	Dietary Fiber	6 g	Vitamin A	943 RE	
Cholesterol	77 mg	Protein	35 g	Vitamin C	125 mg	
Sodium	169 mg	Calcium	69 mg			

DIETARY EXCHANGES: 2 Starch/Bread, 3½ Lean Meat, 2½ Vegetable

THAI BEEF NOODLES

Today more than ever, lean beef can be included in heart-healthy diets. This fabulous dish incorporates many traditional Thai ingredients— without all the fat.

1 pound lean boneless beef top
   sirloin steak, cut 1 inch thick
2 tablespoons reduced sodium
   soy sauce, divided
2 tablespoons rice wine or dry
   sherry
2 teaspoons sugar
1 tablespoon creamy peanut
   butter
2 tablespoons water

2 teaspoons rice wine vinegar
¼ teaspoon crushed red pepper
⅛ teaspoon grated fresh ginger
6 ounces uncooked vermicelli or
   other pasta
   Nonstick cooking spray
1 cup chopped red bell pepper
¾ cup chopped, seeded cucumber
¼ cup diagonally sliced green
   onions

1 Cut steak into 1-inch pieces. Combine 1 tablespoon soy sauce, rice wine and sugar in resealable plastic food storage bag; add beef. Seal bag; turn to coat. Marinate at room temperature 30 minutes or in refrigerator overnight, turning occasionally.

2 Combine remaining 1 tablespoon soy sauce, peanut butter, water, rice wine vinegar, crushed red pepper and ginger in large bowl.

3 Cook pasta according to package directions, omitting salt. Drain and rinse well under hot water. Add pasta to peanut butter mixture; toss to coat evenly. Set aside. Drain beef; discard marinade. Set aside.

4 Spray large nonstick skillet with cooking spray; heat over medium-high heat. Add beef and bell pepper to skillet. Cook 2 to 3 minutes or until desired doneness. Add beef and bell pepper to noodle mixture; toss to coat evenly. Sprinkle with cucumber and green onions.   *Makes 4 servings*

Nutrients per Serving:					
Calories	400 (29% of calories from fat)				
Total Fat	13 g	Carbohydrate	40 g	Iron	5 mg
Saturated Fat	4 g	Dietary Fiber	1 g	Vitamin A	48 RE
Cholesterol	76 mg	Protein	33 g	Vitamin C	52 mg
Sodium	790 mg	Calcium	35 mg		

DIETARY EXCHANGES: 2½ Starch/Bread, 3½ Lean Meat, 1 Vegetable, ½ Fat

PAD THAI

8 ounces uncooked rice noodles,
⅛ inch wide
1½ tablespoons fish sauce*
1 to 2 tablespoons fresh lemon
juice
2 tablespoons rice wine vinegar
1 tablespoon ketchup
2 teaspoons sugar
¼ teaspoon crushed red pepper
1 tablespoon vegetable oil
4 ounces boneless skinless
chicken breast, finely
chopped

2 green onions, thinly sliced
2 cloves garlic, minced
3 ounces raw small shrimp,
peeled and deveined
2 cups fresh bean sprouts
1 medium carrot, shredded
3 tablespoons minced fresh
cilantro
2 tablespoons chopped unsalted
dry-roasted peanuts

1 Place noodles in medium bowl. Cover with lukewarm water and let stand 30 minutes or until soft. Drain and set aside. Whisk together fish sauce, lemon juice, rice wine vinegar, ketchup, sugar and crushed red pepper in small bowl; set aside.

2 Heat oil in wok or large nonstick skillet over medium-high heat. Add chicken, green onions and garlic. Cook and stir until chicken is no longer pink. Stir in noodles; cook 1 minute. Add shrimp and bean sprouts; cook just until shrimp turn opaque, about 3 minutes. Stir in fish sauce mixture; toss to coat evenly. Cook until heated through, about 2 minutes.

3 Arrange noodle mixture on platter; sprinkle with carrot, cilantro and peanuts. Garnish with lemon wedges, tomato wedges and fresh cilantro, if desired.

Makes 5 (1-cup) servings

*Fish sauce is available at most larger supermarkets and Oriental markets.

Nutrients per Serving:

Calories	265 (18% of calories from fat)				
Total Fat	6 g	Carbohydrate	42 g	Iron	2 mg
Saturated Fat	1 g	Dietary Fiber	1 g	Vitamin A	453 RE
Cholesterol	38 mg	Protein	14 g	Vitamin C	13 mg
Sodium	798 mg	Calcium	78 mg		

DIETARY EXCHANGES: 2½ Starch/Bread, ½ Lean Meat, 1 Vegetable, ½ Fat

SOBA STIR-FRY

Among the favorite noodles used in Japanese cooking are thin buckwheat strands called soba. You can find dried soba in Oriental markets.

8 ounces uncooked soba noodles
(Japanese buckwheat pasta)
1 tablespoon olive oil
2 cups sliced fresh shiitake
mushrooms
1 medium red bell pepper, cut
into thin strips
2 whole dried red peppers *or*
¼ teaspoon crushed red
pepper
1 clove garlic, minced

2 cups shredded napa cabbage
½ cup ⅓-less-salt chicken broth
2 tablespoons reduced sodium
tamari or soy sauce
1 tablespoon rice wine or dry
sherry
2 teaspoons cornstarch
1 package (14 ounces) firm tofu,
drained and cut into 1-inch
cubes
2 green onions, thinly sliced

1 Cook noodles according to package directions, omitting salt. Drain and set aside.

2 Heat oil in large nonstick skillet or wok over medium heat. Add mushrooms, bell pepper, dried peppers and garlic. Cook 3 minutes or until mushrooms are tender.

3 Add cabbage. Cover. Cook 2 minutes or until cabbage is wilted.

4 Combine chicken broth, tamari, rice wine and cornstarch in small bowl. Stir sauce into vegetable mixture. Cook 2 minutes or until sauce is bubbly.

5 Stir in tofu and noodles; toss gently until heated through. Sprinkle with green onions. Serve immediately. *Makes 4 (2-cup) servings*

Nutrients per Serving:					
Calories	443 (24% of calories from fat)				
Total Fat	13 g	Carbohydrate	64 g	Iron	13 mg
Saturated Fat	2 g	Dietary Fiber	6 g	Vitamin A	242 RE
Cholesterol	0 mg	Protein	27 g	Vitamin C	40 mg
Sodium	773 mg	Calcium	261 mg		

DIETARY EXCHANGES: 3½ Starch/Bread, 2 Lean Meat, 1 Vegetable, 1 Fat

PLUM CHICKEN

The plum is one of the world's most popular fruits. Choose plums that are firm but not hard, and look for plumpness and full color. Avoid plums with breaks in the skin and brownish discoloration.

6 ounces fresh uncooked Chinese egg noodles

¼ cup plum preserves or jam

3 tablespoons rice wine vinegar

3 tablespoons reduced sodium soy sauce

1 tablespoon cornstarch

3 teaspoons vegetable oil, divided

1 small red onion, thinly sliced

2 cups fresh pea pods, diagonally sliced

12 ounces boneless skinless chicken breasts, cut into thin strips

4 medium plums or apricots, pitted and sliced

1 Cook noodles according to package directions, omitting salt. Drain and keep warm.

2 Stir together plum preserves, rice wine vinegar, soy sauce and cornstarch in small bowl; set aside.

3 Heat 2 teaspoons oil in large nonstick skillet or wok. Add onion and cook 2 minutes or until slightly softened. Add pea pods and cook 3 minutes. Remove vegetables to medium bowl.

4 Heat remaining 1 teaspoon oil in skillet. Add chicken and cook over medium-high heat 2 to 3 minutes or until no longer pink. Push chicken to one side of skillet.

5 Stir sauce; add to skillet. Cook and stir until thick and bubbly. Stir in vegetables and plums; coat evenly. Cook 3 minutes or until heated through. Toss with noodles and serve immediately.

Makes 4 servings

Nutrients per Serving:

Calories	415 (11% of calories from fat)				
Total Fat	5 g	Carbohydrate	73 g	Iron	3 mg
Saturated Fat	1 g	Dietary Fiber	3 g	Vitamin A	33 RE
Cholesterol	43 mg	Protein	21 g	Vitamin C	30 mg
Sodium	307 mg	Calcium	49 mg		

DIETARY EXCHANGES: 3 Starch/Bread, 1½ Lean Meat, 1½ Fruit, 1 Vegetable

CHICKEN CHOW MEIN

Chow mein is a Chinese-American dish of bits of meat and vegetables served over crisp, fried noodles.

6 ounces uncooked fresh
    Chinese egg noodles
    Nonstick cooking spray
½ cup ⅓-less-salt chicken broth
2 tablespoons reduced sodium
    soy sauce
1½ teaspoons cornstarch
½ teaspoon Oriental sesame oil
½ teaspoon ground black pepper
⅛ teaspoon Chinese five-spice
    powder

6 ounces boneless skinless
    chicken breasts, coarsely
    chopped
2 green onions, sliced
2 cups thinly sliced bok choy
1½ cups mixed frozen vegetables,
    thawed and drained
1 can (8 ounces) sliced water
    chestnuts, drained and
    rinsed
1 cup fresh bean sprouts

1 Preheat oven to 400°F. Cook noodles according to package directions, omitting salt. Drain and rinse well under cold water until pasta is cool; drain well. Lightly spray 9-inch cake pan with cooking spray. Spread noodles in pan, pressing firmly. Lightly spray top of noodles with cooking spray. Bake 10 minutes.

2 Invert noodles onto baking sheet or large plate. Carefully slide noodle cake back into cake pan. Bake 10 to 15 minutes or until top is crisp and lightly browned. Transfer to serving platter. Whisk together next 6 ingredients in small bowl until cornstarch is dissolved; set aside.

3 Spray large nonstick skillet with cooking spray. Add chicken and green onions. Cook, stirring frequently, over medium-high heat until chicken is no longer pink, about 5 minutes. Stir in bok choy, mixed vegetables and water chestnuts. Cook 3 minutes or until vegetables are crisp-tender. Push vegetables to one side of skillet; stir in sauce. Cook and stir until thickened, about 2 minutes. Stir in bean sprouts. Spoon over noodle cake.

Makes 4 servings

Nutrients per Serving:

Calories	284 (6% of calories from fat)				
Total Fat	2 g	Carbohydrate	52 g	Iron	3 mg
Saturated Fat	<1 g	Dietary Fiber	3 g	Vitamin A	350 RE
Cholesterol	22 mg	Protein	16 g	Vitamin C	23 mg
Sodium	322 mg	Calcium	57 mg		

DIETARY EXCHANGES: 2 Starch/Bread, 1 Lean Meat, 3 Vegetable

CHICKEN NOODLE ROLL-UPS

Serve this colorful lasagnalike dish for a special occasion!

9 uncooked lasagna noodles
   (about 9 ounces)
8 ounces boneless skinless
   chicken breasts, cut into
   chunks
   Nonstick cooking spray
2 cups finely chopped broccoli
2 cups 1% low fat cottage cheese
1 egg
2 teaspoons minced fresh chives

¼ teaspoon ground nutmeg
¼ teaspoon ground black pepper
1 tablespoon reduced calorie
   margarine
2 tablespoons all-purpose flour
1 cup ⅓-less-salt chicken broth
½ cup skim milk
½ teaspoon dry mustard
1 medium tomato, seeded and
   chopped

1 Cook lasagna noodles according to package directions, omitting salt. Drain and rinse well under cold water. Place in single layer on aluminum foil.

2 Preheat oven to 375°F. Place chicken in food processor or blender; process until finely chopped. Spray large nonstick skillet with cooking spray; place over medium heat. Add chicken; cook 4 minutes or until chicken is no longer pink. Stir in broccoli; cook until broccoli is crisp-tender, about 3 minutes. Cool.

3 Combine cottage cheese, egg, chives, nutmeg and pepper in medium bowl. Stir in chicken mixture. Spread generous ⅓ cup filling over each lasagna noodle. Roll up noodles, starting at short end. Place filled rolls, seam side down, in 12×8-inch baking dish; set aside.

4 Melt margarine in small saucepan over medium heat. Stir in flour; cook 1 minute. Whisk in chicken broth, milk and mustard. Cook, stirring constantly, until thickened. Pour sauce over filled rolls; sprinkle with tomato. Cover dish with foil. Bake 30 to 35 minutes or until filling is set. *Makes 9 servings*

Nutrients per Serving:

Calories	179 (22% of calories from fat)				
Total Fat	4 g	Carbohydrate	17 g	Iron	1 mg
Saturated Fat	1 g	Dietary Fiber	2 g	Vitamin A	95 RE
Cholesterol	46 mg	Protein	18 g	Vitamin C	24 mg
Sodium	291 mg	Calcium	77 mg		

DIETARY EXCHANGES: 1 Starch/Bread, 2 Lean Meat

VEGETABLE SPAGHETTI SAUCE WITH MEATBALLS

Nonstick cooking spray
1½ cups sliced fresh mushrooms
½ cup chopped onion plus
    2 tablespoons finely chopped
    onion
½ cup chopped carrot
½ cup chopped green bell pepper
2 cloves garlic, minced
2 cans (14½ ounces each) no-
    salt-added stewed tomatoes,
    undrained

1 can (6 ounces) no-salt-added
    tomato paste
2½ teaspoons Italian seasoning,
    divided
½ teaspoon salt
¼ teaspoon ground black pepper
1 egg white
2 tablespoons fine dry bread
    crumbs
8 ounces 95% lean ground beef
4 cups hot, cooked spaghetti

1 Preheat oven to 375°F. Coat large saucepan with cooking spray; heat over medium heat until hot. Add mushrooms, ½ cup onion, carrot, bell pepper and garlic. Cook and stir 4 to 5 minutes or until vegetables are crisp-tender. Stir in stewed tomatoes with liquid, tomato paste, 2 teaspoons Italian seasoning, salt and black pepper. Bring to a boil over medium-high heat. Reduce heat to medium-low. Cover; simmer 20 minutes, stirring occasionally.

2 Combine egg white, bread crumbs, remaining 2 tablespoons onion and remaining ½ teaspoon Italian seasoning in medium bowl. Add beef; mix until well blended. Shape to form 16 meatballs. Place in 11×7-inch baking pan. Bake 18 to 20 minutes or until beef is no longer pink. Drain on paper towels.

3 Stir meatballs into sauce. Return sauce to a boil; reduce heat. Simmer, uncovered, about 10 minutes more or until sauce slightly thickens, stirring occasionally. Serve over spaghetti. *Makes 4 servings*

Nutrients per Serving:

Calories	341 (13% of calories from fat)				
Total Fat	5 g	Carbohydrate	56 g	Iron	5 mg
Saturated Fat	2 g	Dietary Fiber	7 g	Vitamin A	593 RE
Cholesterol	25 mg	Protein	21 g	Vitamin C	71 mg
Sodium	381 mg	Calcium	74 mg		

DIETARY EXCHANGES: 3½ Starch/Bread, 1½ Meat, 3 Vegetable

FAJITA STUFFED SHELLS

*Mexican and Italian meet in this enticing entrée. Flavored
with lime, garlic, oregano, cumin and cilantro, it tastes much
more complicated than it is.*

¼ cup fresh lime juice
1 clove garlic, minced
½ teaspoon dried oregano leaves
¼ teaspoon ground cumin
1 (6-ounce) boneless lean beef
    round or flank steak
1 medium green bell pepper,
    halved and seeded
1 medium onion, cut in half

12 uncooked jumbo pasta shells
    (about 6 ounces)
½ cup reduced fat sour cream
2 tablespoons shredded reduced
    fat Cheddar cheese
1 tablespoon minced fresh
    cilantro
⅔ cup bottled chunky salsa
2 cups shredded leaf lettuce

1 Combine lime juice, garlic, oregano and cumin in resealable plastic food
storage bag; add steak, bell pepper and onion. Seal bag; turn to coat.
Marinate in refrigerator 8 hours or overnight, turning occasionally.

2 Preheat oven to 350°F. Cook pasta shells according to package directions,
omitting salt. Drain and rinse well under cold water; set aside.

3 Grill steak and vegetables over medium-hot coals 3 to 4 minutes per side
or until desired doneness; cool slightly. Cut steak into very thin slices. Chop
vegetables. Place steak slices and vegetables in medium bowl. Stir in sour
cream, Cheddar cheese and cilantro. Stuff shells evenly with meat mixture,
mounding slightly.

4 Arrange shells in 8-inch baking dish. Pour salsa over filled shells. Cover
with foil and bake 15 minutes or until heated through. Divide lettuce evenly
among 4 plates; arrange 3 shells on each plate.   *Makes 4 servings*

Nutrients per Serving:

Calories	265 (16% of calories from fat)				
Total Fat	5 g	Carbohydrate	36 g	Iron	3 mg
Saturated Fat	2 g	Dietary Fiber	3 g	Vitamin A	99 RE
Cholesterol	33 mg	Protein	19 g	Vitamin C	38 mg
Sodium	341 mg	Calcium	98 mg		

DIETARY EXCHANGES: 2 Starch/Bread, 1½ Lean Meat, 1 Vegetable

SANTA FE FUSILLI

If you have a taste for something hearty and healthy, this
Texas-style dish is for you.

1 medium red bell pepper*
2 teaspoons cumin seeds
¾ cup chopped seeded tomato
¼ cup chopped onion
1 clove garlic, minced
1 tablespoon chili powder
¼ teaspoon crushed red pepper
¼ teaspoon ground black pepper
1 can (16 ounces) no-salt-added
    tomato purée
⅓ cup water

1 teaspoon sugar
8 ounces uncooked fusilli pasta
1 can (16 ounces) black beans,
    drained and rinsed
1 package (10 ounces) frozen
    corn, thawed and drained
1 can (4 ounces) chopped green
    chilies, drained
⅓ cup low fat sour cream
    Fresh cilantro

1 Roast bell pepper over charcoal or gas flame or place under broiler, turning several times, until skin is charred. Place in paper bag; cool 10 minutes. Peel and discard charred skin. Cut pepper in half; seed, devein and coarsely chop.

2 Place cumin seeds in large nonstick saucepan. Cook and stir over medium heat until lightly toasted, about 3 minutes. Stir in tomato, onion, garlic, chili powder, crushed red pepper and black pepper. Cook until vegetables are tender, about 5 minutes. Stir in tomato purée, water and sugar. Reduce heat to low. Cover and simmer 15 minutes.

3 Cook pasta according to package directions, omitting salt. Drain and set aside. Stir beans, corn and chilies into vegetable mixture. Cook until heated through, about 8 minutes. Stir in pasta. Spoon into individual bowls; top with sour cream and cilantro.   *Makes 8 (1-cup) servings*

*Or, substitute 1 jar (7 ounces) roasted peppers.

Nutrients per Serving:

Calories	228 (9% of calories from fat)				
Total Fat	2 g	Carbohydrate	46 g	Iron	2 mg
Saturated Fat	<1 g	Dietary Fiber	8 g	Vitamin A	189 RE
Cholesterol	3 mg	Protein	12 g	Vitamin C	57 mg
Sodium	215 mg	Calcium	41 mg		

DIETARY EXCHANGES: 2 Starch/Bread, ½ Lean Meat, 2½ Vegetable

CHILI WAGON WHEEL CASSEROLE

Quick and easy is the idea in this tasty baked chili and pasta dish.

8 ounces uncooked wagon wheel
    or other pasta
    Nonstick cooking spray
1 pound 95% lean ground beef or
    ground turkey breast
¾ cup chopped green bell pepper
¾ cup chopped onion
1 can (14½ ounces) no-salt-
    added stewed tomatoes

1 can (8 ounces) no-salt-added
    tomato sauce
½ teaspoon ground black pepper
¼ teaspoon ground allspice
½ cup (2 ounces) shredded
    reduced fat Cheddar cheese

1 Preheat oven to 350°F. Cook pasta according to package directions, omitting salt. Drain and rinse; set aside.

2 Spray large nonstick skillet with cooking spray. Add ground beef, bell pepper and onion; cook 5 minutes or until meat is no longer pink, stirring frequently. (Drain mixture if using ground beef.)

3 Stir in tomatoes, tomato sauce, black pepper and allspice; cook 2 minutes. Stir in pasta. Spoon mixture into 2½-quart casserole. Sprinkle with cheese.

4 Bake 20 to 25 minutes or until heated through. *Makes 6 servings*

Nutrients per Serving:

Calories	340 (32% of calories from fat)					
Total Fat	12 g	Carbohydrate	34 g	Iron	3 mg
Saturated Fat	5 g	Dietary Fiber	3 g	Vitamin A	123 RE
Cholesterol	54 mg	Protein	24 g	Vitamin C	43 mg
Sodium	366 mg	Calcium	125 mg		

DIETARY EXCHANGES: 2 Starch/Bread, 2 Lean Meat, 1½ Vegetable, 1 Fat

EASY TEX-MEX BAKE

Tex-Mex is quickly becoming one of the most requested flavor combinations. If that is the taste you're looking for, you will not be disappointed with this low fat dish.

8 ounces uncooked thin
   mostaccioli
   Nonstick cooking spray
1 pound ground turkey breast
1 package (10 ounces) frozen
   corn, thawed, drained
⅔ cup bottled medium or mild
   salsa
1 container (16 ounces) 1% low
   fat cottage cheese

1 egg
1 tablespoon minced fresh
   cilantro
½ teaspoon ground white pepper
¼ teaspoon ground cumin
½ cup (2 ounces) shredded
   Monterey Jack cheese

1 Cook pasta according to package directions, omitting salt. Drain and rinse well; set aside.

2 Spray large nonstick skillet with cooking spray. Add turkey; cook until no longer pink, about 5 minutes. Stir in corn and salsa. Remove from heat.

3 Preheat oven to 350°F. Combine cottage cheese, egg, cilantro, white pepper and cumin in small bowl.

4 Spoon half of turkey mixture in bottom of 11×7-inch baking dish. Top with pasta. Spoon cottage cheese mixture over pasta. Top with remaining turkey mixture. Sprinkle cheese over casserole.

5 Bake 25 to 30 minutes or until heated through. *Makes 6 servings*

Nutrients per Serving:

Calories	365 (15% of calories from fat)					
Total Fat	6 g	Carbohydrate	39 g	Iron		3 mg
Saturated Fat	3 g	Dietary Fiber	4 g	Vitamin A		166 RE
Cholesterol	99 mg	Protein	38 g	Vitamin C		26 mg
Sodium	800 mg	Calcium	147 mg			

DIETARY EXCHANGES: 2 Starch/Bread, 4 Lean Meat

PASTITSO

Replacing real eggs with egg substitute in this fabulous Greek dish significantly reduces the amount of cholesterol.

8 ounces uncooked elbow
  macaroni
½ cup cholesterol free egg
  substitute
¼ teaspoon ground nutmeg
¾ pound lean ground lamb, beef
  or turkey
½ cup chopped onion
1 clove garlic, minced
1 can (8 ounces) tomato sauce

¾ teaspoon dried mint leaves
½ teaspoon dried oregano leaves
½ teaspoon ground black pepper
⅛ teaspoon ground cinnamon
2 teaspoons reduced calorie
  margarine
3 tablespoons all-purpose flour
1½ cups skim milk
2 tablespoons grated Parmesan
  cheese

1 Cook pasta according to package directions, omitting salt. Drain and transfer to medium bowl; stir in egg substitute and nutmeg.

2 Lightly spray bottom of 9-inch square baking dish with nonstick cooking spray. Spread pasta mixture in bottom of baking dish. Set aside.

3 Preheat oven to 350°F. Cook lamb, onion and garlic in large nonstick skillet over medium heat until lamb is no longer pink. Stir in tomato sauce, mint, oregano, pepper and cinnamon. Reduce heat to low and simmer 10 minutes; spread over pasta.

4 Melt margarine in small nonstick saucepan over medium heat. Add flour. Stir constantly for 1 minute. Whisk in milk. Cook, stirring constantly, until thickened, about 6 minutes; spread over meat mixture. Sprinkle with cheese. Bake 30 to 40 minutes or until set.

Makes 6 servings

Nutrients per Serving:

Calories	280 (15% of calories from fat)				
Total Fat	5 g	Carbohydrate	39 g	Iron	3 mg
Saturated Fat	2 g	Dietary Fiber	1 g	Vitamin A	198 RE
Cholesterol	31 mg	Protein	20 g	Vitamin C	4 mg
Sodium	366 mg	Calcium	134 mg		

DIETARY EXCHANGES: 2½ Starch/Bread, 1½ Lean Meat, ½ Vegetable

DOUBLE SPINACH BAKE

The two basic varieties of spinach, curly leaf and smooth, essentially taste the same. However, the smooth variety is easier to clean, since grit gets caught in the folds of the curly leaf.

8 ounces uncooked spinach
   fettuccine
   Nonstick cooking spray
1 cup fresh mushroom slices
1 green onion with top, finely
   chopped
1 clove garlic, minced
4 to 5 cups fresh spinach,
   coarsely chopped *or* 1
   package (10 ounces) frozen
   spinach, thawed and drained

1 tablespoon water
1 container (15 ounces) nonfat
   ricotta cheese
¼ cup skim milk
1 egg
½ teaspoon ground nutmeg
½ teaspoon ground black pepper
¼ cup (1 ounce) shredded
   reduced fat Swiss cheese

1 Preheat oven to 350°F. Cook pasta according to package directions, omitting salt. Drain and set aside.

2 Spray medium skillet with cooking spray. Add mushrooms, green onion and garlic. Cook and stir over medium heat until mushrooms are softened. Add spinach and water. Cover; cook until spinach is wilted, about 3 minutes.

3 Combine ricotta cheese, milk, egg, nutmeg and black pepper in large bowl. Gently stir in noodles and vegetables; toss to coat evenly.

4 Lightly coat shallow 11×7-inch baking dish with nonstick cooking spray. Spread noodle mixture in casserole. Sprinkle with Swiss cheese.

5 Bake 25 to 30 minutes or until knife inserted halfway to center comes out clean.
Makes 6 (1-cup) servings

Nutrients per Serving:

Calories	235 (9% of calories from fat)				
Total Fat	3 g	Carbohydrate	41 g	Iron	1 mg
Saturated Fat	<1 g	Dietary Fiber	1 g	Vitamin A	280 RE
Cholesterol	46 mg	Protein	19 g	Vitamin C	12 mg
Sodium	110 mg	Calcium	57 mg		

DIETARY EXCHANGES: 2 Starch/Bread, 1½ Lean Meat, ½ Vegetable

SOUTHWESTERN BEEF AND BEAN LASAGNA

½ pound 95% lean ground beef
1 can (16 ounces) pinto beans,
   rinsed and drained
1 teaspoon olive oil
1½ cups chopped onions
1 tablespoon seeded and minced
   jalapeño pepper*
1 clove garlic, minced
4 cups no-salt-added tomato
   sauce
1 can (4 ounces) diced green
   chilies, undrained
2 teaspoons chili powder

1 teaspoon dried oregano leaves
½ teaspoon ground cumin
1 container (8 ounces) nonfat
   cottage cheese
1½ cups (6 ounces) shredded
   reduced fat Cheddar cheese,
   divided
1 egg white
¼ cup chopped fresh cilantro
½ teaspoon salt
¼ teaspoon ground black pepper
8 ounces uncooked lasagna
   noodles

1 Brown beef in skillet; drain fat. Stir in beans; set aside. In large nonstick skillet, heat oil. Add onions, jalapeño and garlic; cook until onions are soft. Add tomato sauce, green chilies, chili powder, oregano and cumin. Bring to a boil; reduce heat. Simmer, uncovered, 20 minutes.

2 Preheat oven to 350°F. Combine cottage cheese, ½ cup Cheddar cheese, egg white, cilantro, salt and black pepper in medium bowl. Spray 13×9-inch baking pan with nonstick cooking spray. Cover bottom with ¾ cup tomato sauce mixture. Place layer of noodles on sauce. Spread half of beef mixture over noodles, then place another layer of noodles on top. Spread cheese mixture over noodles. Spread with remaining beef mixture. Layer with noodles. Pour remaining sauce mixture over all; sprinkle with remaining 1 cup Cheddar cheese. Pour 1 cup water around edges. Cover tightly with foil. Bake 1 hour and 15 minutes or until pasta is tender. Cool 10 minutes before cutting.   *Makes 6 servings*

*Jalapeño peppers can sting and irritate the skin; wear rubber gloves when handling peppers and do not touch eyes. Wash hands after handling.

Nutrients per Serving:

Calories	416 (25% of calories from fat)				
Total Fat	12 g	Carbohydrate	50 g	Iron	3 mg
Saturated Fat	4 g	Dietary Fiber	5 g	Vitamin A	262 RE
Cholesterol	40 mg	Protein	30 g	Vitamin C	36 mg
Sodium	1270 mg	Calcium	271 mg		

DIETARY EXCHANGES: 2½ Starch/Bread, 2 Lean Meat, 3 Vegetable, 1 Fat

CHICKEN AND VEGGIE LASAGNA

*Pasta is a great source of complex carbohydrates. It also contains
six essential amino acids, three B-complex vitamins and iron.
When cooking pasta, make sure the water is at a rolling boil.
This circulates the pasta so that it cooks evenly.*

Tomato-Herb Sauce (page 398)
Nonstick olive oil cooking spray
1½ cups thinly sliced zucchini
1 cup thinly sliced carrots
3 cups washed and torn fresh
   spinach leaves
½ teaspoon salt

1 package (15 ounces) fat free
   ricotta cheese
½ cup grated Parmesan cheese
9 lasagna noodles, cooked and
   drained
2 cups (8 ounces) reduced fat
   shredded mozzarella cheese

1 Prepare Tomato-Herb Sauce.

2 Preheat oven to 350°F. Spray large nonstick skillet with cooking spray; heat over medium heat until hot. Add zucchini and carrots; cook and stir about 5 minutes or until almost tender. Remove from heat; stir in spinach and salt.

3 Combine ricotta and Parmesan cheese in small bowl. Spread 1⅔ cups Tomato-Herb Sauce on bottom of 13×9-inch baking pan. Top with 3 noodles. Spoon half the ricotta cheese mixture over noodles; spread lightly with spatula. Spoon half the zucchini mixture over ricotta cheese mixture; sprinkle with 1 cup mozzarella cheese. Repeat layers; place remaining 3 noodles on top.

4 Spread remaining Tomato-Herb Sauce over noodles. Cover; bake 1 hour or until sauce is bubbly. Let stand 5 to 10 minutes; cut into rectangles. Garnish as desired.

Makes 12 servings

(continued on page 398)

Chicken and Veggie Lasagna, continued

TOMATO–HERB SAUCE

Nonstick olive oil cooking spray
1½ cups chopped onions (about
    2 medium)
4 cloves garlic, minced
1 tablespoon dried basil leaves
1 teaspoon dried oregano leaves
½ teaspoon dried tarragon leaves
¼ teaspoon dried thyme leaves

2½ pounds ripe tomatoes, peeled
    and cut into wedges
1 pound ground chicken, cooked,
    crumbled, drained
¾ cup water
¼ cup no-salt-added tomato paste
½ teaspoon salt
½ teaspoon ground black pepper

1 Spray large nonstick skillet with cooking spray; heat over medium heat until hot. Add onions, garlic, basil, oregano, tarragon and thyme; cook and stir about 5 minutes or until onions are tender.

2 Add tomatoes, chicken, water and tomato paste; heat to a boil. Reduce heat to low and simmer, uncovered, about 20 minutes or until sauce is reduced to 5 cups. Stir in salt and pepper. *Makes 5 cups*

Nutrients per Serving:

includes Tomato-Herb Sauce

Calories	254 (27% of calories from fat)				
Total Fat	8 g	Carbohydrate	26 g	Iron	3 mg
Saturated Fat	2 g	Dietary Fiber	4 g	Vitamin A	480 RE
Cholesterol	51 mg	Protein	22 g	Vitamin C	29 mg
Sodium	431 mg	Calcium	154 mg		

DIETARY EXCHANGES: 1 Starch/Bread, 2 Lean Meat, 2 Vegetable, ½ Fat

Health Note
Recent studies have shown that eating generous amounts of garlic may play a role in protection against heart disease. Results indicate that garlic may cause serum cholesterol levels to drop, help prevent blood clots that lead to heart attacks and strokes and aid in lowering blood pressure.

❖

CHEESE RAVIOLI WITH SPINACH PESTO AND CHICKEN

Pesto is a wonderful, fresh-tasting sauce that originated in Italy and is traditionally made with fresh basil leaves. Spinach is substituted in this recipe; one pound of raw spinach will yield four cups of leaves.

Cheese Ravioli (page 400) *or*
  2 (9-ounce) packages
  refrigerated low fat ravioli
Spinach Pesto (page 400)
Nonstick cooking spray
¾ cup matchstick-size carrot
  strips
¾ cup thinly sliced celery
½ cup chopped onion (about
  1 small)

2 cloves garlic, minced
1 can (14½ ounces) no-salt-
  added stewed tomatoes
1½ pounds chicken tenders, cut
  crosswise into halves
¼ cup dry white wine
2 teaspoons dried rosemary
  leaves
¼ teaspoon salt
⅛ teaspoon ground black pepper

1 Prepare Cheese Ravioli and Spinach Pesto.

2 Spray large nonstick skillet with cooking spray; heat over medium heat. Add carrots, celery, onion and garlic; cook and stir about 5 minutes or until crisp-tender.

3 Add tomatoes, chicken, wine, rosemary, salt and pepper; heat to a boil. Reduce heat to low and simmer, uncovered, about 10 minutes or until vegetables are tender and chicken is no longer pink in center.

4 Arrange Cheese Ravioli on serving plates; spoon chicken and vegetable mixture over ravioli. Top with Spinach Pesto or serve alongside.

Makes 8 servings

(continued on page 400)

Cheese Ravioli with Spinach Pesto and Chicken, continued

CHEESE RAVIOLI

Nonstick cooking spray
¼ cup finely chopped onion
2 cloves garlic, minced
2 tablespoons minced fresh
  parsley
½ teaspoon dried basil leaves
¼ teaspoon dried oregano leaves

¼ teaspoon dried thyme leaves
⅛ teaspoon ground black pepper
½ cup reduced fat ricotta cheese
32 wonton wrappers
1½ quarts plus 2 tablespoons
  water, divided
2 teaspoons cornstarch

1 Spray small nonstick skillet with cooking spray; heat over medium heat until hot. Add onion and garlic; cook and stir 2 to 3 minutes or until tender. Sprinkle with parsley, basil, oregano, thyme and pepper; cook and stir 1 minute. Remove from heat; stir in ricotta cheese.

2 Place 2 teaspoons cheese mixture in center of each of 16 wonton wrappers. Combine 2 tablespoons water and cornstarch in small bowl; brush on edges of wrappers. Top with remaining wonton wrappers; press edges to seal.

3 Place remaining 1½ quarts water in large saucepan. Bring to a boil over medium-high heat. Boil 4 to 6 ravioli at a time, uncovered, 2 to 3 minutes or until ravioli are tender and rise to surface of water. Repeat with remaining ravioli.

Makes 8 servings (2 ravioli per serving)

SPINACH PESTO

2 cups loosely packed fresh
  spinach leaves
2 tablespoons grated Romano
  cheese

2 tablespoons olive oil or
  vegetable oil
1 to 2 tablespoons lemon juice
1 tablespoon dried basil leaves
3 cloves garlic

1 Process all ingredients in food processor or blender until smooth.

Makes about 1 cup

Nutrients per Serving:

includes Cheese Ravioli and Spinach Pesto

Calories	284 (26% of calories from fat)				
Total Fat	8 g	Carbohydrate	28 g	Iron	3 mg
Saturated Fat	1 g	Dietary Fiber	3 g	Vitamin A	356 RE
Cholesterol	74 mg	Protein	23 g	Vitamin C	21 mg
Sodium	173 mg	Calcium	101 mg		

DIETARY EXCHANGES: 1½ Starch/Bread, 2½ Lean Meat, 1½ Vegetable

SWEET POTATO RAVIOLI WITH ASIAGO CHEESE SAUCE

¾ pound sweet potatoes
2 tablespoons plain nonfat
   yogurt
1 teaspoon minced fresh chives
1 tablespoon plus ¼ teaspoon
   minced fresh sage, divided
24 wonton wrappers
1 tablespoon reduced calorie
   margarine

1 tablespoon plus 2 teaspoons
   all-purpose flour
½ cup skim milk
½ cup ⅓-less-salt chicken broth
½ cup (2 ounces) shredded
   Asiago or Cheddar cheese
¼ teaspoon ground nutmeg
¼ teaspoon ground white pepper
⅛ teaspoon ground cinnamon

1 Preheat oven to 350°F. Bake sweet potatoes 40 to 45 minutes or until tender. Cool completely. Peel potatoes and mash pulp. Stir in yogurt, chives and ¼ teaspoon sage.

2 Place wonton wrappers on counter. Spoon 1 rounded teaspoon potato mixture in center of each wonton. Spread filling flat, leaving ½-inch border. Brush edges lightly with water. Fold wontons in half diagonally, pressing lightly to seal. Place filled wontons on baking sheet and cover loosely with plastic wrap.

3 Bring 1½ quarts water to a boil in large saucepan. Reduce heat to medium. Add a few ravioli at a time. (Do not overcrowd.) Cook until tender, about 9 minutes. Transfer to platter with slotted spoon.

4 Melt margarine in small saucepan over medium heat. Stir in flour; cook 1 minute, stirring constantly. Gradually stir in milk and chicken broth. Cook and stir until slightly thickened, about 4 minutes. Stir in cheese, nutmeg, white pepper and cinnamon.

5 Spoon 3 tablespoons sauce onto individual plates. Place 3 ravioli onto each plate. Sprinkle with remaining sage.   *Makes 8 servings*

Nutrients per Serving:

Calories	304 (20% of calories from fat)				
Total Fat	7 g	Carbohydrate	49 g	Iron	2 mg
Saturated Fat	3 g	Dietary Fiber	3 g	Vitamin A	1530 RE
Cholesterol	19 mg	Protein	11 g	Vitamin C	17 mg
Sodium	558 mg	Calcium	174 mg		

DIETARY EXCHANGES: 3 Starch/Bread, ½ Lean Meat, 1 Fat

CHEESE TORTELLINI WITH TUNA

Cheese tortellini and tuna are both good sources of protein. Add a green salad to complete this delicious meal.

1 tuna steak* (about 6 ounces)
1 package (9 ounces)
   refrigerated reduced fat
   cheese tortellini
   Nonstick cooking spray
1 cup finely chopped red bell
   pepper
1 cup finely chopped green bell
   pepper

¼ cup finely chopped onion
¾ teaspoon fennel seeds, crushed
½ cup evaporated skimmed milk
2 teaspoons all-purpose flour
½ teaspoon dry mustard
½ teaspoon ground black pepper

1 Grill or broil tuna 4 inches from heat source until fish just begins to flake, about 7 to 9 minutes, turning once. Remove and discard skin. Cut tuna into chunks; set aside.

2 Cook pasta according to package directions, omitting salt. Drain; set aside.

3 Spray large nonstick skillet with cooking spray. Add bell peppers, onion and fennel seeds; cook over medium heat until crisp-tender.

4 Whisk together milk, flour, mustard and black pepper in small bowl until smooth; add to skillet. Cook until thickened, stirring constantly. Stir in tuna and pasta; reduce heat to low and simmer until heated through, about 3 minutes. Serve immediately. *Makes about 4 (1½-cup) servings*

*Or, substitute 1 can (6 ounces) tuna packed in water, drained, for tuna steak. Omit step 1.

Nutrients per Serving:

Calories	180 (19% of calories from fat)				
Total Fat	4 g	Carbohydrate	21 g	Iron	2 mg
Saturated Fat	2 g	Dietary Fiber	3 g	Vitamin A	397 RE
Cholesterol	21 mg	Protein	16 g	Vitamin C	112 mg
Sodium	160 mg	Calcium	141 mg		

DIETARY EXCHANGES: ½ Starch/Bread, 1½ Lean Meat, ½ Milk, 1 Vegetable

JAMBALAYA

In Italian, orzo means "barley," but it is actually a tiny, rice-shaped pasta. It is ideal for soups and wonderful when served as a substitute for rice, as it is in this spicy dish.

2 teaspoons vegetable oil
4 ounces smoked chicken, cubed
1½ cups chopped green bell peppers
1¼ cups chopped celery
1 cup chopped onion
3 cloves garlic, minced
1 can (16 ounces) no-salt-added tomatoes, cut up

2 bay leaves
½ teaspoon dried thyme leaves
¼ teaspoon dry mustard
¼ teaspoon ground black pepper
3 to 5 dashes hot pepper sauce
1 cup uncooked orzo pasta
1 can (15½ ounces) red kidney beans, rinsed and drained
¼ cup thinly sliced green onions

1 Heat oil in large nonstick saucepan over medium-high heat. Add chicken and cook until lightly browned, about 2 minutes. Add bell peppers, celery, onion and garlic. Cook, stirring frequently, 5 minutes or until vegetables are tender.

2 Add tomatoes, bay leaves, thyme, mustard, black pepper and hot pepper sauce. Bring to a boil; reduce heat to low and simmer 10 minutes or until slightly thickened. Remove bay leaves.

3 Cook pasta according to package directions, omitting salt. Drain, but do not rinse.

4 Stir beans into tomato mixture. Cook 5 minutes or until heated through.

5 Spoon approximately ½ cup pasta into individual bowls. Spoon Jambalaya over pasta. Sprinkle with green onions. Garnish as desired.

Makes 4 servings

Nutrients per Serving:					
Calories	359 (11% of calories from fat)				
Total Fat	5 g	Carbohydrate	62 g	Iron	5 mg
Saturated Fat	1 g	Dietary Fiber	11 g	Vitamin A	156 RE
Cholesterol	24 mg	Protein	20 g	Vitamin C	102 mg
Sodium	728 mg	Calcium	113 mg		

DIETARY EXCHANGES: 3 Starch/Bread, 1 Lean Meat, 3 Vegetable

RED CLAM SAUCE WITH VEGETABLES

This recipe is loaded with nutrients. The tomatoes, bell pepper and squash provide vitamins A and C, the clams provide protein and iron, and the spaghetti contributes carbohydrates and B vitamins.

2 cups sliced fresh mushrooms
1 can (14½ ounces) no-salt-added stewed tomatoes, undrained
1 cup chopped green bell pepper
1 can (8 ounces) no-salt-added tomato sauce
½ cup chopped onion
1½ teaspoons dried basil leaves
¾ teaspoon dried savory leaves

½ teaspoon ground black pepper
2 cans (6½ ounces each) minced clams, drained, reserving liquid
1 small yellow squash, cut lengthwise into halves, then into slices
2 tablespoons cornstarch
3 cups hot, cooked spaghetti

1 Combine mushrooms, tomatoes with liquid, bell pepper, tomato sauce, onion, basil, savory and black pepper in large saucepan. Bring to a boil over medium-high heat. Reduce heat to medium. Cover; cook 5 to 6 minutes or until vegetables are tender.

2 Stir in clams and squash. Stir ½ cup clam liquid into cornstarch in small bowl until smooth. Stir into mixture in saucepan. Cook and stir over medium heat until mixture comes to a boil and thickens. Cook and stir 2 minutes more. Serve over spaghetti.

Makes 4 servings

Nutrients per Serving:

Calories	393 (8% of calories from fat)				
Total Fat	3 g	Carbohydrate	58 g	Iron	30 mg
Saturated Fat	<1 g	Dietary Fiber	7 g	Vitamin A	344 RE
Cholesterol	62 mg	Protein	33 g	Vitamin C	99 mg
Sodium	136 mg	Calcium	148 mg		

DIETARY EXCHANGES: 3 Starch/Bread, 3 Meat, 1 Vegetable

ENLIGHTENED MACARONI AND CHEESE

This twist on an all-time American favorite is guaranteed to make your family smile, and it's low in fat too!

8 ounces uncooked wagon wheel, bow tie or elbow pasta
1 tablespoon all-purpose flour
2 teaspoons cornstarch
¼ teaspoon dry mustard
1 can (12 ounces) evaporated skimmed milk
1 cup (4 ounces) shredded reduced fat medium sharp Cheddar cheese

½ cup (2 ounces) shredded reduced fat Monterey Jack cheese
1 jar (2 ounces) diced pimiento, drained and rinsed
1 teaspoon Worcestershire sauce
¼ teaspoon ground black pepper
1 tablespoon dry bread crumbs
1 tablespoon paprika

1 Preheat oven to 375°F.

2 Cook pasta according to package directions, omitting salt. Drain and set aside.

3 Combine flour, cornstarch and mustard in medium saucepan; stir in milk until smooth. Cook over medium heat, stirring occasionally, until slightly thickened, about 8 minutes.

4 Remove from heat; stir in cheeses, pimiento, Worcestershire sauce and pepper. Add pasta; mix well.

5 Spray 1½-quart casserole with nonstick cooking spray. Spoon mixture into casserole; sprinkle with bread crumbs and paprika.

6 Bake 20 minutes or until bubbly and heated through.

Makes 6 (1-cup) servings

Nutrients per Serving:

Calories	226 (19% of calories from fat)				
Total Fat	6 g	Carbohydrate	35 g	Iron	2 mg
Saturated Fat	3 g	Dietary Fiber	2 g	Vitamin A	125 RE
Cholesterol	18 mg	Protein	18 g	Vitamin C	11 mg
Sodium	200 mg	Calcium	406 mg		

DIETARY EXCHANGES: 2 Starch/Bread, 1 Medium Fat Meat, ½ Milk

STRAW AND HAY

The Italians call a combination of green and white noodles "straw and hay." A delicate sauce of cheese and peas coats the noodles in this recipe.

1 cup skim milk
½ cup nonfat cottage cheese
2 teaspoons cornstarch
¼ teaspoon ground mace
⅛ teaspoon ground black pepper
4 ounces uncooked fettuccine
4 ounces uncooked spinach
   fettuccine
Nonstick cooking spray

4 ounces reduced fat deli-style
   ham, diagonally sliced
2 tablespoons chopped chives
1 cup frozen peas, thawed and
   drained
¼ cup grated Parmesan cheese
⅛ teaspoon paprika

1 Combine milk, cottage cheese, cornstarch, mace and pepper in blender or food processor; process until smooth. Set aside.

2 Cook noodles according to package directions, omitting salt. Drain and set aside. Meanwhile, spray large nonstick skillet with cooking spray. Cook and stir ham and chives over medium heat until ham is lightly browned. Stir in milk mixture and peas; cook over medium heat until thickened.

3 Remove from heat. Combine noodles and milk mixture. Add Parmesan cheese. Toss to coat evenly. Sprinkle with paprika; serve immediately.

Makes 4 (1½-cup) servings

Nutrients per Serving:					
Calories	348 (11% of calories from fat)				
Total Fat	4 g	Carbohydrate	52 g	Iron	2 mg
Saturated Fat	2 g	Dietary Fiber	3 g	Vitamin A	106 RE
Cholesterol	9 mg	Protein	25 g	Vitamin C	6 mg
Sodium	592 mg	Calcium	187 mg		

DIETARY EXCHANGES: 3 Starch/Bread, 2 Lean Meat, ½ Fat

SPICY MEXICAN FRITTATA

Jalapeño peppers pack a mighty flavor wallop without adding many calories or much fat. One pepper has only about 7 calories and just half a gram of fat. The hotness of jalapeño peppers varies by the way they're used. For milder flavor, seed peppers before adding them to a dish. For a very hot dish, use the seeds.

1 fresh jalapeño pepper
1 clove garlic
1 medium tomato, peeled, halved, seeded and quartered
½ teaspoon ground coriander
½ teaspoon chili powder
  Nonstick cooking spray
½ cup chopped onion
1 cup frozen corn

6 egg whites
2 whole eggs
¼ cup skim milk
¼ teaspoon salt
¼ teaspoon ground black pepper
¼ cup (1 ounce) shredded part-skim farmer or mozzarella cheese

1 Add jalapeño pepper and garlic to food processor or blender. Process until finely chopped. Add tomato, coriander and chili powder. Cover; process until tomato is almost smooth.

2 Spray large nonstick skillet with cooking spray; heat skillet over medium heat. Cook and stir onion in skillet until tender. Stir in tomato mixture and corn. Cook 3 to 4 minutes or until liquid is almost evaporated, stirring occasionally.

3 Combine egg whites, eggs, milk, salt and black pepper in medium bowl. Add egg mixture all at once to skillet. Cook, without stirring, 2 minutes until eggs begin to set. Run large spatula around edge of skillet, lifting eggs and tilting skillet to allow uncooked egg mixture to run under cooked egg mixture. Remove skillet from heat when eggs are almost set but surface is still moist.

4 Sprinkle with cheese. Cover; let stand 3 to 4 minutes or until surface is set and cheese melts. Cut into wedges. *Makes 4 servings*

Nutrients per Serving:

Calories	129 (22% of calories from fat)				
Total Fat	3 g	Carbohydrate	14 g	Iron	1 mg
Saturated Fat	1 g	Dietary Fiber	2 g	Vitamin A	104 RE
Cholesterol	108 mg	Protein	12 g	Vitamin C	10 mg
Sodium	371 mg	Calcium	47 mg		

DIETARY EXCHANGES: ½ Starch/Bread, 1 Lean Meat, 1½ Vegetable

PEA AND SPINACH FRITTATA

Tablespoon for tablespoon, grated Romano or Parmesan cheese goes a lot farther than other cheeses toward boosting the flavor of recipes.

1 cup chopped onion
¼ cup water
1 cup frozen peas
1 cup washed and torn spinach
6 egg whites
2 whole eggs
½ cup cooked brown rice
¼ cup skim milk

2 tablespoons grated Romano or Parmesan cheese
1 tablespoon chopped fresh mint *or* 1 teaspoon dried mint leaves
¼ teaspoon ground black pepper
⅛ teaspoon salt

1 Place onion and water in large skillet. Bring to a boil over high heat. Reduce heat to medium. Cover; cook 2 to 3 minutes or until onion is tender. Stir in peas. Cook until peas are heated through; drain liquid from skillet. Stir spinach into pea mixture. Cook and stir about 1 minute or until spinach just starts to wilt.

2 Meanwhile, combine egg whites, eggs, rice, milk, cheese, mint, pepper and salt in medium bowl. Add egg mixture to skillet. Cook, without stirring, 2 minutes until eggs begin to set. Run large spatula around edge of skillet, lifting eggs and tilting skillet to allow uncooked egg mixture to run under cooked egg mixture. Remove skillet from heat when eggs are almost set but surface is still moist.

3 Cover; let stand 3 to 4 minutes or until surface is set. Garnish top with additional cheese, if desired. Cut into wedges.   *Makes 4 servings*

Nutrients per Serving:					
Calories	162 (22% of calories from fat)				
Total Fat	4 g	Carbohydrate	18 g	Iron	2 mg
Saturated Fat	1 g	Dietary Fiber	4 g	Vitamin A	190 RE
Cholesterol	110 mg	Protein	14 g	Vitamin C	14 mg
Sodium	246 mg	Calcium	112 mg		

DIETARY EXCHANGES: 1 Starch/Bread, 1 Lean Meat, 1½ Vegetable

CHEDDAR CHEESE STRATA

This make-ahead marvel is perfect for entertaining. You may make it the night before and have your entrée ready in just one hour the day of your party. To eliminate 53 mg of cholesterol per serving, you may replace the whole eggs and egg whites with 1 cup cholesterol free egg substitute.

1 pound French bread, cut into ½- to ¾-inch slices, crusts removed, divided
2 cups (8 ounces) shredded reduced fat Cheddar cheese, divided
3 egg whites

2 whole eggs
1 quart skim milk
1 teaspoon grated fresh onion
1 teaspoon dry mustard
½ teaspoon salt
Paprika to taste

1 Spray 13×9-inch glass baking dish with nonstick cooking spray. Place half the bread slices in bottom of prepared dish, overlapping slightly if necessary. Sprinkle with 1¼ cups cheese. Place remaining bread slices on top of cheese.

2 Whisk egg whites and eggs in large bowl. Add milk, onion, mustard and salt; whisk until well blended. Pour evenly over bread and cheese. Cover with remaining ¾ cup cheese and sprinkle with paprika. Cover and refrigerate 1 hour or overnight.

3 Preheat oven to 350°F. Bake strata about 45 minutes or until cheese is melted and bread is golden brown. Let stand 5 minutes before serving. Garnish with red bell pepper stars and fresh Italian parsley, if desired.

Makes 8 servings

Nutrients per Serving:

Calories	297 (23% of calories from fat)				
Total Fat	7 g	Carbohydrate	38 g	Iron	143 mg
Saturated Fat	3 g	Dietary Fiber	<1 g	Vitamin A	160 RE
Cholesterol	70 mg	Protein	18 g	Vitamin C	1 mg
Sodium	962 mg	Calcium	406 mg		

DIETARY EXCHANGES: 2 Starch/Bread, 1 Medium Fat Meat, ½ Milk

VEGETABLE-CHEESE PIZZAS

If you are watching the fat in your diet closely, be sure to use pita bread rather than tortillas. You will save about 5 grams of fat per serving.

2½ cups chopped tomatoes
1 cup thinly sliced onion
1 cup chopped green bell pepper
6 tablespoons water, divided
2 cloves garlic, minced
1½ teaspoons Italian seasoning
1 teaspoon sugar
2 tablespoons cornstarch
4 large pita bread rounds, split horizontally *or* 8 (6-inch) flour tortillas

½ cup (2 ounces) shredded part-skim mozzarella cheese
⅓ cup (1½ ounces) shredded reduced fat sharp Cheddar or colby cheese
2 tablespoons grated Parmesan or Romano cheese

1 Preheat oven to 375°F. Combine tomatoes, onion, bell pepper, 2 tablespoons water, garlic, Italian seasoning and sugar in 2-quart saucepan. Bring to a boil over medium-high heat. Reduce heat to medium-low. Cover; simmer 8 to 10 minutes or until onion is tender.

2 Stir remaining 4 tablespoons water into cornstarch in small bowl until smooth. Stir into tomato mixture. Cook and stir until mixture comes to a boil and thickens. Cook and stir 2 minutes more.

3 Meanwhile, place pita bread halves on ungreased baking sheets. Bake 8 to 10 minutes or until edges just start to brown.

4 Spread vegetable mixture over pita bread halves. Sprinkle with mozzarella, Cheddar and Parmesan cheeses. Bake about 5 minutes more or until cheeses melt and pizzas are heated through.   *Makes 4 servings*

Nutrients per Serving:

Calories	268 (21% of calories from fat)				
Total Fat	6 g	Carbohydrate	40 g	Iron	2 mg
Saturated Fat	3 g	Dietary Fiber	4 g	Vitamin A	164 RE
Cholesterol	18 mg	Protein	14 g	Vitamin C	80 mg
Sodium	407 mg	Calcium	273 mg		

DIETARY EXCHANGES: 1½ Starch/Bread, 1 Medium Fat Meat, 3 Vegetable

STUFFED BELL PEPPERS

1 package (8½ ounces) cornbread mix *plus* ingredients for preparation
6 green bell peppers
1 large onion, thinly sliced
1 teaspoon olive oil
1 can (16 ounces) no-salt-added diced tomatoes
1 package (10 ounces) frozen whole kernel corn, thawed and drained
1 can (2¼ ounces) sliced ripe olives, drained
⅓ cup raisins
1 tablespoon chili powder
1 teaspoon ground sage
1 cup (4 ounces) shredded reduced fat Monterey Jack cheese, divided

1 Prepare cornbread according to package directions. Cut into cubes. Reduce oven temperature to 350°F.

2 Slice tops off peppers. Discard stems and seeds. Finely chop tops to equal 1 cup; set aside. Rinse peppers. Bring 2 to 3 inches water in large saucepan to a boil over high heat. Add 1 or more peppers and boil 1 minute, turning peppers with tongs to blanch evenly. Rinse with cold water; drain upside down. Repeat with remaining peppers.

3 Place onion and oil in Dutch oven. Cover; cook over medium-high heat, stirring occasionally, 8 to 10 minutes or until onion is tender and browned. Add 1 to 2 tablespoons water, if needed, to prevent sticking. Add chopped pepper; cook and stir 1 minute more. Remove from heat. Add tomatoes, corn, olives, raisins, chili powder and sage; stir. Stir in cornbread (it will crumble) and ¾ cup cheese.

4 Spoon filling into peppers. Top with remaining ¼ cup cheese. Place peppers in baking dish; bake 20 to 30 minutes or until heated through. Garnish with cherry tomato halves and fresh herbs, if desired.

Makes 6 servings

Nutrients per Serving:

Calories	257 (23% of calories from fat)				
Total Fat	7 g	Carbohydrate	42 g	Iron	2 mg
Saturated Fat	2 g	Dietary Fiber	6 g	Vitamin A	253 RE
Cholesterol	7 mg	Protein	12 g	Vitamin C	169 mg
Sodium	301 mg	Calcium	277 mg		

DIETARY EXCHANGES: 1 Starch/Bread, ½ Lean Meat, ½ Fruit, 3½ Vegetable, 1 Fat

VEGETABLE RISOTTO

This tasty Italian rice dish contains almost no cholesterol.

2 cups broccoli flowerets
1 cup finely chopped zucchini
1 cup finely chopped yellow
squash
1 cup finely chopped red bell
pepper
2½ cups chicken broth
1 tablespoon extra virgin olive oil

2 tablespoons finely chopped
onion
½ cup Arborio or other short-
grain rice
¼ cup dry white wine or water
⅓ cup freshly grated Parmesan
cheese

1 Steam broccoli, zucchini, yellow squash and bell pepper 3 minutes or just until crisp-tender. Rinse with cold water; drain and set aside.

2 Bring chicken broth to a simmer in small saucepan; keep hot over low heat. Heat oil in heavy, large saucepan over medium-high heat. Add onion to oil; reduce heat to medium. Cook and stir about 5 minutes or until onion is translucent. Add rice, stirring to coat with oil. Add wine; cook and stir until almost dry. Add ½ cup hot broth; cook and stir until broth is absorbed. Continue adding broth, ½ cup at a time, allowing broth to be absorbed before each addition and stirring frequently. (Total cooking time for broth absorption is about 20 minutes.)

3 Remove from heat and stir in cheese. Add steamed vegetables and mix well. Serve immediately.

Makes 6 servings

Nutrients per Serving:

Calories	150 (27% of calories from fat)				
Total Fat	5 g	Carbohydrate	20 g	Iron	2 mg
Saturated Fat	1 g	Dietary Fiber	2 g	Vitamin A	93 RE
Cholesterol	4 mg	Protein	7 g	Vitamin C	59 mg
Sodium	253 mg	Calcium	107 mg		

DIETARY EXCHANGES: 1 Starch/Bread, 1 Vegetable, 1 Fat

TWO BEANS AND RICE

For protein and fiber, beans are hard to beat. There are about 5 grams of protein and almost 6 grams of fiber in one ⅓-cup portion of canned kidney beans.

Nonstick cooking spray
1½ cups chopped onions
1 cup chopped green bell pepper
1 cup thinly sliced celery
2 cloves garlic, minced
1 teaspoon olive oil
2 cups chopped seeded tomatoes
1 can (15½ ounces) kidney beans, rinsed, drained and slightly mashed
1 can (15 ounces) black beans, rinsed, drained and slightly mashed

¼ cup water
1 bay leaf
½ teaspoon low sodium chicken bouillon granules
¼ teaspoon ground red pepper
4 cups hot, cooked brown or white rice
¼ cup low fat sour cream
¼ cup chopped fresh cilantro or parsley

1 Spray 3-quart saucepan with cooking spray; heat saucepan over medium heat. Cook and stir onions, bell pepper, celery and garlic in oil until vegetables are tender.

2 Stir in tomatoes, kidney beans, black beans, water, bay leaf, chicken bouillon and red pepper. Bring to a boil over high heat. Reduce heat to medium-low. Simmer 15 minutes, stirring occasionally. Remove bay leaf. Serve bean mixture over rice. Top with sour cream and sprinkle with cilantro.

Makes 4 servings

Nutrients per Serving:

Calories	507 (11% of calories from fat)					
Total Fat	6 g	Carbohydrate	98 g	Iron	4 mg
Saturated Fat	1 g	Dietary Fiber	19 g	Vitamin A	135 RE
Cholesterol	6 mg	Protein	23 g	Vitamin C	85 mg
Sodium	517 mg	Calcium	96 mg		

DIETARY EXCHANGES: 5½ Starch/Bread, 3 Vegetable, 1 Fat

TOSTADAS

Mexico's version of the chef salad, tostadas offer as much room for variety as for flavor. A good source of vitamins A and C, iron, calcium and fiber, this light, meatless meal also provides over one third of your daily requirement of high-quality protein.

½ small avocado (optional)
3 tablespoons plain nonfat yogurt (optional)
1 teaspoon lemon juice (optional)
4 (6-inch) flour tortillas
  Nonstick cooking spray
1 small onion, chopped
1 tablespoon chili powder

2 teaspoons dried oregano leaves
1 can (15 ounces) pinto beans, rinsed and drained
4 cups washed and shredded romaine lettuce
1 cup (4 ounces) shredded reduced fat Cheddar cheese
  Salsa Cruda (page 38)
3 tablespoons sliced ripe olives

1 Preheat oven to 375°F. If desired, combine avocado, yogurt and lemon juice in food processor or blender; process until smooth. Set aside.

2 Place tortillas in single layer on center rack of oven. Bake 5 minutes or until crisp and golden, turning halfway through baking. Set aside.

3 Spray large skillet with cooking spray and heat over medium heat. Add onion; cook and stir 10 minutes or until onion begins to brown. Add chili powder and oregano; cook and stir 1 minute. Remove from heat; stir in beans and ¼ cup water. Mash beans with fork until smooth; if necessary, add more water, 1 tablespoon at a time. Return to heat. Cover and cook, stirring occasionally, 6 minutes or until heated through.

4 Place each tortilla on plate. Spread ⅓ cup bean mixture over each tortilla. Top with 1 cup lettuce, ¼ cup cheese, ¼ cup Salsa Cruda and about 2 teaspoons olives. Garnish with avocado mixture in cherry tomato cup, if desired.

Makes 4 servings

Nutrients per Serving:

Calories	380 (20% of calories from fat)				
Total Fat	9 g	Carbohydrate	55 g	Iron	6 mg
Saturated Fat	2 g	Dietary Fiber	11 g	Vitamin A	317 RE
Cholesterol	10 mg	Protein	23 g	Vitamin C	32 mg
Sodium	509 mg	Calcium	451 mg		

DIETARY EXCHANGES: 3 Starch/Bread, 1 Medium Fat Meat, 2 Vegetable, ½ Fat

BEAN AND VEGETABLE BURRITOS

The combination of amino acids from beans, corn, tortillas and cheese provides a high-quality, complete protein.

1 tablespoon olive oil
1 medium onion, thinly sliced
1 jalapeño pepper,* seeded, minced
1 tablespoon chili powder
3 cloves garlic, minced
2 teaspoons dried oregano leaves
1 teaspoon ground cumin
1 large sweet potato, baked, cooled, peeled and diced *or* 1 can (16 ounces) yams in syrup, rinsed, drained and diced

1 can black beans or pinto beans, rinsed and drained
1 cup frozen whole kernel corn, thawed and drained
1 green bell pepper, chopped
2 tablespoons lime juice
¾ cup (3 ounces) shredded reduced fat Monterey Jack cheese
4 (10-inch) flour tortillas
Low fat sour cream (optional)

1 Preheat oven to 350°F.

2 Heat oil over medium-high heat in large saucepan or Dutch oven. Add onion; cook and stir 10 minutes or until golden. Add jalapeño pepper, chili powder, garlic, oregano and cumin; cook and stir 1 minute more. Add 1 tablespoon water and stir; remove from heat. Stir in sweet potato, beans, corn, bell pepper and lime juice.

3 Spoon 2 tablespoons cheese in center of each tortilla. Top with 1 cup filling. Fold all 4 sides around filling to enclose. Place burritos seam side down on baking sheet. Cover with foil and bake 30 minutes or until heated through. Serve with sour cream, if desired.　　　*Makes 4 servings*

*Jalapeño peppers can sting and irritate the skin; wear rubber gloves when handling peppers and do not touch eyes. Wash hands after handling.

Nutrients per Serving:

Calories	428 (17% of calories from fat)				
Total Fat	9 g	Carbohydrate	75 g	Iron	3 mg
Saturated Fat	2 g	Dietary Fiber	9 g	Vitamin A	147 RE
Cholesterol	7 mg	Protein	22 g	Vitamin C	35 mg
Sodium	617 mg	Calcium	320 mg		

DIETARY EXCHANGES: 4 Starch/Bread, 1 Lean Meat, 2 Vegetable, 1 Fat

SIDE DISHES

RED CABBAGE WITH APPLES

The combination of cabbage and apples in this recipe is a great-tasting way to get extra fiber.

1 small head red cabbage,
  shredded
2 large apples, peeled, cored and
  thinly sliced
½ cup sliced onion
½ cup unsweetened apple juice

¼ cup lemon juice
2 tablespoons raisins
2 tablespoons packed brown
  sugar
Salt and ground black pepper
  to taste (optional)

1 Combine cabbage, apples, onion, apple juice, lemon juice, raisins and brown sugar in large nonstick saucepan.

2 Bring to a boil over high heat. Reduce heat to low. Cover; simmer 30 minutes. Season with salt and pepper, if desired.   *Makes 8 servings*

Nutrients per Serving:

Calories	68 (3% of calories from fat)				
Total Fat	<1 g	Carbohydrate	17 g	Iron	1 mg
Saturated Fat	<1 g	Dietary Fiber	2 g *	Vitamin A	9 RE
Cholesterol	0 mg	Protein	1 g	Vitamin C	33 mg
Sodium	13 mg	Calcium	37 mg		

DIETARY EXCHANGES: ½ Fruit, 1½ Vegetable

BRAISED ORIENTAL CABBAGE

A healthful mixture of both green and Chinese cabbages, this dish has a subtle sweet-sour flavor.

½ small head green cabbage (about ½ pound)
1 small head bok choy (about ¾ pound)
½ cup ⅓-less-salt chicken broth
2 tablespoons reduced sodium soy sauce

2 tablespoons rice wine vinegar
1 tablespoon brown sugar
¼ teaspoon crushed red pepper (optional)
1 tablespoon water
1 tablespoon cornstarch

1 Cut cabbage into 1-inch pieces. Cut woody stems from bok choy leaves; slice stems into ½-inch pieces. Cut tops of leaves into ½-inch slices; set aside.

2 Combine cabbage and bok choy stems in large nonstick skillet. Add chicken broth, soy sauce, vinegar, brown sugar and crushed red pepper, if desired.

3 Bring to a boil over high heat. Reduce heat to medium. Cover and simmer 5 minutes or until vegetables are crisp-tender.

4 Blend water into cornstarch in small bowl until smooth. Stir into skillet. Cook and stir 1 minute or until sauce boils and thickens.

5 Stir in reserved bok choy leaves; cook 1 minute.   *Makes 6 servings*

Nutrients per Serving:

Calories	34 (5% of calories from fat)				
Total Fat	<1 g	Carbohydrate	6 g	Iron	1 mg
Saturated Fat	<1 g	Dietary Fiber	1 g	Vitamin A	90 RE
Cholesterol	0 mg	Protein	2 g	Vitamin C	53 mg
Sodium	170 mg	Calcium	67 mg		

DIETARY EXCHANGES: 1½ Vegetable

CRISPY VEGETABLES WITH ORANGE FLAVOR

Eating tofu is a good way to incorporate protein into your diet without adding lots of fat, cholesterol or sodium.

1 tablespoon vegetable oil
2 cups diagonally sliced celery
1 cup broccoli flowerets
¾ cup red bell pepper, coarsely chopped
¼ cup sliced green onions
4 strips orange peel (2 × ½ inch)
1½ teaspoons ground ginger
1½ cups (about 8 ounces) firm tofu cut into 1-inch pieces

1 tablespoon reduced sodium soy sauce
1½ cups water or no-salt-added tomato juice
1 envelope reduced sodium vegetable bouillon
2 tablespoons cornstarch
6 ounces thin spaghetti, cooked

1 Heat oil in large nonstick skillet or wok over medium-high heat. Add celery, broccoli, bell pepper, onions, orange peel and ginger. Cook 4 to 5 minutes or until vegetables are crisp-tender, stirring occasionally.

2 Meanwhile, combine tofu with soy sauce in medium bowl; set aside. Stir water into bouillon and cornstarch in measuring cup until smooth. Stir cornstarch mixture into vegetable mixture. Cook and stir until mixture comes to a boil and thickens. Cook 1 minute more. Gently stir in tofu mixture; cook 1 minute or until heated through. Serve over cooked spaghetti. Garnish with quartered orange slices, if desired. *Makes 4 servings*

Nutrients per Serving:				
Calories	321 (25% of calories from fat)			
Total Fat	9 g	Carbohydrate	46 g	Iron	9 mg
Saturated Fat	1 g	Dietary Fiber	3 g	Vitamin A	104 RE
Cholesterol	0 mg	Protein	17 g	Vitamin C	67 mg
Sodium	278 mg	Calcium	169 mg		

DIETARY EXCHANGES: 2 Starch/Bread, 1½ Meat, 2 Vegetable, 1 Fat

SWEET AND SOUR VEGETABLES

The flavor of this pretty vegetable medley is enhanced by the addition of pineapple juice. Its vitamin A content soars thanks to generous amounts of broccoli and carrots.

3 cups broccoli flowerets
2 medium carrots, diagonally sliced
1 large red bell pepper, cut into short, thin strips
¼ cup water
2 teaspoons cornstarch

1 teaspoon sugar
⅓ cup unsweetened pineapple juice
1 tablespoon reduced sodium soy sauce
1 tablespoon rice vinegar
½ teaspoon Oriental sesame oil

1 Combine broccoli, carrots and bell pepper in large nonstick skillet with tight-fitting lid. Add water; bring to a boil over high heat. Reduce heat to medium. Cover and steam 4 minutes or until vegetables are crisp-tender.

2 Meanwhile, combine cornstarch and sugar in small bowl. Blend in pineapple juice, soy sauce and vinegar until smooth.

3 Transfer vegetables to colander; drain. Stir pineapple mixture and add to skillet. Cook and stir 2 minutes or until sauce boils and thickens.

4 Return vegetables to skillet; toss with sauce. Stir in oil. Garnish with green onions and fresh cilantro, if desired.   *Makes 4 servings*

Nutrients per Serving:

Calories	65 (11% of calories from fat)				
Total Fat	1 g	Carbohydrate	13 g	Iron	1 mg
Saturated Fat	<1 g	Dietary Fiber	3 g	Vitamin A	1126 RE
Cholesterol	0 mg	Protein	3 g	Vitamin C	86 mg
Sodium	163 mg	Calcium	44 mg		

DIETARY EXCHANGES: 2½ Vegetable

CHINESE VEGETABLES

Seven different vegetables make this classic stir-fry pleasing to the palate and it's loaded with vitamin C, fiber and potassium.

1 pound fresh broccoli
1½ teaspoons vegetable oil
2 medium yellow onions, cut into wedges and separated
2 cloves garlic, minced
1½ tablespoons minced fresh ginger
8 ounces fresh spinach, coarsely chopped
4 ribs celery, diagonally cut into ½-inch pieces

8 ounces fresh snow peas *or* 1 package (6 ounces) thawed frozen snow peas, trimmed and strings removed
4 medium carrots, sliced
8 green onions, diagonally cut into thin slices
¾ cup ⅓-less-salt chicken broth
1 tablespoon reduced sodium soy sauce

1 Cut broccoli tops into flowerets. Cut stalks into 2×¼-inch strips.

2 Heat oil in wok or large nonstick skillet over high heat. Add broccoli stalks, yellow onions, garlic and ginger; stir-fry 1 minute. Add broccoli flowerets, spinach, celery, snow peas, carrots and green onions; toss lightly.

3 Add chicken broth and soy sauce to vegetables; toss to coat. Bring to a boil; cover and cook 2 to 3 minutes until vegetables are crisp-tender.

Makes 4 servings

Nutrients per Serving:

Calories	154 (15% of calories from fat)				
Total Fat	3 g	Carbohydrate	28 g	Iron	5 mg
Saturated Fat	<1 g	Dietary Fiber	10 g	Vitamin A	2626 RE
Cholesterol	0 mg	Protein	9 g	Vitamin C	153 mg
Sodium	277 mg	Calcium	191 mg		

DIETARY EXCHANGES: 5 Vegetable, ½ Fat

MOO SHU VEGETABLES

You won't even miss the meat in this nutritious all-vegetable version of classic moo shu. Wrapping the savory filling in flour tortillas makes preparation a snap.

½ package dried Chinese black
  mushrooms (6 or
  7 mushrooms)
2 tablespoons vegetable oil
2 cloves garlic, minced
2 cups shredded napa cabbage or
  green cabbage *or*
  preshredded cabbage or
  coleslaw mix

1 red bell pepper, cut into short,
  thin strips
1 cup fresh or rinsed, drained
  canned bean sprouts
2 large green onions, cut into
  short, thin strips
1 tablespoon teriyaki sauce
⅓ cup plum sauce
8 (6-inch) flour tortillas, warmed

1 Place mushrooms in small bowl; cover with warm water. Soak 20 minutes to soften. Drain; squeeze out excess water. Discard stems; slice caps.

2 Heat oil in wok or large nonstick skillet over medium heat. Add garlic; stir-fry 30 seconds.

3 Add cabbage, mushrooms and bell pepper; stir-fry 3 minutes. Add bean sprouts and onions; stir-fry 2 minutes. Add teriyaki sauce; stir-fry 30 seconds or until mixture is hot.

4 Spread about 2 teaspoons plum sauce on each tortilla. Spoon heaping ¼ cupful of vegetable mixture over sauce. Fold bottom of tortilla up over filling, then fold sides over filling.

Makes 8 servings

Nutrients per Serving:

Calories	147 (22% of calories from fat)					
Total Fat	4 g	Carbohydrate	26 g	Iron	2 mg
Saturated Fat	1 g	Dietary Fiber	2 g	Vitamin A	18 RE
Cholesterol	0 mg	Protein	4 g	Vitamin C	22 mg
Sodium	207 mg	Calcium	62 mg		

DIETARY EXCHANGES: 1½ Starch/Bread, 1 Vegetable, ½ Fat

ZUCCHINI SHANGHAI STYLE

4 dried Chinese black
   mushrooms
½ cup ⅓-less-salt chicken broth
2 tablespoons ketchup
2 teaspoons dry sherry
1 teaspoon reduced sodium soy
   sauce
1 teaspoon red wine vinegar
¼ teaspoon sugar
1½ teaspoons vegetable oil,
   divided
1 teaspoon minced fresh ginger

1 clove garlic, minced
1 large tomato, peeled, seeded
   and chopped
1 green onion, finely chopped
4 tablespoons water, divided
1 teaspoon cornstarch
1 pound zucchini (about 3
   medium), diagonally cut into
   1-inch pieces
½ small yellow onion, cut into
   wedges and separated

1 Soak mushrooms in warm water 20 minutes. Drain, reserving ¼ cup liquid. Squeeze out excess water. Discard stems; slice caps. Combine reserved ¼ cup mushroom liquid, chicken broth, ketchup, sherry, soy sauce, vinegar and sugar in small bowl.

2 Heat 1 teaspoon oil in large saucepan over medium heat. Add ginger and garlic; stir-fry 10 seconds. Add mushrooms, tomato and green onion; stir-fry 1 minute. Add broth mixture; bring to a boil over high heat. Reduce heat to medium; simmer 10 minutes.

3 Combine 1 tablespoon water and cornstarch in small bowl. Heat remaining ½ teaspoon oil in large nonstick skillet over medium heat. Add zucchini and yellow onion; stir-fry 30 seconds. Add remaining 3 tablespoons water. Cover and cook 3 to 4 minutes until vegetables are crisp-tender, stirring occasionally. Add tomato mixture to skillet. Stir cornstarch mixture and add to skillet. Cook and stir until sauce boils and thickens.

Makes 4 servings

Nutrients per Serving:					
Calories	72 (23% of calories from fat)				
Total Fat	2 g	Carbohydrate	12 g	Iron	1 mg
Saturated Fat	<1 g	Dietary Fiber	3 g	Vitamin A	73 RE
Cholesterol	0 mg	Protein	3 g	Vitamin C	19 mg
Sodium	156 mg	Calcium	26 mg		

DIETARY EXCHANGES: 2 Vegetable, 1 Fat

MARINATED VEGETABLES

Serve this colorful medley of zesty vegetables at your next party. In addition to great flavor, guests will benefit from healthy doses of fiber, beta-carotene and other vitamins and minerals.

1 tablespoon vegetable oil
4 tablespoons rice wine vinegar
3 tablespoons reduced sodium
    soy sauce
1 clove garlic, minced
1 teaspoon minced fresh ginger
2 tablespoons fresh lemon juice
½ teaspoon sugar

2 cups broccoli flowerets
2 cups cauliflower flowerets
2 cups diagonally sliced carrots
    (½-inch pieces)
½ pound whole fresh mushrooms
1 large red bell pepper, cut into
    1-inch pieces
Lettuce leaves

1 Combine oil, vinegar, soy sauce, garlic, ginger, lemon juice and sugar in large bowl.

2 To blanch broccoli, cauliflower and carrots, cook 1 minute in salted boiling water to cover. Remove and plunge into cold water, then drain immediately. Toss with oil mixture while still warm. Cool to room temperature.

3 Add mushrooms and bell pepper to bowl; toss to coat. Cover and marinate in refrigerator at least 4 hours or up to 24 hours. Drain vegetables; reserve marinade.

4 Arrange vegetables on lettuce-lined platter. Serve chilled or at room temperature with wooden picks. If desired, serve reserved marinade in small cup for dipping.

Makes 12 servings

Nutrients per Serving:					
Calories	37 (28% of calories from fat)				
Total Fat	1 g	Carbohydrate	6 g	Iron	1 mg
Saturated Fat	<1 g	Dietary Fiber	2 g	Vitamin A	543 RE
Cholesterol	0 mg	Protein	2 g	Vitamin C	35 mg
Sodium	146 mg	Calcium	20 mg		

DIETARY EXCHANGES: 1 Vegetable

GRILLED VEGETABLES

Most vegetables require no preparation at all before grilling other than slicing them to a uniform thickness. However, eggplant is better if sprinkled with a little salt after slicing and drained for an hour before grilling to remove bitterness.

¼ cup minced fresh herbs, such as parsley, thyme, rosemary, oregano or basil

1 small eggplant (about ¾ pound), cut into ¼-inch-thick slices

½ teaspoon salt
    Nonstick cooking spray

1 *each* red, green and yellow bell pepper, quartered and seeded

2 zucchini, cut lengthwise into ¼-inch-thick slices

1 fennel bulb, cut lengthwise into ¼-inch-thick slices

1 Combine herbs in small bowl; let stand 3 hours or overnight.

2 Place eggplant in large colander over bowl; sprinkle with salt. Drain 1 hour.

3 Heat grill until coals are glowing red, but not flaming. Spray vegetables with cooking spray and sprinkle with herb mixture. Grill 10 to 15 minutes or until fork-tender and lightly browned on both sides, turning occasionally. Or, place vegetables on rack of broiler pan. Broil 10 to 15 minutes or until fork-tender and lightly browned on both sides, turning occasionally. (Cooking times vary depending on vegetable; remove vegetables as they are done to avoid overcooking.)   *Makes 6 servings*

Variation: Cut vegetables into 1-inch cubes and thread onto skewers. Spray with cooking spray and sprinkle with herb mixture. Grill or broil as directed above.

Nutrients per Serving:

Calories	34 (6% of calories from fat)				
Total Fat	<1 g	Carbohydrate	8 g	Iron	1 mg
Saturated Fat	<1 g	Dietary Fiber	2 g	Vitamin A	54 RE
Cholesterol	0 mg	Protein	1 g	Vitamin C	43 mg
Sodium	190 mg	Calcium	24 mg		

DIETARY EXCHANGES: 1½ Vegetable

HARVARD BEETS

Not only are beets low in calories, they're loaded with fiber. One cup of beets contains 3.4 grams of fiber, which is about the same amount found in 1½ cups of cooked oatmeal.

2 teaspoons cornstarch
¼ teaspoon salt (optional)
   Dash ground black pepper
   Dash ground allspice
¼ teaspoon grated orange peel

2 tablespoons cider vinegar
1 can (16 ounces) sliced beets,
   drained, reserving ⅓ cup
   liquid
1 tablespoon orange juice

 Microwave Directions: Combine cornstarch, salt, if desired, pepper, allspice and orange peel in 1-quart microwavable casserole. Blend in vinegar, reserved beet liquid and orange juice.

 Microwave at HIGH 1¾ to 2½ minutes or until clear and thickened, stirring every minute. Add beets. Microwave at HIGH 2 to 4 minutes or until beets are thoroughly heated.   *Makes 4 servings*

Nutrients per Serving:

Calories	42 (3% of calories from fat)					
Total Fat	<1 g	Carbohydrate	10 g	Iron	2 mg
Saturated Fat	<1 g	Dietary Fiber	3 g	Vitamin A	2 RE
Cholesterol	0 mg	Protein	1 g	Vitamin C	10 mg
Sodium	312 mg	Calcium	18 mg		

DIETARY EXCHANGES: 2 Vegetable

❖

Health Note

Beets are rich in folic acid, which is essential for preventing some anemias. In addition, beets are a good source of fiber, both soluble and insoluble.

❖

SESAME HONEY VEGETABLE CASSEROLE

The frozen mixed vegetables here let you forgo some chopping and slicing without sacrificing nutrients. In fact, frozen vegetables can contain more nutrients than fresh ones that are past their peak of freshness.

1 package (16 ounces) frozen mixed vegetables, such as baby carrots, broccoli, onions and red peppers, thawed and drained

3 tablespoons honey
1 tablespoon Oriental sesame oil
1 tablespoon reduced sodium soy sauce
2 teaspoons sesame seeds

 Heat oven to 350°F. Place mixed vegetables in shallow 1½-quart casserole dish or quiche dish.

 Combine honey, oil, soy sauce and sesame seeds; mix well. Drizzle evenly over vegetables. Bake 20 to 25 minutes or until vegetables are hot, stirring after 15 minutes.

Makes 4 side-dish servings

Nutrients per Serving:

Calories	176 (27% of calories from fat)				
Total Fat	5 g	Carbohydrate	28 g	Iron	<1 mg
Saturated Fat	1 g	Dietary Fiber	3 g	Vitamin A	532 RE
Cholesterol	0 mg	Protein	4 g	Vitamin C	23 mg
Sodium	173 mg	Calcium	3 mg		

DIETARY EXCHANGES: 3 Vegetable, 1 Fruit, 1 Fat

❖

Cook's Note
When measuring sticky liquids, such as honey and molasses, spray the measuring spoon or cup with nonstick cooking spray before adding the liquid. This makes their removal easier.

❖

HONEY GLAZED CARROTS AND PARSNIPS

This root vegetable combination is high in Vitamin A and can be made more quickly by cutting the carrots and parsnips into ¼-inch rounds instead of into matchstick-sized pieces. They look fancier when julienned, but it is not essential for the great flavor!

½ pound carrots, peeled and cut
    into julienned strips
½ pound parsnips, peeled and cut
    into julienned strips

¼ cup chopped fresh parsley
2 tablespoons honey

1 Steam carrots and parsnips 3 to 4 minutes until crisp-tender. Rinse under cold running water; drain and set aside.

2 Just before serving, combine carrots, parsnips, parsley and honey in large saucepan or skillet. Cook over medium heat just until heated through. Garnish with fresh Italian parsley, if desired. Serve immediately.

Makes 6 (⅔-cup) servings

Nutrients per Serving:

Calories	69 (2% of calories from fat)				
Total Fat	<1 g	Carbohydrate	17 g	Iron	1 mg
Saturated Fat	<1 g	Dietary Fiber	3 g	Vitamin A	1076 RE
Cholesterol	0 mg	Protein	1 g	Vitamin C	12 mg
Sodium	19 mg	Calcium	28 mg		

DIETARY EXCHANGES: 2½ Vegetable

Cook's Note

Most carrots are sold in plastic bags with their tops removed. When purchasing carrots, look to see that the bag contains fresh-looking, smooth and well-shaped carrots of a bright or deep orange color. If you buy fresh carrots that are not packaged, look for those with fresh green tops and well-shaped brightly-colored roots.

COLD ASPARAGUS WITH LEMON-MUSTARD DRESSING

This easy-to-make, no cholesterol dish may also be served as an appetizer.

12 fresh asparagus spears
2 tablespoons fat free
   mayonnaise
1 tablespoon sweet brown
   mustard

1 tablespoon fresh lemon juice
1 teaspoon grated lemon peel,
   divided

1 Steam asparagus until crisp-tender and bright green; immediately drain and run under cold water. Cover and refrigerate until chilled.

2 Combine mayonnaise, mustard and lemon juice in small bowl; blend well. Stir in ½ teaspoon lemon peel; set aside.

3 Divide asparagus between 2 plates. Spoon 2 tablespoons dressing over each serving; sprinkle each with ¼ teaspoon lemon peel. Garnish with carrot strips and edible flowers, such as pansies, violets or nasturtiums, if desired.

Makes 2 servings

Nutrients per Serving:

Calories	39 (14% of calories from fat)				
Total Fat	1 g	Carbohydrate	7 g	Iron	1 mg
Saturated Fat	<1 g	Dietary Fiber	2 g	Vitamin A	71 RE
Cholesterol	0 mg	Protein	3 g	Vitamin C	15 mg
Sodium	294 mg	Calcium	33 mg		

DIETARY EXCHANGES: 1½ Vegetable

Health Note

Asparagus is a great source of glutathione, a powerful antioxidant. Studies have shown that glutathione acts against at least 30 carcinogens.

RATATOUILLE

This classic Mediterranean dish is made with a medley of vegetables.

½ pound eggplant, cut into
    ½-inch cubes
1 small onion, sliced and
    separated into rings
1 small zucchini, thinly sliced
1 tomato, cut into wedges
1 rib celery, chopped
½ medium green bell pepper,
    chopped

1 tablespoon grated Parmesan
    cheese
¼ teaspoon salt (optional)
¼ teaspoon dried chervil leaves
¼ teaspoon dried oregano leaves
⅛ teaspoon instant minced garlic
⅛ teaspoon dried thyme leaves
    Dash ground black pepper

1 Microwave Directions: Combine all ingredients in 2-quart microwavable casserole; cover. Microwave at HIGH 7 to 10 minutes or until eggplant is translucent, stirring every 3 minutes.   *Makes 6 servings*

Nutrients per Serving:

Calories	29 (15% of calories from fat)					
Total Fat	1 g	Carbohydrate	6 g	Iron	<1 mg
Saturated Fat	<1 g	Dietary Fiber	2 g	Vitamin A	29 RE
Cholesterol	1 mg	Protein	1 g	Vitamin C	13 mg
Sodium	29 mg	Calcium	28 mg		

DIETARY EXCHANGES: 1 Vegetable

Cook's Note

Since ancient times, eggplant has been a popular vegetable in Middle Eastern and Mediterranean countries, as well as the Orient. Thomas Jefferson is said to have introduced it to America, but Westerners considered it poisonous until the nineteenth century. Eggplant comes in a variety of shapes, colors and sizes—the small Thai eggplant is round and white and actually resembles an egg!

ITALIAN BROCCOLI WITH TOMATOES

Broccoli is one of the few vegetables that contains calcium, which is important for healthy bones and teeth.

4 cups broccoli flowerets
½ cup water
2 medium tomatoes, cut into wedges
½ teaspoon Italian seasoning

½ teaspoon dried parsley flakes
¼ teaspoon salt (optional)
⅛ teaspoon ground black pepper
½ cup (2 ounces) shredded part-skim mozzarella cheese

 Microwave Directions: Place broccoli and water in 2-quart microwavable casserole; cover. Microwave at HIGH 5 to 8 minutes or until crisp-tender. Drain. Stir in tomatoes, Italian seasoning, parsley, salt, if desired, and pepper.

 Microwave, uncovered, at HIGH 2 to 4 minutes or until tomatoes are hot. Sprinkle with cheese. Microwave 1 minute or until cheese melts.

Makes 6 servings

Nutrients per Serving:

Calories	50 (30% of calories from fat)				
Total Fat	2 g	Carbohydrate	5 g	Iron	1 mg
Saturated Fat	1 g	Dietary Fiber	2 g	Vitamin A	136 RE
Cholesterol	5 mg	Protein	4 g	Vitamin C	63 mg
Sodium	64 mg	Calcium	94 mg		

DIETARY EXCHANGES: ½ Lean Meat, 1 Vegetable

❖

Health Note

For best flavor and texture, keep fresh broccoli cold and humid and use as soon as possible. Rinse and trim leaves and stalk ends just before using.

❖

PESTO-PASTA STUFFED TOMATOES

*This makes a wonderfully light accompaniment to any
chicken or fish entrée.*

3 ounces uncooked star or other
　　small pasta
4 large tomatoes
1 cup loosely packed fresh basil
1 clove garlic, minced
3 tablespoons reduced calorie
　　mayonnaise

1 tablespoon skim milk
¼ teaspoon ground black pepper
1 cup shredded zucchini
4 teaspoons grated Parmesan
　　cheese

1 Cook pasta according to package directions, omitting salt. Drain and
rinse; set aside.

2 Cut tops from tomatoes. Scoop out and discard all but ½ cup tomato pulp.
Chop tomato pulp and add to pasta. Place tomatoes, cut side down, on paper
towels; let drain 5 minutes.

3 Preheat oven to 350°F.

4 Place basil and garlic in blender or food processor; process until finely
chopped. Add mayonnaise, milk and black pepper. Process until smooth.

5 Combine pasta mixture, zucchini and basil mixture; toss to coat evenly.
Place tomatoes, cut side up, in 8-inch baking dish. Divide pasta mixture
evenly among tomatoes, mounding filling slightly. Sprinkle with cheese.

6 Bake 10 to 15 minutes or until heated through.   *Makes 4 servings*

Nutrients per Serving:

Calories	155 (28% of calories from fat)				
Total Fat	6 g	Carbohydrate	22 g	Iron	1 mg
Saturated Fat	1 g	Dietary Fiber	3 g	Vitamin A	195 RE
Cholesterol	2 mg	Protein	6 g	Vitamin C	27 mg
Sodium	154 mg	Calcium	66 mg		

DIETARY EXCHANGES: 1 Starch/Bread, 1½ Vegetable, 1 Fat

PASTA WITH ONION AND GOAT CHEESE

Goats, as well as cows, provide milk. Goat's milk is usually made into goat cheese, which tends to be lower in fat than regular cheeses. It delivers a delightfully tart flavor that easily distinguishes it from other cheeses.

2 teaspoons olive oil
4 cups thinly sliced sweet onions
3 ounces goat cheese
¼ cup skim milk
6 ounces uncooked baby bow tie or other small pasta
1 clove garlic, minced
2 tablespoons dry white wine or ⅓-less-salt chicken broth

1½ teaspoons chopped fresh sage or ½ teaspoon dried sage leaves
½ teaspoon salt
¼ teaspoon ground black pepper
2 tablespoons chopped toasted walnuts

1 Heat oil in large nonstick skillet over medium heat. Add onions and cook slowly until golden and caramelized, about 20 to 25 minutes, stirring occasionally.

2 Combine goat cheese and milk in small bowl; mix until well blended. Set aside.

3 Cook pasta according to package directions, omitting salt. Drain and set aside.

4 Add garlic to onions in skillet; cook until softened, about 3 minutes. Add wine, sage, salt and pepper; cook until liquid is evaporated. Remove from heat; add pasta and goat cheese mixture, stirring to melt cheese. Sprinkle with walnuts.

Makes 8 (½-cup) servings

Nutrients per Serving:

Calories	150 (28% of calories from fat)				
Total Fat	5 g	Carbohydrate	21 g	Iron	1 mg
Saturated Fat	<1 g	Dietary Fiber	2 g	Vitamin A	18 RE
Cholesterol	9 mg	Protein	5 g	Vitamin C	5 mg
Sodium	107 mg	Calcium	34 mg		

DIETARY EXCHANGES: 1 Starch/Bread, 1 Vegetable, 1 Fat

LEMON TOSSED LINGUINE

Lemon is rapidly becoming an appealing substitute for high fat sauces. Once you've tried this exceptional combination, you may never go back to your original sauces.

8 ounces uncooked linguine
    noodles
3 tablespoons fresh lemon juice
2 teaspoons reduced calorie
    margarine
2 tablespoons minced chives
⅓ cup skim milk
1 teaspoon cornstarch
1 tablespoon minced fresh dill *or*
    1 teaspoon dried dill weed

1 tablespoon minced fresh
    parsley *or* 1 teaspoon dried
    parsley
2 teaspoons grated lemon peel
¼ teaspoon ground white pepper
3 tablespoons grated Romano or
    Parmesan cheese

1 Cook noodles according to package directions, omitting salt. Drain well. Place in medium bowl; pour lemon juice over noodles.

2 Meanwhile, melt margarine in small saucepan over medium heat. Add chives and cook until chives are soft. Stir milk into cornstarch in small bowl until smooth; stir into saucepan. Cook and stir until thickened. Stir in dill, parsley, lemon peel and white pepper.

3 Pour milk mixture over noodles. Sprinkle with cheese; toss to coat evenly. Garnish with lemon slices and dill sprigs, if desired. Serve immediately.

Makes 6 (½-cup) servings

Nutrients per Serving:

Calories	173 (18% of calories from fat)				
Total Fat	3 g	Carbohydrate	27 g	Iron	1 mg
Saturated Fat	1 g	Dietary Fiber	2 g	Vitamin A	51 RE
Cholesterol	7 mg	Protein	8 g	Vitamin C	6 mg
Sodium	110 mg	Calcium	104 mg		

DIETARY EXCHANGES: 1½ Starch/Bread, ½ Lean Meat, ½ Fat

SOUTHERN GREENS AND PASTA

If you are unfamiliar with chicory's bitter-tasting leaves, then you may want to try the more subtle, yet still pungent, mustard greens.

2 teaspoons olive oil
1 cup chopped green bell pepper
½ cup chopped onion
½ cup peeled and chopped jicama
⅓ cup chopped celery
1 clove garlic, minced
1 can (about 14 ounces) ⅓-less-salt chicken broth
2 tablespoons tomato paste
1 teaspoon dried oregano leaves

¼ teaspoon ground black pepper
1 package (10 ounces) frozen black-eyed peas
4 ounces uncooked radiatore or other medium pasta
1 head chicory or 1 bunch mustard greens or kale, washed, ribs removed, thinly sliced
2 to 3 drops hot pepper sauce

1 Heat oil in large saucepan. Add bell pepper, onion, jicama, celery and garlic. Cook over medium heat 3 minutes. Stir in chicken broth, tomato paste, oregano and black pepper. Bring to a boil; stir in black-eyed peas. Cover and simmer over low heat 20 minutes or until peas are tender.

2 Cook pasta according to package directions, omitting salt. Drain and set aside.

3 Add chicory to saucepan; cover and cook on low until wilted, about 3 minutes. Stir in pasta. Cook until heated through. Season to taste with hot pepper sauce. Garnish as desired.   *Makes 12 (½-cup) servings*

Nutrients per Serving:					
Calories	88 (13% of calories from fat)				
Total Fat	1 g	Carbohydrate	15 g	Iron	1 mg
Saturated Fat	<1 g	Dietary Fiber	3 g	Vitamin A	80 RE
Cholesterol	0 mg	Protein	4 g	Vitamin C	24 mg
Sodium	39 mg	Calcium	31 mg		

DIETARY EXCHANGES: 1 Starch/Bread, ½ Vegetable

TOASTED SESAME ORZO

Iron, found in spinach, is needed by the body to aid in the proper function of the immune system and in the production of connective tissue.

1 tablespoon sesame seeds
⅔ cup uncooked orzo pasta
1 teaspoon reduced calorie
   margarine
1½ cups fresh spinach, washed
   and coarsely chopped
1 clove garlic, minced
3 tablespoons skim milk

2 tablespoons grated Parmesan
   cheese
1½ teaspoons fresh oregano *or*
   ½ teaspoon dried oregano
   leaves
½ teaspoon paprika
¼ teaspoon ground black pepper

1 Place sesame seeds in small skillet. Cook over medium heat until golden brown, stirring constantly. Set aside.

2 Cook pasta according to package directions, omitting salt. Drain and set aside.

3 Melt margarine in medium skillet. Add spinach and garlic; cook over medium heat until spinach is wilted. Stir in milk, cheese, oregano, paprika, pepper and pasta. Cook over low heat until heated through. Sprinkle with sesame seeds; serve immediately.　　　*Makes 5 (½-cup) servings*

Nutrients per Serving:

Calories	116 (19% of calories from fat)					
Total Fat	2 g	Carbohydrate	19 g	Iron		1 mg
Saturated Fat	1 g	Dietary Fiber	1 g	Vitamin A		110 RE
Cholesterol	2 mg	Protein	5 g	Vitamin C		4 mg
Sodium	72 mg	Calcium	68 mg			

DIETARY EXCHANGES: 1 Starch/Bread, 1 Vegetable, ½ Fat

GINGER NOODLES WITH SESAME EGG STRIPS

Even though this recipe gets most of its protein from eggs, it's virtually cholesterol free. Only the egg whites are used, thus eliminating the fat and cholesterol contained in the yolks.

1 tablespoon sesame seeds

5 egg whites

6 teaspoons teriyaki sauce, divided

1 teaspoon Oriental sesame oil

½ cup ⅓-less-salt chicken broth

1 tablespoon minced fresh ginger

6 ounces uncooked Chinese rice noodles or vermicelli, cooked and well drained

⅓ cup sliced green onions

1 Place sesame seeds in small skillet. Cook over medium heat until golden brown, stirring constantly. Set aside.

2 Beat together egg whites, 2 teaspoons teriyaki sauce and 1 teaspoon sesame seeds.

3 Heat oil in large nonstick skillet over medium heat. Pour egg mixture into skillet; cook 1½ to 2 minutes or until bottom of omelet is set. Turn omelet over; cook 30 seconds to 1 minute. Slide onto plate; cool and cut into ½-inch strips.

4 Place chicken broth, ginger and remaining 4 teaspoons teriyaki sauce in skillet. Bring to a boil over high heat; reduce heat to medium. Add noodles; heat through. Add omelet strips and onions; heat through. Sprinkle with remaining 2 teaspoons sesame seeds.

Makes 4 servings

Nutrients per Serving:					
Calories	111 (19% of calories from fat)				
Total Fat	2 g	Carbohydrate	16 g	Iron	2 mg
Saturated Fat	1 g	Dietary Fiber	<1 g	Vitamin A	31 RE
Cholesterol	0 mg	Protein	7 g	Vitamin C	3 mg
Sodium	226 mg	Calcium	15 mg		

DIETARY EXCHANGES: 1 Starch/Bread, ½ Lean Meat, ½ Fat

VEGETABLE LO MEIN

Noodles, tofu and vegetables are seasoned with garlic, ginger and a touch of plum preserves in this delightful low calorie dish.

8 ounces uncooked vermicelli or thin spaghetti, cooked and drained
¾ teaspoon Oriental sesame oil
½ teaspoon vegetable oil
3 cloves garlic, minced
1 teaspoon grated fresh ginger
2 cups sliced bok choy
½ cup sliced green onions

2 cups shredded carrots
6 ounces firm tofu, drained and cubed
6 tablespoons rice wine vinegar
¼ cup plum preserves
¼ cup water
1 teaspoon reduced sodium soy sauce
½ teaspoon crushed red pepper

1 Toss vermicelli with sesame oil in large bowl until well coated.

2 Heat vegetable oil in large nonstick skillet over medium heat. Stir in garlic and ginger; stir-fry 10 seconds.

3 Add bok choy and onions; stir-fry 3 to 4 minutes until crisp-tender. Add carrots and tofu; stir-fry 2 to 3 minutes until carrots are crisp-tender.

4 Combine vinegar, preserves, water, soy sauce and crushed red pepper in small saucepan. Heat over medium heat until preserves are melted, stirring constantly.

5 Combine noodles, vegetable mixture and sauce in large bowl; mix well.

Makes 6 servings

Nutrients per Serving:

Calories	248 (13% of calories from fat)				
Total Fat	4 g	Carbohydrate	45 g	Iron	5 mg
Saturated Fat	<1 g	Dietary Fiber	2 g	Vitamin A	1112 RE
Cholesterol	<1 mg	Protein	9 g	Vitamin C	21 mg
Sodium	791 mg	Calcium	109 mg		

DIETARY EXCHANGES: 2 Starch/Bread, ½ Lean Meat, 2 Vegetable, ½ Fat

BEAN THREADS WITH TOFU AND VEGETABLES

Bean threads, or cellophane noodles, are dry, fine, white noodles made from powdered mung beans. When cooked, they become transparent and appear to be made of cellophane.

8 ounces firm tofu, drained and cubed

1 tablespoon Oriental sesame oil

3 teaspoons reduced sodium soy sauce, divided

1 can (about 14 ounces) ⅓-less-salt chicken broth

1 package (3¾ ounces) bean threads

1 package (16 ounces) frozen mixed vegetable medley, such as broccoli, carrots and red pepper, thawed

¼ cup rice wine vinegar

½ teaspoon crushed red pepper

1 Place tofu on shallow plate; drizzle with oil and 1½ teaspoons soy sauce.

2 Combine chicken broth and remaining 1½ teaspoons soy sauce in deep skillet or large saucepan. Bring to a boil over high heat; reduce heat. Add bean threads; simmer, uncovered, 7 minutes or until noodles absorb liquid, stirring occasionally to separate noodles.

3 Stir in vegetables and vinegar; heat through. Stir in tofu mixture and crushed red pepper; heat through about 1 minute.   *Makes 6 servings*

Nutrients per Serving:

Calories	167 (30% of calories from fat)				
Total Fat	6 g	Carbohydrate	23 g	Iron	5 mg
Saturated Fat	1 g	Dietary Fiber	3 g	Vitamin A	615 RE
Cholesterol	0 mg	Protein	8 g	Vitamin C	27 mg
Sodium	130 mg	Calcium	111 mg		

DIETARY EXCHANGES: 1 Starch/Bread, ½ Lean Meat, 1 Vegetable, 1 Fat

ROASTED VEGETABLES WITH NOODLES

One of the vegetables in this delicious recipe is eggplant, which has almost as much fiber per serving as oat bran.

5 tablespoons soy sauce, divided
3 tablespoons peanut oil
2 tablespoons rice vinegar
2 cloves garlic, minced
1 teaspoon sugar
2 small Oriental eggplants, cut into ½-inch slices
1 medium zucchini, cut lengthwise into halves, then cut into 1-inch slices
1 medium yellow squash, cut lengthwise into halves, then cut into 1-inch slices

1 red bell pepper, cut into 1-inch pieces
1 yellow bell pepper, cut into 1-inch pieces
½ pound large fresh mushrooms
4 ounces shallots
8 ounces uncooked Chinese egg noodles or vermicelli, cooked and drained
1 tablespoon Oriental sesame oil

1 Preheat oven to 425°F. Combine 2 tablespoons soy sauce, peanut oil, vinegar, garlic and sugar in small bowl; mix well. Combine vegetables in shallow roasting pan (do not line pan with foil). Toss with soy sauce mixture to coat well. Roast vegetables 20 minutes or until browned and tender, stirring well after 10 minutes.

2 Place noodles in large bowl. Toss hot noodles with remaining 3 tablespoons soy sauce and sesame oil. Toss roasted vegetables with noodle mixture; serve warm or at room temperature. *Makes 6 servings*

Nutrients per Serving:

Calories	273 (30% of calories from fat)					
Total Fat	10 g	Carbohydrate	42 g	Iron	2 mg
Saturated Fat	1 g	Dietary Fiber	2 g	Vitamin A	272 RE
Cholesterol	0 mg	Protein	6 g	Vitamin C	35 mg
Sodium	867 mg	Calcium	34 mg		

DIETARY EXCHANGES: 2 Starch/Bread, 2 Vegetable, 2 Fat

TEX-MEX NOODLE CAKE

Noodle cakes are typically Oriental, but try this Tex-Mex version using angel hair pasta and you will insist it comes from the Southwest!

8 ounces uncooked angel hair pasta
½ cup finely chopped red bell pepper
1 whole egg
1 egg white
2 tablespoons skim milk
3 tablespoons grated Asiago or Parmesan cheese

2 teaspoons chili powder
½ teaspoon cumin
¼ teaspoon ground black pepper
Nonstick cooking spray
Plain nonfat yogurt
Minced fresh cilantro

1 Cook pasta according to package directions, omitting salt. Drain and cool slightly, but do not rinse. Place pasta in medium bowl with bell pepper.

2 Combine whole egg, egg white, milk, cheese, chili powder, cumin and black pepper in small bowl; pour over pasta, tossing to coat evenly.

3 Spray large nonstick skillet with cooking spray. Add pasta mixture, spreading evenly and pressing firmly. Cook over medium-low heat until bottom is golden brown, about 7 to 8 minutes.

4 Slide noodle cake onto large plate, invert and return noodle cake to skillet. Cook until brown, 3 to 5 minutes.

5 Cut into wedges; serve warm, topped with yogurt and cilantro.

Makes 6 servings

Nutrients per Serving:

Calories	183 (20% of calories from fat)					
Total Fat	4 g	Carbohydrate	27 g	Iron	2 mg
Saturated Fat	<1 g	Dietary Fiber	2 g	Vitamin A	67 RE
Cholesterol	36 mg	Protein	9 g	Vitamin C	18 mg
Sodium	136 mg	Calcium	23 mg		

DIETARY EXCHANGES: 2 Starch/Bread, ½ Lean Meat, ½ Fat

ORIENTAL PILAF

Snow peas and carrots lend crunch, color and vitamin A to this delicious rice dish. Vitamin A promotes good vision and healthy skin.

1 tablespoon vegetable oil	¼ cup water*
1 cup chopped onion	3 ounces (1 cup) fresh snow
2 cloves garlic, minced	peas, cut lengthwise into
1 cup uncooked white rice	thin strips
1 can (about 14 ounces) ⅓-less-	2 medium carrots, coarsely
salt chicken broth	shredded

1 Heat oil in medium saucepan over medium heat. Add onion and garlic; cook and stir 4 minutes or until tender. Add rice; cook and stir 1 minute.

2 Add chicken broth and water. Bring to a boil over high heat. Reduce heat to low. Cover and simmer 18 minutes. Stir in snow peas and carrots. Cover and simmer 2 minutes or until liquid is absorbed.

3 Remove from heat. Let stand, covered, 5 minutes; fluff with fork before serving.

Makes 4 servings

*If using converted rice, increase water to ½ cup.

Nutrients per Serving:

Calories	242 (15% of calories from fat)				
Total Fat	4 g	Carbohydrate	46 g	Iron	3 mg
Saturated Fat	1 g	Dietary Fiber	3 g	Vitamin A	1015 RE
Cholesterol	0 mg	Protein	5 g	Vitamin C	16 mg
Sodium	31 mg	Calcium	43 mg		

DIETARY EXCHANGES: 2½ Starch/Bread, 1 Vegetable, 1 Fat

VEGETABLE FRIED RICE

Fried rice comes alive with a vibrant mix of broccoli, red bell pepper and carrot. The vegetables also boost the amount of vitamins and minerals in this traditional Chinese favorite.

1 teaspoon vegetable oil
1½ cups small broccoli flowerets
½ cup chopped red bell pepper
2 cups chilled, cooked white rice

1 tablespoon reduced sodium soy
   sauce
½ cup shredded carrot

1 Heat oil in large nonstick skillet over medium heat. Add broccoli and bell pepper; stir-fry 3 minutes or until crisp-tender.

2 Add rice and soy sauce; stir-fry 2 minutes. Add carrot; heat through. Serve on kale-lined plates, if desired.

Makes 4 servings

Nutrients per Serving:

Calories	193 (8% of calories from fat)				
Total Fat	2 g	Carbohydrate	40 g	Iron	2 mg
Saturated Fat	<1 g	Dietary Fiber	5 g	Vitamin A	526 RE
Cholesterol	0 mg	Protein	5 g	Vitamin C	143 mg
Sodium	278 mg	Calcium	47 mg		

DIETARY EXCHANGES: 2 Starch/Bread, 2 Vegetable

Cook's Note
Don't throw away those broccoli stems after removing the flowerets for this recipe. Instead, peel the stems with a vegetable peeler, cut them crosswise into thin slices and steam until crisp-tender.

VEGETABLE-BARLEY PILAF

Besides adding a nutty, chewy quality to this pilaf, the quick-cooking barley supplies fiber, potassium and phosphorus.

Nonstick cooking spray
¾ cup chopped onion
¾ cup chopped celery
¾ cup sliced fresh mushrooms
1 cup water
¾ cup sliced yellow summer squash
½ cup quick-cooking barley

½ cup sliced carrot
¼ cup chopped fresh parsley
2 teaspoons chopped fresh basil *or* ½ teaspoon dried basil leaves
½ teaspoon chicken bouillon granules
⅛ teaspoon ground black pepper

1 Coat large skillet with cooking spray. Add onion, celery and mushrooms; cook and stir over medium heat until vegetables are tender.

2 Stir in water, squash, barley, carrot, parsley, basil, chicken bouillon granules and pepper. Bring to a boil over high heat. Reduce heat to medium-low. Cover; simmer 10 to 12 minutes or until barley and vegetables are tender.

Makes 4 servings

Nutrients per Serving:

Calories	111 (10% of calories from fat)				
Total Fat	1 g	Carbohydrate	22 g	Iron	2 mg
Saturated Fat	<1 g	Dietary Fiber	5 g	Vitamin A	429 RE
Cholesterol	0 mg	Protein	4 g	Vitamin C	9 mg
Sodium	147 mg	Calcium	37 mg		

DIETARY EXCHANGES: 1 Starch/Bread, 1½ Vegetable

BAKED SPANISH RICE AND BARLEY

When it comes to good nutrition, this two-grain combo stacks up pretty well: 72% of its calories come from carbohydrate, 9% from protein and 16% from fat. There are even 3 grams of fiber per serving.

½ cup chopped onion
½ cup chopped green bell pepper
2 cloves garlic, minced
2 teaspoons vegetable oil
1 cup coarsely chopped seeded
   tomatoes

1 cup ⅓-less-salt chicken broth
½ cup uncooked white rice
3 tablespoons quick-cooking
   barley
¼ teaspoon ground black pepper
⅛ teaspoon salt

1 Preheat oven to 350°F. Coat 1½-quart casserole with nonstick cooking spray. Cook and stir onion, bell pepper and garlic in oil in medium saucepan over medium heat until vegetables are tender. Stir in tomatoes, chicken broth, rice, ½ cup water, barley, black pepper and salt. Bring to a boil over high heat.

2 Pour mixture into prepared casserole. Cover; bake 25 to 30 minutes or until rice and barley are tender and liquid is absorbed. Fluff rice mixture with fork.

Makes 4 servings

Nutrients per Serving:

Calories	167 (16% of calories from fat)				
Total Fat	3 g	Carbohydrate	32 g	Iron	2 mg
Saturated Fat	<1 g	Dietary Fiber	3 g	Vitamin A	52 RE
Cholesterol	0 mg	Protein	4 g	Vitamin C	38 mg
Sodium	83 mg	Calcium	24 mg		

DIETARY EXCHANGES: 1½ Starch/Bread, 1½ Vegetable, ½ Fat

CAKES & PIES

NORTHWOODS BUTTERMILK CAKE

2 cups all-purpose flour
1 cup whole wheat flour
2 teaspoons baking soda
1 teaspoon ground cinnamon
½ teaspoon salt
½ teaspoon ground nutmeg
½ cup reduced calorie margarine
1 cup firmly packed light brown
  sugar

5 egg whites
⅔ cup unsweetened applesauce
1 teaspoon vanilla
1 cup low fat buttermilk
2 cups cooked wild rice
  Powdered sugar (optional)

1 Preheat oven to 350°F. Spray 13×9-inch baking pan with nonstick cooking spray; dust lightly with flour. Combine flours, baking soda, cinnamon, salt and nutmeg in medium bowl.

2 Beat together margarine and brown sugar in large bowl with electric mixer until well blended. Beat in egg whites. Blend in applesauce and vanilla.

3 Add flour mixture to margarine mixture alternately with buttermilk, beating well after each addition. Stir in wild rice.

4 Pour mixture into prepared pan. Bake 45 to 50 minutes or until wooden toothpick inserted in center comes out clean. (*Do not overbake.*) Cool completely. Sprinkle with powdered sugar, if desired.   *Makes 16 servings*

Nutrients per Serving:

Calories	197 (16% of calories from fat)					
Total Fat	4 g	Carbohydrate	37 g	Iron		2 mg
Saturated Fat	1 g	Dietary Fiber	2 g	Vitamin A		77 RE
Cholesterol	1 mg	Protein	5 g	Vitamin C		<1 mg
Sodium	233 mg	Calcium	39 mg			

DIETARY EXCHANGES: 2 Starch/Bread, ½ Fruit, ½ Fat

SCRUMPTIOUS APPLE CAKE

Apples produce ethylene, a gas which accelerates the ripening of fruit.
Place an apple with any unripe fruit in a closed paper bag; the fruit should
be ripe within a few days.

3 egg whites
1½ cups granulated sugar
1 cup unsweetened applesauce
1 teaspoon vanilla
2 cups all-purpose flour
2 teaspoons ground cinnamon

1 teaspoon baking soda
½ teaspoon salt
4 cups cored peeled tart apple
   slices (McIntosh or Crispin)
Yogurt Glaze (recipe follows)

1 Preheat oven to 350°F. Spray 13×9-inch baking pan or 9-inch round springform pan with nonstick cooking spray. Beat egg whites in large bowl with electric mixer until slightly foamy. Add sugar; beat well. Blend in applesauce and vanilla. Combine flour, cinnamon, baking soda and salt in medium bowl. Add to applesauce mixture; mix well.

2 Place apples in prepared pan; cover with batter. Bake 35 to 40 minutes or until toothpick inserted in center comes out clean; cool completely.

3 Prepare Yogurt Glaze; spoon over cake. Sprinkle with additional cinnamon, if desired.

Makes 15 servings

YOGURT GLAZE

1½ cups plain or vanilla nonfat
   yogurt
3 tablespoons firmly packed
   brown sugar

1 teaspoon vanilla or lemon juice

1 Combine yogurt, brown sugar and vanilla in medium bowl; stir until smooth.

Makes about 2 cups

Nutrients per Serving:

Calories	186 (2% of calories from fat)				
Total Fat	<1 g	Carbohydrate	43 g	Iron	1 mg
Saturated Fat	<1 g	Dietary Fiber	1 g	Vitamin A	3 RE
Cholesterol	<1 mg	Protein	4 g	Vitamin C	2 mg
Sodium	156 mg	Calcium	57 mg		

DIETARY EXCHANGES: 1 Starch/Bread, 2 Fruit

BERRY BUNDT CAKE

*A cup of fresh, delicious blueberries or raspberries supplies about
one third of your daily vitamin C requirement. This fantastic
Bundt cake contains 4 cups of berries!*

2 cups all-purpose flour
1 tablespoon baking powder
1 teaspoon baking soda
¼ teaspoon salt
1 cup sugar
¾ cup buttermilk

½ cup cholesterol free egg
    substitute
¼ cup vegetable oil
2 cups raspberries
2 cups blueberries

1 Preheat oven to 350°F. Spray 6-cup Bundt pan with nonstick cooking
spray. Set aside.

2 Combine flour, baking powder, baking soda and salt in large bowl.
Combine sugar, buttermilk, egg substitute and oil in medium bowl. Add sugar
mixture to flour mixture; stir just until moistened.

3 Fold in raspberries and blueberries. Pour batter into prepared pan. Bake
1 hour or until wooden pick inserted in center comes out clean. Cool in pan
on wire rack. Serve with additional berries, if desired.   *Makes 12 servings*

Nutrients per Serving:

Calories	215 (21% of calories from fat)				
Total Fat	5 g	Carbohydrate	39 g	Iron	1 mg
Saturated Fat	1 g	Dietary Fiber	2 g	Vitamin A	58 RE
Cholesterol	1 mg	Protein	4 g	Vitamin C	6 mg
Sodium	262 mg	Calcium	46 mg		

DIETARY EXCHANGES: 2 Starch/Bread, ½ Fruit, 1 Fat

PINEAPPLE-COCONUT UPSIDE-DOWN CAKE

*If you love the taste of piña coladas, this extraordinary cake
will not disappoint you!*

2 tablespoons light corn syrup
6 tablespoons margarine,
    softened, divided
½ cup firmly packed light brown
    sugar
2 tablespoons flaked coconut
1 can (8 ounces) sliced
    pineapple in light syrup,
    drained
1⅓ cups all-purpose flour

2 teaspoons baking powder
¼ teaspoon salt
¾ cup granulated sugar
1 egg
1 teaspoon vanilla
⅔ cup skim milk
10 tablespoons thawed reduced
    fat frozen nondairy whipped
    topping

1 Heat corn syrup and 1 tablespoon margarine in small skillet over medium heat until margarine is melted. Stir in brown sugar; cook over medium heat until mixture is bubbly. Pour mixture into ungreased 9-inch round cake pan; sprinkle coconut evenly over top. Arrange pineapple slices on top of coconut.

2 Preheat oven to 350°F. Combine flour, baking powder and salt in medium bowl. Set aside. Beat remaining 5 tablespoons margarine in large bowl until fluffy; beat in granulated sugar, egg and vanilla. Add flour mixture to margarine mixture alternately with milk, beating well after each addition. Pour batter over prepared topping in cake pan.

3 Bake about 40 minutes or until wooden pick inserted in center comes out clean. Cool in pan on wire rack 2 to 3 minutes; loosen side of cake with knife and invert onto serving plate. Cut cake into wedges. Serve warm or cool, topped with whipped topping. Garnish, if desired.

Makes 10 servings

Nutrients per Serving:

Calories	272 (27% of calories from fat)				
Total Fat	8 g	Carbohydrate	47 g	Iron	1 mg
Saturated Fat	2 g	Dietary Fiber	1 g	Vitamin A	108 RE
Cholesterol	22 mg	Protein	3 g	Vitamin C	1 mg
Sodium	224 mg	Calcium	57 mg		

DIETARY EXCHANGES: 3 Starch/Bread, 1½ Fat

LEMON POPPY SEED CAKE

What a classic combination—lemon and poppy seed. Once you taste this luscious cake, you won't believe it's low fat!

6 tablespoons margarine, softened
½ cup firmly packed light brown sugar
½ cup plain low fat yogurt
1 whole egg
2 egg whites
3 teaspoons fresh lemon juice

1¾ cups all-purpose flour
1 teaspoon baking powder
½ teaspoon baking soda
¼ teaspoon salt
⅓ cup skim milk
2 tablespoons poppy seed
1 tablespoon grated lemon peel

LEMON GLAZE

1 cup powdered sugar
2 tablespoons plus 1½ teaspoons lemon juice

½ teaspoon poppy seed

1 Preheat oven to 350°F. Grease and flour 6-cup Bundt pan. Beat margarine in large bowl with electric mixer until fluffy. Beat in brown sugar, yogurt, whole egg, egg whites and lemon juice. Set aside.

2 Combine flour, baking powder, baking soda and salt in medium bowl. Add flour mixture to margarine mixture alternately with milk, beating well after each addition. Mix in 2 tablespoons poppy seed and lemon peel. Pour batter into prepared pan.

3 Bake about 40 minutes or until cake is golden brown and wooden pick inserted in center comes out clean. Cool in pan on wire rack 10 minutes; remove cake from pan and cool on wire rack.

4 For glaze, mix powdered sugar with lemon juice until desired consistency. Spoon glaze over cake; sprinkle with ½ teaspoon poppy seed.

Makes 12 servings

Nutrients per Serving:

Calories	217 (29% of calories from fat)				
Total Fat	7 g	Carbohydrate	34 g	Iron	1 mg
Saturated Fat	1 g	Dietary Fiber	1 g	Vitamin A	83 RE
Cholesterol	18 mg	Protein	4 g	Vitamin C	2 mg
Sodium	219 mg	Calcium	69 mg		

DIETARY EXCHANGES: 2½ Starch/Bread, 1 Fat

HONEY CARROT CAKE

The pineapple in this recipe gives the cake a fabulous flavor and also helps to keep it moist without adding fat. In addition, the frosting contains almost no fat since it is made with Neufchâtel cheese, a lighter version of cream cheese.

2 cups all-purpose flour
2 teaspoons baking powder
1½ teaspoons ground cinnamon
1 cup firmly packed dark brown sugar
½ cup honey
⅓ cup vegetable oil
1 whole egg
3 egg whites

3 cups shredded carrots
1 can (8 ounces) crushed pineapple in juice, drained
¼ cup chopped toasted pecans
6 ounces Neufchâtel cheese, softened
¾ cup powdered sugar
1 tablespoon cornstarch
1½ teaspoons vanilla extract

1 Preheat oven to 350°F. Spray 13×9-inch baking pan with nonstick cooking spray; set aside. Combine flour, baking powder and cinnamon in small bowl; set aside. Beat together brown sugar, honey, oil, whole egg and egg whites in large bowl with electric mixer. Gradually beat flour mixture into sugar mixture on low speed until well blended. Stir in carrots, pineapple and pecans.

2 Pour batter into prepared pan. Bake 40 to 45 minutes until toothpick inserted in center comes out clean. Cool completely in pan on wire rack.

3 To prepare frosting, beat Neufchâtel cheese, powdered sugar, cornstarch and vanilla in small bowl until smooth. Spread frosting over top of cake, reserving some frosting to tint with food coloring and pipe into carrot shapes for garnish. Store in refrigerator. *Makes 16 servings*

Variation: Instead of folding pecans into batter, sprinkle pecans over frosted cake.

Nutrients per Serving:

Calories	272 (29% of calories from fat)				
Total Fat	9 g	Carbohydrate	45 g	Iron	1 mg
Saturated Fat	2 g	Dietary Fiber	1 g	Vitamin A	623 RE
Cholesterol	22 mg	Protein	4 g	Vitamin C	3 mg
Sodium	112 mg	Calcium	42 mg		

DIETARY EXCHANGES: 2½ Starch/Bread, ½ Fruit, 1½ Fat

ORANGE SOUR CREAM POUND CAKE WITH MANDARIN SAUCE

In this time-honored recipe, sour cream provides the traditional rich flavor and smooth dense texture.

6 tablespoons margarine, softened
1 cup sugar, divided
1 cup low fat sour cream
1 whole egg
2 egg whites
1 tablespoon frozen orange juice concentrate

1 tablespoon grated orange peel
2½ cups cake flour
½ teaspoon baking soda
¼ teaspoon salt
⅓ cup orange juice
Mandarin Sauce (page 504)

1 Preheat oven to 350°F. Grease and flour 9×5-inch loaf pan. Beat margarine in large bowl with electric mixer until fluffy; beat in ⅔ cup sugar. Beat in sour cream, whole egg, egg whites, orange juice concentrate and orange peel until smooth. Set aside.

2 Combine flour, baking soda and salt in medium bowl; add to margarine mixture. Beat at medium speed until smooth. Pour batter into prepared pan.

3 Bake 40 minutes or until cake is golden brown and wooden pick inserted in center comes out clean. Cool in pan on wire rack 5 minutes.

4 Combine orange juice and remaining ⅓ cup sugar in small saucepan; bring to a boil. Remove from heat; cool slightly. Drizzle warm syrup over warm cake in pan; let stand 10 minutes. Remove cake from pan; cool on wire rack. Prepare Mandarin Sauce.

5 Serve cake slices with Mandarin Sauce.

Makes 12 servings

(continued on page 504)

Orange Sour Cream Pound Cake with Mandarin Sauce, continued

MANDARIN SAUCE

1¼ cups orange juice, divided   1 tablespoon honey
1 tablespoon cornstarch
2 cans (11 ounces each)
    mandarin orange segments,
    drained

 Bring 1 cup orange juice to a boil in small saucepan. Mix cornstarch and remaining ¼ cup orange juice in cup; stir into boiling juice. Boil until thickened, about 1 minute, stirring constantly. Stir in mandarin segments and honey; cook 1 minute. Serve warm.   *Makes about 1¾ cups sauce*

Nutrients per Serving:
cake plus 2 tablespoons sauce

Calories	260 (26% of calories from fat)					
Total Fat	8 g	Carbohydrate	44 g	Iron		2 mg
Saturated Fat	1 g	Dietary Fiber	1 g	Vitamin A		164 RE
Cholesterol	24 mg	Protein	4 g	Vitamin C		31 mg
Sodium	191 mg	Calcium	47 mg			

DIETARY EXCHANGES: 2½ Starch/Bread, ½ Fruit, 1 Fat

Cook's Tip
When measuring liquids, use a standard glass or clear plastic measuring cup. Place the cup on a level surface and fill to the desired amount. Bend down to read the marking, don't lift the cup off the surface to read. When measuring dry ingredients, use a measuring cup that is the exact capacity you wish to measure. Spoon the ingredient into the cup and level with the flat edge of a spatula.

CHOCOLATE CAKE WITH ALMOND FROSTING

Substituting puréed prunes for oil in this ultra-rich chocolate cake provides true low fat snacking.

1 tablespoon instant coffee granules
1 cup boiling water
1 cup unsweetened cocoa powder
2 cups all-purpose flour
2 cups sugar
2 teaspoons baking soda
1 teaspoon baking powder
¼ teaspoon salt
1 cup skim milk
3 jars (2½ ounces each) puréed prunes
4 egg whites
1 tablespoon vanilla
½ teaspoon almond extract
Almond Frosting (page 506)

1 Preheat oven to 350°F. Spray 13×9-inch baking pan with nonstick cooking spray. Set aside.

2 Combine coffee granules and boiling water in measuring cup. Stir until coffee is completely dissolved. Set aside.

3 Sift cocoa into large bowl. Add flour, sugar, baking soda, baking powder and salt; mix well. In another large bowl, combine prepared coffee, milk, prunes, egg whites, vanilla and almond extract; mix well. Add coffee mixture to cocoa mixture; mix well.

4 Pour batter into prepared pan. Bake 30 minutes or until wooden pick inserted in center of cake comes out clean. Cool in pan on wire rack 10 minutes. Invert cake onto serving plate; cool completely.

5 Prepare Almond Frosting; spread onto top and sides of cake. Garnish with toasted sliced almonds, if desired. *Makes 12 servings*

(continued on page 506)

Chocolate Cake with Almond Frosting, continued

ALMOND FROSTING

3 egg whites*
1½ cups firmly packed light brown
    sugar
¼ cup water

1 teaspoon cream of tartar
2 teaspoons vanilla
1 teaspoon almond extract

 Combine egg whites, brown sugar, water and cream of tartar in top of double boiler. Place over simmering water. Using electric hand mixer, beat until stiff peaks form, about 5 minutes.

 Add vanilla and almond extract; beat 2 minutes. Remove from heat; cool.

*Use only clean, uncracked Grade A eggs.

Nutrients per Serving:

1 piece frosted cake

Calories	285 (2% of calories from fat)				
Total Fat	1 g	Carbohydrate	68 g	Iron	3 mg
Saturated Fat	0 g	Dietary Fiber	1 g	Vitamin A	13 RE
Cholesterol	0 mg	Protein	5 g	Vitamin C	1 mg
Sodium	274 mg	Calcium	58 mg		

DIETARY EXCHANGES: 4 Starch/Bread

❖

Cook's Tip

Separate eggs while they are cold, as the yolk is firm and less likely to break. Let the whites sit at room temperature for 30 minutes before beating in order to achieve their highest volume. Adding cream of tartar to beaten egg whites prevents them from collapsing.

❖

OLD-FASHIONED GINGERBREAD

Molasses contributes a wonderful flavor to this spicy, moist cake. For an added bonus, it's also rich in iron.

2 tablespoons margarine, melted and cooled
⅓ cup firmly packed light brown sugar
¼ cup cholesterol free egg substitute
¼ cup buttermilk
2 cups all-purpose flour
1½ teaspoons baking soda
1½ teaspoons ground ginger
1 teaspoon ground cinnamon

½ teaspoon salt
1 tablespoon instant coffee granules
1 cup hot water
½ cup molasses
¼ cup honey
1 jar (2½ ounces) puréed prunes
Thawed reduced fat frozen nondairy whipped topping (optional)

1 Preheat oven to 350°F. Spray 9-inch square or 11×7-inch baking pan with nonstick cooking spray; set aside.

2 Combine margarine, brown sugar, egg substitute and buttermilk in medium bowl; set aside. Combine flour, baking soda, ginger, cinnamon and salt in large bowl; set aside. Dissolve coffee granules in hot water in small bowl. Stir in molasses, honey and puréed prunes.

3 Add flour mixture alternately with coffee mixture to margarine mixture, mixing well after each addition. *(Batter will be lumpy. Do not overmix.)*

4 Pour batter into prepared pan. Bake 40 to 45 minutes or until wooden pick inserted in center comes out clean. Cool in pan on wire rack. Before serving, top with whipped topping, if desired.

Makes 8 servings

Nutrients per Serving:					
Calories	265 (11% of calories from fat)				
Total Fat	3 g	Carbohydrate	56 g	Iron	5 mg
Saturated Fat	1 g	Dietary Fiber	1 g	Vitamin A	77 RE
Cholesterol	<1 mg	Protein	4 g	Vitamin C	1 mg
Sodium	447 mg	Calcium	174 mg		

DIETARY EXCHANGES: 3½ Starch/Bread, ½ Fat

RASPBERRY SHORTCAKE

1½ cups frozen raspberries,
    thawed, divided
6 tablespoons sugar, divided
1 cup all-purpose flour
1 teaspoon baking powder
¼ teaspoon baking soda

1 tablespoon cold margarine
1 egg white
⅓ cup evaporated skimmed milk
¼ teaspoon almond extract
¾ cup 1% low fat cottage cheese
1 teaspoon lemon juice

1 Preheat oven to 450°F. Spray cookie sheet with nonstick cooking spray. Combine 1¼ cups raspberries and 2 tablespoons plus 1½ teaspoons sugar in small bowl; cover and refrigerate until ready to serve.

2 Combine flour, 2 tablespoons sugar, baking powder and baking soda in medium bowl. Cut in margarine using 2 knives or pastry blender until mixture forms coarse crumbs; set aside.

3 In separate small bowl, beat together egg white, milk and almond extract until well blended. Add to dry ingredients; mix lightly. Place dough on lightly floured board; knead about 5 minutes or until dough is no longer sticky to the touch. Roll out dough to ½-inch thickness. Using 2½-inch biscuit cutter, cut out 8 biscuits from dough; place on cookie sheet. Bake 10 minutes or until tops are lightly browned. Remove to wire rack; cool.

4 Place cottage cheese, remaining 1 tablespoon plus 1½ teaspoons sugar and lemon juice in food processor or blender container; process until smooth. Transfer mixture to medium bowl. Gently stir in remaining ¼ cup raspberries.

5 Split biscuits horizontally in half; place bottom halves on individual serving plates. Cover each biscuit half with about 2 tablespoons reserved raspberry mixture and 1 tablespoon cottage cheese mixture; cover with biscuit top. Top with remaining reserved raspberry and cottage cheese mixtures.

Makes 8 servings

Nutrients per Serving:

Calories	140 (14% of calories from fat)					
Total Fat	2 g	Carbohydrate	24 g	Iron	1 mg
Saturated Fat	1 g	Dietary Fiber	1 g	Vitamin A	37 RE
Cholesterol	2 mg	Protein	6 g	Vitamin C	6 mg
Sodium	189 mg	Calcium	61 mg		

DIETARY EXCHANGES: 1 Starch/Bread, ½ Lean Meat, ½ Fruit, ½ Fat

RASPBERRY-APPLESAUCE COFFEE CAKE

Since this fruity coffee cake has just a touch of margarine and no egg yolks, it's perfect for a low fat diet.

1½ cups raspberries
¼ cup water
7 tablespoons sugar, divided
2 tablespoons cornstarch
½ teaspoon ground nutmeg, divided
1¾ cups all-purpose flour, divided
3 tablespoons margarine

1 tablespoon finely chopped walnuts
1½ teaspoons baking powder
½ teaspoon baking soda
⅛ teaspoon ground cloves
2 egg whites
1 cup unsweetened applesauce

1 Preheat oven to 350°F. Spray 8-inch square baking pan with nonstick cooking spray. Combine raspberries and water in small saucepan. Bring to a boil over high heat. Reduce heat to medium. Combine 2 tablespoons sugar, cornstarch and ¼ teaspoon nutmeg in small bowl. Stir into raspberry mixture. Cook and stir until mixture boils and thickens. Cook and stir 2 minutes more; set aside.

2 Combine ¾ cup flour and remaining 5 tablespoons sugar in medium bowl. Cut in margarine with pastry blender until mixture resembles coarse crumbs; set aside ½ cup crumb mixture for topping.

3 Add remaining 1 cup flour, walnuts, baking powder, baking soda, remaining ¼ teaspoon nutmeg and cloves to remaining crumb mixture. Add egg whites and applesauce; beat until well combined. Spread half of batter into prepared baking pan. Spread raspberry mixture over batter. Drop remaining batter into small mounds on top. Sprinkle with reserved topping.

4 Bake 40 to 45 minutes or until edges start to pull away from sides of pan. Serve warm or cool.

Makes 9 servings

Nutrients per Serving:					
Calories	196 (21% of calories from fat)				
Total Fat	5 g	Carbohydrate	35 g	Iron	1 mg
Saturated Fat	1 g	Dietary Fiber	2 g	Vitamin A	50 RE
Cholesterol	0 mg	Protein	4 g	Vitamin C	6 mg
Sodium	158 mg	Calcium	21 mg		

DIETARY EXCHANGES: 1 Starch/Bread, 1½ Fruit, 1 Fat

RASPBERRY TORTONI CAKE ROLL

Raspberry Tortoni Filling
(page 516)
3 eggs, separated
¾ cup granulated sugar
¼ cup skim milk
1 teaspoon vanilla extract

¾ cup all-purpose flour
1½ teaspoons baking powder
¼ teaspoon salt
¼ teaspoon cream of tartar
1 tablespoon powdered sugar

1 Prepare Raspberry Tortoni Filling; set aside.

2 Lightly grease 15×10-inch jelly-roll pan and line with waxed paper; lightly grease and flour paper. Preheat oven to 400°F. Beat egg yolks in medium bowl with electric mixer at high speed 1 minute; gradually beat in granulated sugar until yolks are thick and lemon colored, about 5 minutes. Beat in milk and vanilla; mix in flour, baking powder and salt.

3 Beat egg whites in another medium bowl at high speed until foamy. Add cream of tartar; beat until stiff peaks form. Stir about ⅓ of egg white mixture into cake batter; gently fold in remaining egg white mixture. Spread batter evenly into prepared pan.

4 Bake 8 to 10 minutes or until top begins to brown. Immediately invert onto clean towel that has been sprinkled with powdered sugar. Peel off waxed paper; roll cake up in towel. Cool on wire rack 10 minutes.

5 Gently unroll cake; spread with Raspberry Tortoni Filling. Roll cake up; wrap in plastic wrap or aluminum foil. Freeze until firm, at least 8 hours or overnight.

6 Remove cake from freezer; unwrap. Trim ends, if uneven. Place cake on serving plate. Sprinkle with additional powdered sugar and garnish with fresh raspberries and mint, if desired.   *Makes 12 servings*

(continued on page 516)

Raspberry Tortoni Cake Roll, continued

RASPBERRY TORTONI FILLING

2 cups fresh or frozen
    unsweetened raspberries,
    thawed, drained and divided
1 tablespoon sugar
2 envelopes (1.3 ounces each)
    whipped topping mix

1 cup 1% low fat milk
½ teaspoon rum or sherry extract
    (optional)
¼ cup pistachio nuts or coarsely
    chopped blanched almonds

1 Place 1 cup raspberries in food processor or blender; process until smooth. Strain and discard seeds. Sprinkle sugar over remaining 1 cup raspberries.

2 Beat whipped topping mix with milk in medium bowl at high speed until stiff peaks form; fold in raspberry purée and rum, if desired. Fold in sugared raspberries and nuts.

Makes 4 cups

Nutrients per Serving:

Calories	174 (8% of calories from fat)						
Total Fat	3 g	Carbohydrate	30 g	Iron		1 mg
Saturated Fat	1 g	Dietary Fiber	2 g	Vitamin A		52 RE
Cholesterol	54 mg	Protein	4 g	Vitamin C		6 mg
Sodium	125 mg	Calcium	53 mg			

DIETARY EXCHANGES: 2 Starch/Bread, ½ Fat

Health Tip

Raspberries are a good source of fiber, potassium
and vitamin C. They also contain a small amount of
vitamin A and iron.

LOW FAT CHEESECAKE

This incredibly delicious cheesecake is so rich and creamy you won't believe that it's so low in fat!

1 cup whole grain toasted oat cereal
½ cup zwieback crumbs
1 cup plus 2 tablespoons sugar, divided
2 tablespoons water
2 teaspoons margarine, melted
3 cups nonfat ricotta cheese

1½ cups reduced fat cream cheese
1 cup low fat sour cream
2 egg whites
3 tablespoons cornstarch
1 tablespoon vanilla
1 teaspoon grated lemon peel
   Blueberry Sauce or Pineapple Sauce (page 518, optional)

1 Preheat oven to 325°F. Spray 10-inch springform pan with nonstick cooking spray. Combine cereal, zwieback crumbs and 2 tablespoons sugar in food processor or blender; process until fine crumbs form. Gradually add water and margarine; process until moistened. Press crumb mixture onto bottom and 1 inch up side of prepared pan. Set aside.

2 Place ricotta cheese in food processor or blender; process 2 minutes or until smooth. Add cream cheese, remaining 1 cup sugar, sour cream, egg whites, cornstarch, vanilla and lemon peel; process until smooth. Pour batter into prepared crust.

3 Bake 1 hour or until center is almost set. Turn off oven; leave cheesecake in oven with door closed 30 minutes. Remove from oven; cool completely on wire rack. Carefully loosen cheesecake from side of pan; remove side. Cover cheesecake with plastic wrap; refrigerate at least 4 hours or up to 2 days. Prepare Blueberry Sauce; spoon over cheesecake.   *Makes 12 servings*

Nutrients per Serving:

Calories	266 (24% of calories from fat)				
Total Fat	7 g	Carbohydrate	39 g	Iron	1 mg
Saturated Fat	3 g	Dietary Fiber	1 g	Vitamin A	453 RE
Cholesterol	22 mg	Protein	14 g	Vitamin C	<1 mg
Sodium	296 mg	Calcium	191 mg		

DIETARY EXCHANGES: 2 Starch/Bread, ½ Milk, 1½ Fat

(continued on page 518)

Low Fat Cheesecake, continued

BLUEBERRY SAUCE

6 tablespoons blueberry jam

2 tablespoons lemon juice

2 tablespoons water

2 teaspoons cornstarch

1 teaspoon grated lemon peel

1 cup fresh or frozen blueberries, thawed, drained

1 Heat jam and lemon juice in medium saucepan over low heat. Stir together water and cornstarch; add to jam mixture. Cook until slightly thickened; cool. Stir in blueberries.   *Makes about 2 cups*

Nutrients per Serving:
2 tablespoons

Calories	21 (0% of calories from fat)				
Total Fat	0 g	Carbohydrate	4 g	Iron	0 mg
Saturated Fat	0 g	Dietary Fiber	<1 g	Vitamin A	1 RE
Cholesterol	0 mg	Protein	0 g	Vitamin C	2 mg
Sodium	<1 mg	Calcium	3 mg		

DIETARY EXCHANGES: ½ Fruit

PINEAPPLE SAUCE

1 can (8¼ ounces) crushed pineapple in juice, drained (reserve juice)

1½ tablespoons cornstarch

1 tablespoon sugar

2 tablespoons spiced rum *or* 1½ teaspoons rum extract

½ teaspoon grated lemon or lime peel

1 Combine reserved pineapple juice and cornstarch in small saucepan; stir in sugar. Heat over medium heat until slightly thickened. Stir in rum; cool. Stir in crushed pineapple and lemon peel.   *Makes about 2 cups*

Nutrients per Serving:
2 tablespoons

Calories	13 (0% of calories from fat)				
Total Fat	0 g	Carbohydrate	4 g	Iron	0 mg
Saturated Fat	0 g	Dietary Fiber	0 g	Vitamin A	1 RE
Cholesterol	0 mg	Protein	0 g	Vitamin C	1 mg
Sodium	8 mg	Calcium	2 mg		

DIETARY EXCHANGES: ½ Fruit

CALORIE WATCHERS' "CHEESECAKE"

By substituting low fat cottage cheese and yogurt for the traditional cream cheese used in cheesecakes, the fat content in this recipe is cut by more than half.

1 envelope unflavored gelatin
¼ cup skim milk
1 container (16 ounces) 1% low fat cottage cheese with pineapple
1 container (8 ounces) vanilla low fat yogurt, divided

¼ cup sugar
¼ teaspoon salt
4 tablespoons graham cracker crumbs, divided

1 Sprinkle gelatin over milk in small saucepan; let stand 5 minutes to soften. Cook over low heat, stirring constantly, until gelatin dissolves, 3 to 5 minutes. Remove from heat; cool slightly.

2 Place cottage cheese, ½ cup yogurt, sugar and salt in food processor or blender container; process until smooth. Gradually add gelatin mixture, processing until well blended.

3 Spoon 1½ teaspoons crumbs into each of four large dessert or wine glasses. Spoon an equal amount of cottage cheese mixture over crumbs in each glass; sprinkle each with another 1½ teaspoons crumbs. Cover and refrigerate until firm, about 2 hours.

4 When ready to serve, top desserts with remaining yogurt. Garnish with fresh strawberries, if desired.

Makes 4 servings

Nutrients per Serving:

Calories	251 (15% of calories from fat)				
Total Fat	4 g	Carbohydrate	32 g	Iron	1 mg
Saturated Fat	2 g	Dietary Fiber	0 g	Vitamin A	33 RE
Cholesterol	13 mg	Protein	21 g	Vitamin C	1 mg
Sodium	683 mg	Calcium	182 mg		

DIETARY EXCHANGES: 2 Starch/Bread, 2 Lean Meat, 1 Milk

RASPBERRY SWIRL CHEESECAKE

Raspberries are not only a good source of fiber, but also of vitamin C.

2 tablespoons vanilla wafer
  crumbs
2 containers (12 ounces each)
  fat free cream cheese,
  softened
⅔ cup sugar

2 eggs
2 tablespoons cornstarch
2 teaspoons vanilla
1 cup low fat sour cream
1 pint raspberries, divided

1 Preheat oven to 400°F. Spray bottom and 1 inch up side of 9-inch springform pan with nonstick cooking spray; coat with wafer crumbs. Beat cream cheese in large bowl with electric mixer until fluffy. Beat in sugar. Add eggs, cornstarch and vanilla; beat until smooth. Blend in sour cream. Pour batter into prepared pan.

2 Place 1 cup raspberries in food processor or blender container; process until smooth. Strain purée; discard seeds. Spoon purée over batter in pan; gently swirl with knife to marbleize.

3 Bake 45 to 50 minutes or until cheesecake is set around edge but slightly soft in center. Turn off oven; let cheesecake cool in oven about 3 hours with oven door slightly opened.

4 Refrigerate cheesecake overnight. Carefully loosen cheesecake from side of pan; remove side. Top with remaining 1 cup raspberries. Garnish with mint, if desired.

Makes 14 servings

Nutrients per Serving:

Calories	136 (19% of calories from fat)				
Total Fat	3 g	Carbohydrate	17 g	Iron	<1 mg
Saturated Fat	<1 g	Dietary Fiber	1 g	Vitamin A	16 RE
Cholesterol	46 mg	Protein	9 g	Vitamin C	4 mg
Sodium	326 mg	Calcium	8 mg		

DIETARY EXCHANGES: 1 Starch/Bread, 1 Lean Meat

PUMPKIN CHEESECAKE

Try this delicious low fat cheesecake as an alternative to your traditional pumpkin pie for Thanksgiving dinner.

⅓ cup graham cracker crumbs
1 can (16 ounces) solid pack pumpkin
2 cups low fat ricotta cheese
1 cup sugar
3 tablespoons all-purpose flour
1 tablespoon nonfat dry milk powder

1 tablespoon ground cinnamon
1 teaspoon ground allspice
1 egg white
¾ cup canned evaporated skimmed milk
1 tablespoon vegetable oil
1 tablespoon vanilla

1 Preheat oven to 400°F. Spray 9-inch springform pan with nonstick cooking spray. Coat with graham cracker crumbs. Set aside.

2 Combine pumpkin and ricotta cheese in food processor or blender; process until smooth. Add sugar, flour, milk powder, cinnamon, allspice, egg white, evaporated skimmed milk, oil and vanilla; process until smooth.

3 Pour mixture into prepared pan. Bake 15 minutes. Reduce oven temperature to 275°F; bake 1 hour and 15 minutes. Turn off oven; leave cheesecake in oven without opening door 1 hour. Remove from oven; cool completely on wire rack. Carefully loosen cheesecake from side of pan; remove side. Cover cheesecake with plastic wrap; refrigerate at least 4 hours or up to 2 days. Garnish with fresh fruit, if desired. *Makes 16 servings*

Nutrients per Serving:					
Calories	121 (15% of calories from fat)				
Total Fat	2 g	Carbohydrate	22 g	Iron	1 mg
Saturated Fat	0 g	Dietary Fiber	1 g	Vitamin A	662 RE
Cholesterol	4 mg	Protein	4 g	Vitamin C	2 mg
Sodium	56 mg	Calcium	89 mg		

DIETARY EXCHANGES: 1½ Starch/Bread, ½ Fat

CRANBERRY APPLE PIE WITH SOFT GINGERSNAP CRUST

The cranberry is a tart fruit that is a member of the berry family. Choose good quality fresh cranberries by picking ones that are plump and unblemished. Discard soft or bruised berries.

20 gingersnaps
1 tablespoons reduced calorie margarine
2 tart apples (McIntosh or Crispin), cored
1 cup fresh cranberries

5 tablespoons firmly packed dark brown sugar
¼ teaspoon vanilla
¼ teaspoon ground cinnamon
1 teaspoon granulated sugar

1 Preheat oven to 375°F. Place gingersnaps and margarine in food processor or blender container; process until mixture forms crumbs. Place gingersnap mixture in 8-inch pie plate; press onto bottom and up side of plate to form crust. (If desired, use slightly smaller pie plate to press crust down uniformly.) Bake 5 to 8 minutes or until crust is golden brown. Cool.

2 Slice apples in food processor. Add cranberries, brown sugar, vanilla and cinnamon; process just until combined.

3 Spoon apple mixture into separate pie plate or casserole dish; sprinkle with granulated sugar. Bake 35 minutes or until apples are tender. Spoon into crust. Garnish, if desired. Serve warm.

Makes 8 servings

Nutrients per Serving:

Calories	141 (16% of calories from fat)					
Total Fat	3 g	Carbohydrate	30 g	Iron	1 mg
Saturated Fat	<1 g	Dietary Fiber	1 g	Vitamin A	19 RE
Cholesterol	0 mg	Protein	1 g	Vitamin C	4 mg
Sodium	135 mg	Calcium	24 mg		

DIETARY EXCHANGES: 1 Starch/Bread, 1 Fruit, ½ Fat

STRAWBERRY CREAM PIE

Feature this cool combination of low fat cream cheese and fresh strawberries at your next party.

1 cup plus 1½ teaspoons all-purpose flour, divided

¼ cup plus 1 teaspoon sugar, divided

¼ teaspoon salt

¼ cup cold margarine, cut into pieces

¾ teaspoon white or cider vinegar

3 tablespoons ice water, divided

6 ounces fat free cream cheese

2 ounces Neufchâtel cheese

¼ cup vanilla nonfat yogurt

2 egg whites

½ teaspoon vanilla

1½ cups fresh strawberries, cut in half lengthwise

¼ cup strawberry jelly

1 Combine 1 cup flour, 1 teaspoon sugar and salt in medium bowl. Cut in margarine using 2 knives or pastry blender until small crumbs form. Add vinegar and 2 tablespoons ice water; stir until flour mixture is moistened. If necessary, add remaining 1 tablespoon ice water. Shape dough into ball.

2 Preheat oven to 450°F. Roll out dough to 12-inch circle on lightly floured surface. Place dough in 9-inch glass pie plate. Bake 10 to 12 minutes or until lightly browned. Place on wire rack to cool. Meanwhile, *reduce oven temperature to 325°F.*

3 Combine cream cheese, Neufchâtel cheese, remaining ¼ cup sugar and 1½ teaspoons flour in large bowl. Beat with electric mixer until creamy. Beat in yogurt, egg whites and vanilla. Pour batter into pie crust. Bake 25 minutes or until center is set. Cool completely on wire rack.

4 Place strawberries on top of pie. Melt jelly in small saucepan over low heat. Carefully brush glaze over strawberries, allowing glaze to run onto pie. Refrigerate 3 hours or overnight.

Makes 8 servings

Nutrients per Serving:

Calories	220 (31% of calories from fat)					
Total Fat	7 g	Carbohydrate	31 g	Iron	1 mg
Saturated Fat	2 g	Dietary Fiber	1 g	Vitamin A	163 RE
Cholesterol	8 mg	Protein	7 g	Vitamin C	16 mg
Sodium	333 mg	Calcium	181 mg		

DIETARY EXCHANGES: 2 Starch/Bread, 1½ Fat

LEMON MERINGUE PIE

Serve this cholesterol free pie as a refreshing finale to any meal.

1 cup graham cracker crumbs
¼ cup powdered sugar
2 tablespoons margarine, melted
1 tablespoon water
1½ cups granulated sugar, divided
⅓ cup cornstarch
1½ cups hot water

¼ cup cholesterol free egg substitute
1½ teaspoons grated lemon peel
½ cup fresh lemon juice
3 egg whites
½ teaspoon vanilla
¼ teaspoon cream of tartar

1 Preheat oven to 375°F. Combine graham cracker crumbs and powdered sugar in small bowl. Stir in margarine and water until all crumbs are moistened. Press crumb mixture onto bottom and up side of 9-inch pie plate. Bake 6 to 9 minutes or until edges are golden brown. Place on wire rack to cool. Meanwhile, *reduce oven temperature to 350°F.*

2 Combine ½ cup granulated sugar and cornstarch in medium saucepan over low heat. Gradually stir in hot water until smooth. Add egg substitute. Bring to a boil, stirring constantly with wire whisk. Boil 1 minute. Remove from heat; stir in lemon peel and lemon juice. Pour hot filling into crust.

3 Beat egg whites, vanilla and cream of tartar in large bowl until soft peaks form. Gradually add remaining 1 cup granulated sugar, beating until stiff peaks form. Spread meringue over filling, sealing carefully to edge of crust.

4 Bake 12 to 15 minutes or until meringue is golden brown. Cool completely before serving.

Makes 8 servings

Nutrients per Serving:

Calories	284 (14% of calories from fat)					
Total Fat	4 g	Carbohydrate	59 g	Iron		1 mg
Saturated Fat	1 g	Dietary Fiber	0 g	Vitamin A		73 RE
Cholesterol	0 mg	Protein	3 g	Vitamin C		7 mg
Sodium	144 mg	Calcium	9 mg			

DIETARY EXCHANGES: 3½ Starch/Bread, 1 Fat

GRASSHOPPER PIE

This incredible pie uses liqueurs for its unique minty flavor, but you may substitute 1 teaspoon mint extract and 1 teaspoon vanilla for the liqueurs, if desired.

2 cups graham cracker crumbs
4 tablespoons unsweetened
    cocoa powder
¼ cup margarine, melted
8 ounces fat free cream cheese
1 cup 1% low fat milk
2 tablespoons green creme de
    menthe liqueur

2 tablespoons white creme de
    cacao liqueur
1½ teaspoons vanilla
1 container (4 ounces) thawed
    frozen nondairy whipped
    topping

1 Spray 9-inch pie plate with nonstick cooking spray. Combine cracker crumbs, cocoa and margarine in medium bowl; press onto bottom and up side of prepared pie plate. Refrigerate.

2 Beat cream cheese in large bowl with electric mixer until fluffy. Gradually beat in milk until smooth. Stir in both liqueurs and vanilla. Fold in whipped topping. Chill 20 minutes. Spoon into crust. Freeze 4 hours or until filling is set. Garnish with fresh mint, if desired. *Makes 8 servings*

Nutrients per Serving:

Calories	310 (31% of calories from fat)				
Total Fat	11 g	Carbohydrate	28 g	Iron	2 mg
Saturated Fat	3 g	Dietary Fiber	0 g	Vitamin A	81 RE
Cholesterol	<1 mg	Protein	3 g	Vitamin C	<1 mg
Sodium	196 mg	Calcium	23 mg		

DIETARY EXCHANGES: 2 Starch/Bread, 2 Fat

CHOCOLATE PIE

On a low fat diet, there's no need to deny yourself a chocolate treat. This pie is as rich as a candy bar—with only 18% of calories from fat!!

1¼ cups sugar
½ cup reduced fat biscuit mix
3 tablespoons unsweetened
  cocoa powder, sifted

2 tablespoons margarine, melted
1 whole egg
3 egg whites
1½ teaspoons vanilla

1 Preheat oven to 350°F. Spray 9-inch pie plate with nonstick cooking spray. Set aside.

2 Combine sugar, biscuit mix and cocoa in large bowl; mix well. Add margarine, egg, egg whites and vanilla; mix well. Pour mixture into prepared plate.

3 Bake 40 minutes or until knife inserted in center comes out clean. Garnish with powdered sugar, if desired.   *Makes 8 servings*

Nutrients per Serving:

Calories	194 (18% of calories from fat)				
Total Fat	4 g	Carbohydrate	38 g	Iron	1 mg
Saturated Fat	1 g	Dietary Fiber	0 g	Vitamin A	47 RE
Cholesterol	27 mg	Protein	3 g	Vitamin C	0 mg
Sodium	177 mg	Calcium	12 mg		

DIETARY EXCHANGES: 2 Starch/Bread, ½ Fat

Cook's Tip
Unsweetened cocoa powder is a great way to add rich chocolate flavor to your diet without all the extra fat and calories. One tablespoon of cocoa contains only a half gram of fat per tablespoon and is naturally very low in sodium and cholesterol free.

DESSERTS

APRICOT CRUMB BARS

Apricots are a good source of potassium and are rich in beta-carotene, the substance that the body transforms into vitamin A.

1 package (18.25 ounces) light yellow cake mix
1 teaspoon ground cinnamon
½ teaspoon ground nutmeg
6 tablespoons cold margarine, cut into pieces
¾ cup uncooked multigrain oatmeal cereal or quick oats

1 whole egg
2 egg whites
1 tablespoon water
1 jar (10 ounces) apricot fruit spread
2 tablespoons firmly packed light brown sugar

1 Preheat oven to 350°F. Combine cake mix, cinnamon and nutmeg in medium bowl. Cut in margarine with pastry blender or 2 knives until mixture forms coarse crumbs. Stir in cereal. Reserve 1 cup crumb mixture; mix whole egg, egg whites and water into remaining crumb mixture.

2 Spread batter evenly onto bottom of ungreased 13×9-inch baking pan; top with fruit spread. Sprinkle reserved 1 cup cereal mixture over fruit; top with brown sugar.

3 Bake 35 to 40 minutes or until top is golden brown. Cool in pan on wire rack; cut into bars.

Makes 15 servings

Nutrients per Serving:

Calories	267 (25% of calories from fat)					
Total Fat	7 g	Carbohydrate	48 g	Iron	1 mg
Saturated Fat	14 g	Dietary Fiber	1 g	Vitamin A	62 RE
Cholesterol	2 mg	Protein	2 g	Vitamin C	0 mg
Sodium	299 mg	Calcium	59 mg		

DIETARY EXCHANGES: 3 Starch/Bread, 1½ Fat

CALIFORNIA APRICOT-CHERRY CORNMEAL COBBLER

Sweet, delicious cherries, which are low in calories, fat and sodium, provide potassium for good blood maintenance.

2 cups sliced pitted halved fresh apricots
⅓ cup sugar
2 cups pitted fresh cherries
1 cup plus 1 tablespoon all-purpose flour, divided
½ cup yellow cornmeal
¼ teaspoon salt
1 tablespoon plus 2½ teaspoons sugar
2 teaspoons baking powder
5 tablespoons cold margarine
½ teaspoon grated orange peel
¾ cup 2% low fat milk

1 Preheat oven to 375°F. Combine apricots and ⅓ cup sugar in small bowl. Combine cherries and 1 tablespoon flour in separate bowl; set aside.

2 Combine remaining 1 cup flour, cornmeal, salt, 1 tablespoon plus 1½ teaspoons sugar and baking powder in large bowl. Cut in margarine until mixture forms coarse crumbs; stir in orange peel. Add milk; stir just until dry ingredients are moistened.

3 Place fruit in 1½-quart baking dish; top with batter. Sprinkle with remaining 1 teaspoon sugar. Bake 25 to 30 minutes or until golden brown. Cool slightly before serving.

Makes 8 servings

Nutrients per Serving:

Calories	252 (29% of calories from fat)				
Total Fat	8 g	Carbohydrate	42 g	Iron	1 mg
Saturated Fat	2 g	Dietary Fiber	3 g	Vitamin A	259 RE
Cholesterol	2 mg	Protein	4 g	Vitamin C	8 mg
Sodium	246 mg	Calcium	61 mg		

DIETARY EXCHANGES: 2 Starch/Bread, 1 Fruit, 1½ Fat

CHERRY COBBLER

The "cobbled" or bumpy appearance of the rich biscuit topping gives this favorite fruit dessert its unique name.

1 cup all-purpose flour
¾ cup sugar, divided
2 tablespoons instant nonfat dry milk powder
2 teaspoons baking powder
¼ teaspoon baking soda
¼ teaspoon salt
2 tablespoons vegetable oil
7 tablespoons low fat buttermilk

2 tablespoons cornstarch
½ cup water
1 package (16 ounces) frozen unsweetened cherries thawed and drained
½ teaspoon vanilla
Fat free frozen yogurt (optional)

1 Preheat oven to 400°F. Combine flour, ¼ cup sugar, milk powder, baking powder, baking soda and salt in medium bowl. Stir in oil until mixture becomes crumbly. Add buttermilk; stir until moistened. Set aside.

2 Combine cornstarch, remaining ½ cup sugar and water in medium saucepan. Stir until cornstarch is dissolved. Cook over medium heat, stirring constantly, until thickened. Add cherries and vanilla; stir until cherries are completely coated. Pour into 8-inch square baking pan; spoon biscuit mixture over cherries.

3 Bake 25 minutes or until topping is golden brown. Serve warm with fat free frozen yogurt, if desired.

Makes 8 servings

Nutrients per Serving:					
Calories	204 (17% of calories from fat)				
Total Fat	4 g	Carbohydrate	40 g	Iron	1 mg
Saturated Fat	1 g	Dietary Fiber	1 g	Vitamin A	58 RE
Cholesterol	1 mg	Protein	3 g	Vitamin C	1 mg
Sodium	209 mg	Calcium	53 mg		

DIETARY EXCHANGES: 2 Starch/Bread, ½ Fruit, ½ Fat

NO-BAKE FRUIT CRISP

When purchasing granola cereal, be sure to read the label. Even though most people consider granola to be a healthy food, it can be loaded with fat.

1 cup low fat granola cereal
¼ cup toasted sliced almonds
1 tablespoon reduced calorie margarine
2 tablespoons firmly packed light brown sugar

1 teaspoon ground cinnamon
½ cup fat free vanilla yogurt
¼ teaspoon ground nutmeg
2 cans (16 ounces each) chunky mixed fruit in juice or extra light syrup, drained

1 Combine granola and almonds in medium bowl.

2 Melt margarine in small saucepan. Add brown sugar and cinnamon; cook, stirring frequently, until sugar dissolves, about 2 minutes. Add to granola mixture; toss to coat. Cool.

3 When ready to serve, combine yogurt and nutmeg in small bowl. Spoon approximately ½ cup chunky mixed fruit onto each serving plate; top with yogurt mixture. Sprinkle with granola mixture.   *Makes 6 servings*

Nutrients per Serving:

Calories	224 (26% of calories from fat)				
Total Fat	7 g	Carbohydrate	39 g	Iron	1 mg
Saturated Fat	3 g	Dietary Fiber	2 g	Vitamin A	69 RE
Cholesterol	<1 mg	Protein	5 g	Vitamin C	4 mg
Sodium	80 mg	Calcium	79 mg		

DIETARY EXCHANGES: 1 Starch/Bread, 2 Fruit, 1 Fat

PEACH AND BLUEBERRY CRISP

Rich in antioxidant vitamins A and C, this colorful combination of peaches and blueberries helps strengthen your body's immune system.

3 cups fresh or thawed frozen
    sliced peeled peaches,
    undrained
1 cup fresh or thawed frozen
    blueberries, undrained
2 tablespoons granulated sugar
¼ teaspoon ground nutmeg
2 tablespoons uncooked quick
    oats

2 tablespoons crisp rice cereal
2 tablespoons all-purpose flour
1 tablespoon firmly packed light
    brown sugar
1 tablespoon reduced calorie
    margarine, melted
⅛ teaspoon ground cinnamon

1 Preheat oven to 375°F. Combine peaches and blueberries in ungreased 8-inch round baking pan. Combine granulated sugar and nutmeg in small bowl. Sprinkle over fruit; toss gently to coat.

2 Combine oats, rice cereal, flour, brown sugar, margarine and cinnamon in small bowl. Sprinkle over fruit. Bake, uncovered, 35 to 40 minutes or until peaches are tender and topping is golden brown. *Makes 4 servings*

Nutrients per Serving:

Calories	153 (11% of calories from fat)				
Total Fat	2 g	Carbohydrate	34 g	Iron	1 mg
Saturated Fat	<1 g	Dietary Fiber	3 g	Vitamin A	104 RE
Cholesterol	0 mg	Protein	2 g	Vitamin C	13 mg
Sodium	46 mg	Calcium	15 mg		

DIETARY EXCHANGES: 1 Starch/Bread, 1½ Fruit

PEAR BROWN BETTY

Hungry for something warm and crunchy? Then this is the dessert for you. Pear Brown Betty features a spicy pear filling with a crunchy topping.

8 medium pears, cored, peeled and sliced
¾ cup frozen unsweetened apple juice concentrate, thawed
½ cup golden raisins
¼ cup plus 3 tablespoons all-purpose flour, divided

1 teaspoon ground cinnamon
⅓ cup uncooked quick oats
3 tablespoons firmly packed dark brown sugar
3 tablespoons margarine, melted

1 Preheat oven to 375°F. Spray 11×7-inch baking dish with nonstick cooking spray. Set aside.

2 Combine sliced pears, apple juice concentrate, raisins, 3 tablespoons flour and cinnamon in large bowl; mix well. Spoon mixture into prepared baking dish.

3 Combine remaining ¼ cup flour, oats, brown sugar and margarine in medium bowl; stir until mixture forms coarse crumbs. Sprinkle evenly over pear mixture. Bake 1 hour or until golden brown. Cool in pan on wire rack.

Makes 12 (½-cup) servings

Nutrients per Serving:

Calories	179 (17% of calories from fat)				
Total Fat	4 g	Carbohydrate	38 g	Iron	1 mg
Saturated Fat	1 g	Dietary Fiber	3 g	Vitamin A	37 RE
Cholesterol	0 mg	Protein	2 g	Vitamin C	5 mg
Sodium	40 mg	Calcium	28 mg		

DIETARY EXCHANGES: ½ Starch/Bread, 2 Fruit, ½ Fat

TEMPTING APPLE TRIFLES

Each serving of this rich-tasting trifle contains only 246 calories,
2 grams of fat and almost no cholesterol.

½ cup skim milk
1½ teaspoons cornstarch
4½ teaspoons dark brown sugar
1 egg white
½ teaspoon vegetable oil
½ teaspoon vanilla
½ teaspoon rum extract, divided
4 tablespoons unsweetened
   apple cider, divided

2 tablespoons raisins
½ teaspoon ground cinnamon
1 cup peeled and chopped
   Golden Delicious apple
1 cup ½-inch angel food cake
   cubes, divided

1 To prepare custard, combine milk and cornstarch in small heavy saucepan; stir until cornstarch is completely dissolved. Add brown sugar, egg white and oil; blend well. Bring to a boil over medium-low heat until thickened, stirring constantly with whisk. Remove from heat; stir in vanilla and ¼ teaspoon rum extract. Set aside to cool completely.

2 Combine 2 tablespoons cider, raisins and cinnamon in medium saucepan; bring to a boil over medium-low heat. Add apple; cook until apple is fork-tender and all liquid has been absorbed, stirring frequently. Remove from heat; set aside to cool.

3 To assemble, place ¼ cup cake cubes in bottom of each of 2 small trifle or dessert dishes. Combine remaining 2 tablespoons cider and ¼ teaspoon rum extract in small bowl; mix well. Spoon 1½ teaspoons cider mixture over cake in each dish. Spoon ¼ of custard mixture over each dish, then top each with ¼ cup cooked apple mixture. Repeat layers. Serve immediately. Garnish with fresh mint, if desired.

Makes 2 servings

Nutrients per Serving:

Calories	246 (6% of calories from fat)				
Total Fat	2 g	Carbohydrate	53 g	Iron	1 mg
Saturated Fat	<1 g	Dietary Fiber	2 g	Vitamin A	41 RE
Cholesterol	1 mg	Protein	6 g	Vitamin C	5 mg
Sodium	117 mg	Calcium	104 mg		

DIETARY EXCHANGES: 2 Starch/Bread, 1½ Fruit

CRANBERRY-APPLE STRUDEL

Butter-flavored nonstick
cooking spray
1 tablespoon margarine
1 tablespoon firmly packed light
brown sugar
2 medium Golden Delicious
apples, cored, peeled and
diced

¼ cup raisins
1 can (16 ounces) whole-berry
cranberry sauce
6 sheets phyllo dough
3 tablespoons graham cracker
crumbs, divided
¼ cup toasted slivered almonds,
chopped

1 Preheat oven to 375°F. Spray cookie sheet with cooking spray. Set aside. Melt margarine in large saucepan over medium heat. Add brown sugar; bring to a boil. Add apples and raisins; cook 10 minutes or until apples can be pierced easily with fork. Remove from heat. Add cranberry sauce; mix well. Set aside.

2 Place 1 sheet of phyllo, narrow side facing away, on piece of parchment paper. Spray phyllo with cooking spray; sprinkle with 1½ teaspoons graham cracker crumbs. Overlap second sheet of phyllo over first sheet about 1 inch down from top. Spray with cooking spray; sprinkle with 1½ teaspoons crumbs. Continue overlapping with remaining phyllo and crumbs, spraying with cooking spray between layers.

3 Spoon cooled cranberry mixture into center of phyllo; sprinkle with chopped almonds. Fold bottom and sides of phyllo to cover mixture, forming an envelope. With floured hands, roll filled phyllo, jelly-roll fashion starting at short end, to form strudel. Place on prepared cookie sheet. Spray top with cooking spray. Make 8 diagonal cuts across top of strudel. Bake 12 to 15 minutes or until lightly browned.

4 Cool on wire rack 30 minutes. Cut crosswise into 8 pieces. Garnish, if desired.

Makes 8 servings

Nutrients per Serving:

Calories	215 (20% of calories from fat)				
Total Fat	5 g	Carbohydrate	43 g	Iron	1 mg
Saturated Fat	1 g	Dietary Fiber	2 g	Vitamin A	20 RE
Cholesterol	0 mg	Protein	2 g	Vitamin C	4 mg
Sodium	118 mg	Calcium	21 mg		

DIETARY EXCHANGES: ½ Starch/Bread, 2 Fruit, 1 Fat

BLACKBERRY STRUDEL CUPS

Blackberries are a great source of fiber—two thirds of that fiber is insoluble, which helps keep your digestive tract running smoothly.

6 sheets frozen phyllo dough, thawed
Nonstick cooking spray
1 pint blackberries
2 tablespoons sugar

1 cup thawed frozen reduced fat nondairy whipped topping
1 container (6 ounces) custard-style apricot or peach low fat yogurt

1 Preheat oven to 400°F. Cut each sheet of phyllo crosswise into 4 pieces. Coat 1 piece lightly with cooking spray; place in large custard cup. Coat remaining 3 pieces lightly with cooking spray; place over first piece, alternating corners. Repeat with remaining phyllo dough to form 6 strudel cups.

2 Place custard cups on cookie sheet. Bake about 15 minutes or until pastry is golden. Let cool to room temperature.

3 Meanwhile, combine blackberries and sugar in small bowl; let stand 15 minutes.

4 Combine whipped topping and yogurt in medium bowl. Reserve ½ cup blackberries for garnish; gently stir remaining blackberries into whipped topping mixture. Spoon into cooled pastry cups. Top with reserved blackberries. Garnish with mint, if desired.   *Makes 6 servings*

Nutrients per Serving:				
Calories	126 (22% of calories from fat)			
Total Fat	4 g	Carbohydrate	25 g	Iron	<1 mg
Saturated Fat	<1 g	Dietary Fiber	3 g	Vitamin A	25 RE
Cholesterol	3 mg	Protein	3 g	Vitamin C	10 mg
Sodium	22 mg	Calcium	55 mg		

DIETARY EXCHANGES: 1½ Fruit, 1 Fat

RASPBERRY NAPOLEONS

4 sheets phyllo dough, divided
  Butter-flavored nonstick
    cooking spray
1 container (15 ounces) low fat
  ricotta cheese
1 container (8 ounces) nonfat
  ricotta cheese

3 tablespoons sugar
1 teaspoon vanilla
½ teaspoon lemon extract
2 cups fresh or frozen thawed
  and drained raspberries,
  divided

1 Preheat oven to 375°F. Spray cookie sheet with butter-flavored nonstick cooking spray. Set aside.

2 Place 1 sheet of phyllo on waxed paper. Cover remaining sheets with damp kitchen towel to prevent dough from drying out. Set aside. Spray phyllo with cooking spray. Cut phyllo lengthwise into thirds. Carefully fold one third in half; spray with cooking spray. Fold in half again; spray. Fold in half a third time, forming rectangle; spray top with cooking spray. Place on prepared cookie sheet. Repeat folding and spraying with remaining two thirds. Repeat with remaining phyllo dough.

3 Bake 7 to 9 minutes or until phyllo is golden brown. Cool on wire rack. Place both ricotta cheeses, sugar, vanilla and lemon extract in food processor or blender; process until smooth.

4 Spread 2 tablespoons ricotta cheese mixture onto each of 4 phyllo rectangles. Place, cheese side up, on dessert plates; top each with ¼ cup raspberries.

5 Spread 2 tablespoons ricotta cheese mixture onto each of 4 more phyllo rectangles. Place, cheese side down, on top of raspberry layer. Spread top of each stack with 2 tablespoons ricotta cheese mixture. Top each with ¼ cup raspberries, reserving 4 raspberries for garnish.

6 Spread each of 4 remaining rectangles with 2 tablespoons ricotta cheese mixture. Place, cheese side down, on raspberry layer. Top each stack with 1 tablespoon cheese mixture and 1 raspberry. *Makes 4 servings*

Nutrients per Serving:

Calories	243 (15% of calories from fat)				
Total Fat	4 g	Carbohydrate	34 g	Iron	1 mg
Saturated Fat	0 g	Dietary Fiber	3 g	Vitamin A	209 RE
Cholesterol	21 mg	Protein	19 g	Vitamin C	16 mg
Sodium	18 mg	Calcium	275 mg		

DIETARY EXCHANGES: 1 Starch/Bread, 2 Lean Meat, 1 Fruit

CRÈME CARAMEL

This wonderfully refreshing French dessert will cool your taste buds after a spicy main dish.

½ cup sugar, divided
1 tablespoon hot water
2 cups skim milk
⅛ teaspoon salt

½ cup cholesterol free egg
  substitute
½ teaspoon vanilla
⅛ teaspoon maple extract

1 Heat ¼ cup sugar in heavy saucepan over low heat, stirring constantly until melted and straw colored. Remove from heat; stir in hot water. Return to heat; stir 5 minutes until mixture is a dark caramel color. Divide melted sugar evenly among 6 custard cups. Set aside.

2 Preheat oven to 350°F. Combine milk, remaining ¼ cup sugar and salt in medium bowl. Add egg substitute, vanilla and maple extract; mix well. Pour ½ cup mixture into each custard cup. Place cups in heavy pan; pour hot water into pan to 1- to 2-inch depth.

3 Bake 40 to 45 minutes until knife inserted near edge of cup comes out clean. Cool on wire rack. Refrigerate at least 4 hours or overnight.

4 When ready to serve, run knife around edge of custard cup. Invert custard onto serving plate; remove cup.

Makes 6 servings

Nutrients per Serving:

Calories	103 (1% of calories from fat)				
Total Fat	<1 g	Carbohydrate	21 g	Iron	0 mg
Saturated Fat	0 g	Dietary Fiber	0 g	Vitamin A	153 RE
Cholesterol	1 mg	Protein	5 g	Vitamin C	1 mg
Sodium	114 mg	Calcium	108 mg		

DIETARY EXCHANGES: 1 Starch/Bread, ½ Milk

CHOCOLATE MOUSSE

This fabulous, nearly fat free mousse is lighter and airier than most chocolate desserts and is so quick and easy to make!

½ cup plus 2 tablespoons sugar, divided

¼ cup unsweetened cocoa powder

1 envelope unflavored gelatin

2 tablespoons coffee-flavored liqueur

2 cups skim milk

¼ cup cholesterol free egg substitute

2 egg whites

⅛ teaspoon cream of tartar

½ cup thawed frozen reduced fat nondairy whipped topping

1 Combine ½ cup sugar, cocoa and gelatin in medium saucepan. Add coffee-flavored liqueur; let stand 2 minutes to soften gelatin.

2 Add milk; cook and stir over medium heat until sugar and gelatin dissolve. Stir in egg substitute. Remove from heat and set aside.

3 Beat egg whites in medium bowl with electric mixer until foamy. Add cream of tartar; beat until soft peaks form. Gradually add remaining 2 tablespoons sugar, beating until stiff peaks form.

4 Gently fold egg white mixture into cocoa mixture; fold in whipped topping. Divide mixture evenly among 8 dessert dishes. Refrigerate until thickened.

Makes 8 servings

Nutrients per Serving:

Calories	118 (3% of calories from fat)				
Total Fat	<1 g	Carbohydrate	23 g	Iron	1 mg
Saturated Fat	<1 g	Dietary Fiber	0 g	Vitamin A	78 RE
Cholesterol	1 mg	Protein	5 g	Vitamin C	1 mg
Sodium	60 mg	Calcium	83 mg		

DIETARY EXCHANGES: 1½ Starch/Bread

ALMOND-PUMPKIN CHIFFON PUDDING

Just ½ cup pumpkin contains five times a full day's supply of vitamin A, which is good for vision and also helps boost your body's immune system.

1 envelope unflavored gelatin
1 cup 2% low fat milk
1 cup solid pack pumpkin
½ teaspoon pumpkin pie spice
1 container (8 ounces) plain low fat yogurt

3 egg whites
Dash salt
⅔ cup firmly packed light brown sugar
½ cup chopped toasted slivered almonds, divided

1 Grease 6-cup mold. Sprinkle gelatin over milk in small saucepan; let stand 5 minutes to soften gelatin. Cook and stir over low heat until gelatin dissolves, 3 to 5 minutes. Remove from heat. Stir in pumpkin and pumpkin pie spice. Cool to room temperature.

2 Stir yogurt into pumpkin mixture; refrigerate until mixture begins to thicken. Beat egg whites and salt in medium bowl with electric mixer until soft peaks form. Gradually add brown sugar, beating until stiff peaks form; fold into pumpkin mixture.

3 Sprinkle 1 tablespoon almonds onto bottom of prepared mold. Fold remaining almonds into pumpkin mixture; spoon into mold. Refrigerate until firm. Unmold to serve.

Makes 8 servings

Nutrients per Serving:

Calories	170 (27% of calories from fat)				
Total Fat	5 g	Carbohydrate	25 g	Iron	1 mg
Saturated Fat	1 g	Dietary Fiber	1 g	Vitamin A	700 RE
Cholesterol	4 mg	Protein	7 g	Vitamin C	2 mg
Sodium	65 mg	Calcium	136 mg		

DIETARY EXCHANGES: 1½ Starch/Bread, ½ Milk, ½ Fat

OLD-FASHIONED BREAD PUDDING

*The history of bread pudding dates back to the 1800s in England.
Then, it was eaten by the poor to make use of stale bread. Today
we think of bread pudding as a rich treat.*

2 cups skim milk
4 egg whites
3 tablespoons sugar
2 tablespoons margarine, melted
1 tablespoon vanilla

2 teaspoons ground cinnamon
12 slices whole wheat bread, cut
    into ½-inch squares
½ cup raisins
½ cup chopped dried apples

1 Preheat oven to 350°F. Spray 2-quart casserole with nonstick cooking spray. Set aside.

2 Combine milk, egg whites, sugar, margarine, vanilla and cinnamon in large bowl; mix well. Stir in bread, raisins and apples; let stand 5 minutes.

3 Pour mixture into prepared casserole. Bake 35 minutes or until browned. Cool in pan on wire rack.

Makes 12 servings

Nutrients per Serving:

Calories	150 (19% of calories from fat)				
Total Fat	3 g	Carbohydrate	26 g	Iron	1 mg
Saturated Fat	1 g	Dietary Fiber	1 g	Vitamin A	48 RE
Cholesterol	1 mg	Protein	6 g	Vitamin C	1 mg
Sodium	214 mg	Calcium	80 mg		

DIETARY EXCHANGES: 1 Starch/Bread, ½ Fruit, ½ Fat

REFRIGERATOR COOKIES

Become a cookie artist—test your decorating skills with these simple, light cookies.

½ cup sugar
¼ cup light corn syrup
¼ cup margarine, softened
¼ cup cholesterol free egg
    substitute

1 teaspoon vanilla
1¾ cups all-purpose flour
¼ teaspoon baking soda
¼ teaspoon salt
Cookie decorations (optional)

1 Beat sugar, corn syrup and margarine in large bowl. Add egg substitute and vanilla; mix well. Set aside.

2 Combine flour, baking soda and salt in medium bowl. Add to sugar mixture; mix well. Shape dough into 2 (1½-inch-wide) rolls. Wrap in plastic wrap. Freeze 1 hour.

3 Preheat oven to 350°F. Cover baking sheets with parchment paper. Cut dough into ¼-inch-thick slices; place, 1 inch apart, on prepared cookie sheets. Sprinkle with cookie decorations, if desired.

4 Bake 8 to 10 minutes or until edges of cookies begin to turn golden brown. Cool on wire racks.

Makes 4 dozen cookies

Variation: Add 2 tablespoons unsweetened cocoa powder to batter for chocolate cookies.

Nutrients per Serving:

(1 cookie)

Calories	39 (23% of calories from fat)					
Total Fat	1 g	Carbohydrate	7 g	Iron	0 mg
Saturated Fat	0 g	Dietary Fiber	0 g	Vitamin A	18 RE
Cholesterol	0 mg	Protein	0 g	Vitamin C	0 mg
Sodium	32 mg	Calcium	2 mg		

DIETARY EXCHANGES: ½ Starch/Bread

MOCHA COOKIES

These delicious cookies have a taste reminiscent of mocha cappuccino.

2 tablespoons plus 1½ teaspoons
    instant coffee granules
1 tablespoon plus 1½ teaspoons
    skim milk
⅓ cup firmly packed light brown
    sugar
¼ cup granulated sugar

¼ cup margarine
1 egg
½ teaspoon almond extract
2 cups all-purpose flour, sifted
¼ cup wheat flake cereal
½ teaspoon ground cinnamon
¼ teaspoon baking powder

1 Preheat oven to 350°F. Spray cookie sheets with nonstick cooking spray.

2 Combine coffee granules and milk in small bowl. Beat together sugars and margarine in large bowl with electric mixer until well blended. Blend in egg, almond extract and coffee mixture.

3 Combine flour, cereal, cinnamon and baking powder in medium bowl. Gradually add to sugar mixture, beating until well blended.

4 Drop teaspoonfuls of dough, 2 inches apart, onto prepared cookie sheets; flatten with back of fork. Bake 8 to 10 minutes or until set. Cool on wire rack.

Makes 3½ dozen cookies

Nutrients per Serving:
(1 cookie)

Calories	48 (25% of calories from fat)					
Total Fat	1 g	Carbohydrate	8 g	Iron	<1 mg
Saturated Fat	<1 g	Dietary Fiber	<1 g	Vitamin A	19 RE
Cholesterol	5 mg	Protein	1 g	Vitamin C	<1 mg
Sodium	20 mg	Calcium	6 mg		

DIETARY EXCHANGES: ½ Starch/Bread, ½ Fat

MOCHA CRINKLES

These decadent chocolate-coffee flavored cookies will remind you of rich fudgy brownies, but with only a small portion of the fat and calories!

1⅓ cups firmly packed light brown sugar
½ cup vegetable oil
¼ cup low fat sour cream
1 egg
1 teaspoon vanilla
1¾ cups all-purpose flour
¾ cups unsweetened cocoa powder

2 teaspoons instant espresso or coffee granules
1 teaspoon baking soda
¼ teaspoon salt
⅛ teaspoon ground black pepper
½ cup powdered sugar

1 Beat brown sugar and oil in medium bowl with electric mixer. Mix in sour cream, egg and vanilla. Set aside.

2 Mix flour, cocoa, espresso, baking soda, salt and pepper in another medium bowl.

3 Add flour mixture to brown sugar mixture; mix well. Refrigerate dough until firm, 3 to 4 hours.

4 Preheat oven to 350°F. Place powdered sugar in shallow bowl. Cut dough into 1-inch pieces; roll into balls. Coat with powdered sugar. Place on ungreased cookie sheets.

5 Bake 10 to 12 minutes or until tops of cookies are firm to touch. *(Do not overbake.)* Cool on wire racks.

Makes 6 dozen cookies

Nutrients per Serving:					
(1 cookie)					
Calories	44 (30% of calories from fat)				
Total Fat	1 g	Carbohydrate	7 g	Iron	1 mg
Saturated Fat	<1 g	Dietary Fiber	0 g	Vitamin A	4 RE
Cholesterol	3 mg	Protein	0 g	Vitamin C	0 mg
Sodium	28 mg	Calcium	7 mg		

DIETARY EXCHANGES: ½ Starch/Bread

WHOLE WHEAT OATMEAL COOKIES

Few things will produce a smile as quickly as a plate full of homemade oatmeal cookies!

1 cup whole wheat flour
1 teaspoon ground cinnamon
1 teaspoon baking powder
½ teaspoon baking soda
½ teaspoon salt
1 cup firmly packed light brown sugar

¼ cup unsweetened applesauce
2 egg whites
2 tablespoons margarine
1½ teaspoons vanilla
1⅓ cups uncooked quick oats
½ cup raisins

1 Preheat oven to 375°F. Lightly spray cookie sheets with nonstick cooking spray. Set aside.

2 Combine flour, cinnamon, baking powder, baking soda and salt in medium bowl; mix well.

3 Combine brown sugar, applesauce, egg whites, margarine and vanilla in large bowl; stir until mixture forms coarse crumbs. Add flour mixture; mix well. Stir in oats and raisins.

4 Drop rounded teaspoonfuls of dough, 2 inches apart, onto prepared cookie sheets. Bake 10 to 12 minutes or until golden brown. Cool on wire racks.

Makes 3½ dozen cookies

Nutrients per Serving:
(1 cookie)

Calories	55 (14% of calories from fat)					
Total Fat	1 g	Carbohydrate	11 g	Iron	0 mg	
Saturated Fat	0 g	Dietary Fiber	0 g	Vitamin A	0 RE	
Cholesterol	0 mg	Protein	1 g	Vitamin C	0 mg	
Sodium	56 mg	Calcium	10 mg			

DIETARY EXCHANGES: 1 Starch/Bread

PEACH OATMEAL COOKIES

The whole wheat flour used in this recipe not only provides more fiber but also more nutrients than all-purpose flour.

¾ cup granulated sugar
¾ cup firmly packed light brown
    sugar
⅔ cup margarine
2 eggs
1½ teaspoons vanilla
1½ cups whole wheat flour

2 teaspoons baking powder
1 teaspoon salt
2½ cups uncooked quick oats
1½ cups diced pitted halved
    peeled fresh peaches
1 cup raisins

1 Preheat oven to 350°F. Spray cookie sheets with nonstick cooking spray. Beat sugars, margarine, eggs and vanilla in large mixing bowl with electric mixer at medium speed until well blended.

2 Combine flour, baking powder and salt in medium bowl. Add to egg mixture; beat at low speed 2 to 3 minutes or until well blended. Stir in oats, peaches and raisins.

3 Drop tablespoonfuls of dough, 2 inches apart, onto prepared cookie sheet. Bake 10 to 15 minutes or until golden brown. Cool on wire racks.

Makes 3 dozen cookies

Nutrients per Serving:
(1 cookie)

Calories	121 (29% of calories from fat)					
Total Fat	4 g	Carbohydrate	20 g	Iron	1 mg
Saturated Fat	1 g	Dietary Fiber	1 g	Vitamin A	52 RE
Cholesterol	12 mg	Protein	2 g	Vitamin C	1 mg
Sodium	123 mg	Calcium	17 mg		

DIETARY EXCHANGES: ½ Starch/Bread, ½ Fruit, 1 Fat

HAZELNUT BISCOTTI

*These crunchy Italian cookies are traditionally served with
a cup of hot cappuccino.*

6 raw hazelnuts
2 tablespoons margarine
¼ cup sugar
2 egg whites, lightly beaten
1½ teaspoons vanilla

1½ cups all-purpose flour
½ teaspoon baking powder
⅛ teaspoon salt
½ teaspoon grated orange peel

1 Preheat oven to 375°F. Place hazelnuts in shallow baking pan; bake 7 to 8 minutes or until rich golden brown. (Watch nuts carefully. They burn easily.) Set nuts aside. *Reduce oven temperature to 325°F.* Spray cookie sheet with nonstick cooking spray. Set aside.

2 Combine margarine and sugar in medium bowl; mix well. Add egg whites and vanilla; mix well. Combine flour, baking powder, salt and orange peel in large bowl; mix well. Finely chop toasted hazelnuts; stir into flour mixture. Add egg white mixture; blend well.

3 Divide dough in half. Shape half of dough into log on lightly floured surface. (Dough will be fairly soft.) Repeat with remaining half of dough to form second log. Place both logs on prepared cookie sheet. Bake 25 minutes or until wooden pick inserted in centers comes out clean. Cool on wire rack. *Reduce oven temperature to 300°F.*

4 As soon as logs are cool enough to handle, cut each log into 8 (½-inch-thick) slices. Return to cookie sheet. Bake 12 minutes; turn slices over. Bake 12 minutes or more until golden brown. Cool on wire racks.

Makes 16 biscotti

Nutrients per Serving:					
(1 cookie)					
Calories	76 (25% of calories from fat)				
Total Fat	2 g	Carbohydrate	12 g	Iron	1 mg
Saturated Fat	<1 g	Dietary Fiber	<1 g	Vitamin A	17 RE
Cholesterol	0 mg	Protein	2 g	Vitamin C	0 mg
Sodium	50 mg	Calcium	6 mg		

DIETARY EXCHANGES: 1 Starch/Bread, ½ Fat

ALMOND BISCOTTI

These no cholesterol, low fat Italian cookies are the perfect guilt-free snack to satisfy any sweet tooth.

¼ cup finely chopped slivered almonds
½ cup sugar
2 tablespoons margarine

4 egg whites, lightly beaten
2 teaspoons almond extract
2 cups all-purpose flour
2 teaspoons baking powder

1 Preheat oven to 375°F. Place almonds in small baking pan. Bake 7 to 8 minutes or until golden brown. *(Watch almonds carefully. They burn easily.)* Set aside.

2 Beat sugar and margarine in medium bowl with electric mixer until smooth. Add egg whites and almond extract; mix well. Combine flour, baking powder and salt in large bowl; mix well. Stir egg white mixture and almonds into flour mixture until well blended.

3 Spray two 9×5-inch loaf pans with nonstick cooking spray. Evenly divide dough between prepared pans; spread dough evenly onto bottoms of pans with wet fingertips. Bake 15 minutes or until knife inserted in centers comes out clean. Remove from oven; turn out onto cutting board.

4 As soon as loaves are cool enough to handle, cut each loaf into 16 (½-inch-thick) slices. Place slices on baking sheets covered with parchment paper or sprayed with cooking spray. Bake 5 minutes; turn over. Bake 5 minutes more or until golden brown. Serve warm or cool completely and store in airtight container.

Makes 32 biscotti

Nutrients per Serving:					
(1 cookie)					
Calories	56 (21% of calories from fat)				
Total Fat	1 g	Carbohydrate	9 g	Iron	<1 mg
Saturated Fat	<1 g	Dietary Fiber	<1 g	Vitamin A	9 RE
Cholesterol	0 mg	Protein	1 g	Vitamin C	<1 mg
Sodium	53 mg	Calcium	8 mg		

DIETARY EXCHANGES: ½ Starch/Bread, ½ Fat

OATMEAL ALMOND BALLS

Toasting almonds releases their full flavor and gives these cookies a rich, nutty taste.

¼ cup sliced almonds
⅓ cup honey
2 egg whites

½ teaspoon ground cinnamon
⅛ teaspoon salt
1½ cups uncooked quick oats

1 Preheat oven to 350°F. Place almonds on cookie sheet; bake 8 to 10 minutes or until golden brown. Set aside. *Do not turn oven off.*

2 Combine honey, egg whites, cinnamon and salt in large bowl; mix well. Add oats and toasted almonds; mix well.

3 Drop rounded teaspoonfuls of dough, 2 inches apart, onto ungreased nonstick cookie sheet. Bake 12 minutes or until lightly browned. Cool on wire rack.

Makes 2 dozen cookies

Nutrients per Serving:

(1 cookie)

Calories	42 (19% of calories from fat)				
Total Fat	1 g	Carbohydrate	7 g	Iron	0 mg
Saturated Fat	0 g	Dietary Fiber	0 g	Vitamin A	0 RE
Cholesterol	0 mg	Protein	1 g	Vitamin C	0 mg
Sodium	16 mg	Calcium	7 mg		

DIETARY EXCHANGES: ½ Starch/Bread

Cook's Tip
Store unopened packages of nuts in a cool dark place. Store opened packages in an airtight container in the refrigerator for up to six months or in the freezer for up to two years.

❖

BUTTERSCOTCH CRISPIES

Even though walnuts are high in fat, it is primarily polyunsaturated fat, which has been shown to lower "bad" cholesterol levels in the blood.

2 cups sifted all-purpose flour
1 teaspoon baking soda
1 teaspoon salt
½ cup margarine
2½ cups firmly packed light brown sugar

2 eggs
1 teaspoon vanilla
2 cups uncooked quick oats
2 cups puffed rice cereal
½ cup chopped walnuts

1 Preheat oven to 350°F. Spray cookie sheets with nonstick cooking spray.

2 Sift flour, baking soda and salt onto waxed paper. Beat margarine and brown sugar in large bowl with electric mixer until well blended. Beat in eggs, one at a time. Blend in vanilla. Add flour mixture, ½ cup at a time, beating well after each addition. Stir in oats, rice cereal and walnuts.

3 Drop teaspoonfuls of dough, about 1 inch apart, onto prepared cookie sheets. Bake 10 minutes or until cookies are firm and lightly browned. Cool on wire racks.

Makes 8½ dozen cookies

Nutrients per Serving:					
(1 cookie)					
Calories	50 (26% of calories from fat)				
Total Fat	1 g	Carbohydrate	9 g	Iron	<1 mg
Saturated Fat	<1 g	Dietary Fiber	<1 g	Vitamin A	13 RE
Cholesterol	4 mg	Protein	1 g	Vitamin C	<1 mg
Sodium	48 mg	Calcium	7 mg		

DIETARY EXCHANGES: ½ Starch/Bread, ½ Fat

PEANUT MERINGUE COOKIES

Create a virtually fat free snack by serving these scrumptious meringue cookies with fresh fruit.

4 egg whites
½ teaspoon cream of tartar

1 cup sugar
¼ cup ground peanuts

1 Preheat oven to 250°F. Cover cookie sheet with parchment paper. Set aside.

2 Beat egg whites in large bowl with electric mixer until foamy. Add cream of tartar; beat until soft peaks form. Gradually add sugar, beating until stiff peaks form. Fold in peanuts.

3 Drop teaspoonfuls of egg white mixture onto prepared cookie sheet. Bake 20 minutes or until lightly browned. Cool on wire racks.

Makes 3 dozen cookies

Nutrients per Serving:
(1 cookie)

Calories	16 (15% of calories from fat)					
Total Fat	<1 g	Carbohydrate	3 g	Iron	0 mg
Saturated Fat	0 g	Dietary Fiber	0 g	Vitamin A	0 RE
Cholesterol	0 mg	Protein	0 g	Vitamin C	0 mg
Sodium	3 mg	Calcium	1 mg		

DIETARY EXCHANGES: ½ Starch/Bread

Cook's Tip

Store cooled meringue cookies in an airtight container at room temperature for two to three days. Freeze cookies in an airtight container for up to two weeks. Thaw, uncovered, at room temperature for 30 minutes.

WILD RICE APPLESAUCE BARS

Low in fat, but full of fiber, protein, B vitamins and minerals, wild rice is very nutritious.

2 cups cooked wild rice
1⅓ cups unsweetened applesauce
1 cup low fat buttermilk, divided
2½ cups all-purpose flour
1 teaspoon baking soda
1 teaspoon salt
1 teaspoon ground cinnamon

⅓ cup shortening
1 cup firmly packed light brown sugar
6 egg whites
2 teaspoons vanilla
1 cup chopped nuts (optional)
Powdered sugar (optional)

1 Preheat oven to 350°F. Spray 15×10-inch jelly-roll pan with nonstick cooking spray. Combine wild rice, applesauce and ½ cup buttermilk in medium bowl; set aside.

2 Combine flour, baking soda, salt and cinnamon in medium bowl; set aside.

3 Beat together shortening and brown sugar in large bowl with electric mixer until well blended. Add egg whites; beat well. Blend in remaining ½ cup buttermilk and vanilla. Gradually add flour mixture, beating until well blended. Stir in wild rice mixture and nuts.

4 Pour batter into prepared pan. Bake 20 to 25 minutes or until toothpick inserted in center comes out clean. Cool completely. Sprinkle with powdered sugar, if desired.

Makes 48 servings

Nutrients per Serving:

Calories	68 (20% of calories from fat)					
Total Fat	2 g	Carbohydrate	12 g	Iron	1 mg
Saturated Fat	<1 g	Dietary Fiber	<1 g	Vitamin A	1 RE
Cholesterol	<1 mg	Protein	2 g	Vitamin C	<1 mg
Sodium	76 mg	Calcium	12 mg		

DIETARY EXCHANGES: ½ Starch/Bread, ½ Fruit

BROWNIES

Moist and chocolatey, these cakelike brownies are sure to please the most devoted chocoholic.

½ cup boiling water
½ cup unsweetened cocoa
    powder
1¼ cups all-purpose flour
¾ cup granulated sugar
¾ cup firmly packed light brown
    sugar

1 teaspoon baking powder
¼ teaspoon salt
4 egg whites, lightly beaten
⅓ cup vegetable oil
1½ teaspoons vanilla
½ cup chopped unsalted mixed
    nuts (optional)

1 Preheat oven to 350°F.

2 Spray 13×9-inch baking pan with nonstick cooking spray. Combine boiling water and cocoa in large bowl; mix until completely dissolved. Add flour, granulated sugar, brown sugar, baking powder, salt, egg whites, oil and vanilla; mix well. Fold in chopped nuts, if desired.

3 Pour batter into prepared pan. Bake 25 minutes or until brownies spring back when lightly touched. (*Do not overbake.*) Cool in pan on wire rack; cut into bars.

Makes 32 servings

Nutrients per Serving:

Calories	81 (26% of calories from fat)					
Total Fat	2 g	Carbohydrate	14 g	Iron	0 mg
Saturated Fat	<1 g	Dietary Fiber	0 g	Vitamin A	0 RE
Cholesterol	0 mg	Protein	1 g	Vitamin C	0 mg
Sodium	37 mg	Calcium	9 mg		

DIETARY EXCHANGES: 1 Starch/Bread, ½ Fat

MERINGUE-FILLED PEARS

In the United States, the Bartlett pear is the most popular variety of pear.

1 can (29 ounces) Bartlett pear halves, undrained
2 tablespoons firmly packed light brown sugar
1 teaspoon grated lemon peel
½ teaspoon ground nutmeg

2 egg whites
Dash salt
2 tablespoons granulated sugar
2 tablespoons slivered almonds (optional)

1 Preheat oven to 325°F. Drain pears, reserving ⅓ cup liquid. Place pears, cut side up, in 8-inch square baking pan. Pour reserved pear liquid over pears.

2 Combine brown sugar, lemon peel and nutmeg in small bowl; mix well. Sprinkle mixture evenly over pears.

3 For meringue, beat together egg whites and salt in small bowl with electric mixer until soft peaks form. Gradually add granulated sugar, beating until stiff peaks form.

4 Spoon meringue evenly over pear halves; sprinkle with almonds, if desired. Bake 15 to 20 minutes or until pears are thoroughly heated and meringue is golden brown. Serve warm.

Makes 4 servings

Nutrients per Serving:

Calories	176 (1% of calories from fat)				
Total Fat	<1 g	Carbohydrate	44 g	Iron	1 mg
Saturated Fat	<1 g	Dietary Fiber	4 g	Vitamin A	<1 RE
Cholesterol	0 mg	Protein	2 g	Vitamin C	3 mg
Sodium	40 mg	Calcium	18 mg		

DIETARY EXCHANGES: 3 Fruit

NECTARINE MERINGUE CROWNS

Cranberry juice has been used to help fight infections of the urinary tract.

2 egg whites
⅛ teaspoon cream of tartar
⅛ teaspoon ground nutmeg
⅔ cup sugar
1 can (6 ounces) frozen
    cranberry juice concentrate,
    thawed

½ cup water
1 tablespoon plus 1½ teaspoons
    cornstarch
5 fresh nectarines, halved, pitted
    and sliced

1 Preheat oven to 250°F.

2 For meringue, beat together egg whites, cream of tartar and nutmeg in small bowl with electric mixer until foamy. Gradually add sugar, beating until stiff peaks form. Divide meringue into 6 equal mounds on baking sheet. Shape into round tarts using back of spoon. Bake 1 hour; cool.

3 Pour cranberry juice concentrate into medium saucepan. Stir in water and cornstarch. Cook, stirring constantly, until sauce thickens and becomes translucent; cool.

4 Fill each meringue tart with about ½ cup nectarine slices; drizzle with sauce.

Makes 6 servings

Nutrients per Serving:

Calories	203 (2% of calories from fat)				
Total Fat	1 g	Carbohydrate	50 g	Iron	<1 mg
Saturated Fat	<1 g	Dietary Fiber	2 g	Vitamin A	84 RE
Cholesterol	0 mg	Protein	2 g	Vitamin C	28 mg
Sodium	20 mg	Calcium	10 mg		

DIETARY EXCHANGES: 3½ Fruit

FANTASY IN BERRIES

This unique, beautiful and delicious dessert is also very healthful. The berries are high in vitamin C and ricotta cheese is higher in calcium than any other cheese. It is also fun to make. You might even want to put your "pastry cream" in plastic squeeze bottles and let the guests decorate their own "Fantasy."

1 bag (12 ounces) frozen unsweetened raspberries, thawed
¼ cup plus 2 tablespoons sugar, divided
1 tablespoon fresh lemon juice

2 cups sliced fresh strawberries
1 cup fresh raspberries
1 cup fresh blueberries
1 cup low fat ricotta cheese
1 teaspoon vanilla
¼ teaspoon almond extract

1 To prepare raspberry sauce, place thawed raspberries, ¼ cup sugar and lemon juice in blender or food processor container; process until smooth. Strain to remove seeds. Spoon 3 tablespoons raspberry sauce onto each of 8 dessert plates. Tilt each plate, rotating to spread raspberry mixture over bottom of plate.

2 Arrange ¼ cup sliced strawberries, 2 tablespoons raspberries and 2 tablespoons blueberries on top of sauce in desired pattern on each plate.

3 Place ricotta cheese, remaining 2 tablespoons sugar, vanilla and almond extract in clean blender or food processor container; process until smooth. Spoon ricotta cheese mixture into pastry bag; pipe onto berries, using about 2 tablespoons mixture on each serving. (Use star tip to make rosettes or various sizes of writing tips to drizzle mixture over berries.) Before serving, garnish with mint and edible flowers, such as pansies, violets or nasturtiums, if desired.

Makes 8 servings

Nutrients per Serving:

Calories	104 (10% of calories from fat)				
Total Fat	1 g	Carbohydrate	21 g	Iron	1 mg
Saturated Fat	<1 g	Dietary Fiber	5 g	Vitamin A	26 RE
Cholesterol	4 mg	Protein	4 g	Vitamin C	37 mg
Sodium	25 mg	Calcium	56 mg		

DIETARY EXCHANGES: ½ Lean Meat, 1½ Fruit

FIRE AND ICE

This whimsical, southwestern dessert is designed to represent all of the colors of the Mexican flag. It is a perfect finale for a fiesta and it's fun to decorate each serving with a little Mexican flag.

2 cups vanilla ice milk or
  reduced fat ice cream
2 teaspoons finely chopped
  jalapeño pepper*
1 teaspoon grated lime peel,
  divided

1 cup water
¼ cup sugar
1 cup chopped peeled kiwifruit
1 tablespoon lime juice
1 cup fresh raspberries

1 Soften ice milk slightly in small bowl. Stir in jalapeño pepper and ½ teaspoon lime peel. Freeze until firm.

2 Combine water, sugar and remaining ½ teaspoon lime peel in small saucepan; bring to a boil. Boil, uncovered, 5 minutes or until reduced by about one third. Remove from heat; cool to room temperature.

3 Place kiwifruit and lime juice in blender or food processor container; process until blended. Stir in water mixture. Pour through fine strainer to remove kiwifruit seeds and lime peel, pressing liquid through strainer with back of spoon. Refrigerate kiwifruit mixture until cold.

4 Pour ¼ cup kiwifruit mixture into each of 6 chilled bowls. Scoop ⅓ cup jalapeño ice milk into each bowl. Sprinkle raspberries evenly on top. Garnish with lime peel strips, if desired.

Makes 6 servings

*Jalapeño peppers can sting and irritate the skin; wear rubber gloves when handling peppers and do not touch eyes. Wash hands after handling.

Nutrients per Serving:

Calories	152 (11% of calories from fat)					
Total Fat	2 g	Carbohydrate	32 g	Iron	<1 mg
Saturated Fat	1 g	Dietary Fiber	3 g	Vitamin A	32 RE
Cholesterol	7 mg	Protein	4 g	Vitamin C	62 mg
Sodium	58 mg	Calcium	112 mg		

DIETARY EXCHANGES: 1½ Starch/Bread, 1 Fruit

LIME SURPRISE

This exceptionally flavorful treat is surprisingly simple to prepare!

2 whole eggs
6 egg whites
3 tablespoons margarine
1¼ cups sugar

1 tablespoon grated lime peel
¾ cup fresh lime juice
8 ounces ladyfingers, divided

1 Combine whole eggs and egg whites in medium bowl; beat until foamy. Set aside. Combine margarine and sugar in top of double boiler; heat over simmering water until margarine is melted. Add lime peel and lime juice; mix well.

2 Add egg mixture to margarine mixture; cook and stir until thickened, about 6 minutes. Remove from heat; cool completely.

3 Split ladyfingers in half lengthwise. Line bottom of 1½-quart soufflé dish or casserole dish with ladyfingers. Cover with 1 cup lime mixture. Continue layering until all ladyfingers are used, ending with layer of lime sauce.

4 Cover tightly; refrigerate 6 hours or overnight. Garnish with grated lime peel, if desired.

Makes 12 servings

Nutrients per Serving:

Calories	200 (24% of calories from fat)				
Total Fat	5 g	Carbohydrate	34 g	Iron	1 mg
Saturated Fat	1 g	Dietary Fiber	0 g	Vitamin A	82 RE
Cholesterol	104 mg	Protein	5 g	Vitamin C	6 mg
Sodium	99 mg	Calcium	17 mg		

DIETARY EXCHANGES: 2 Starch/Bread, 1 Fat

LEMON CHEESE QUESADILLAS WITH MANGO SAUCE

4 (7-inch) flour tortillas
1 cup part-skim ricotta cheese
⅓ cup vanilla nonfat yogurt
4 tablespoons lemon juice, divided
1 tablespoon plus 1½ teaspoons sugar
2 teaspoons grated lemon peel
1 teaspoon vanilla
1 large ripe mango

2 tablespoons lightly packed fresh mint, fresh cilantro or fresh basil
½ jalapeño pepper, seeded, minced (optional)*
1 firm ripe banana, cut into ¼-inch-thick slices
½ pint fresh strawberries, quartered

1 Preheat oven to 375°F.

2 Place tortillas on center oven rack. Bake 6 to 7 minutes or until golden. Place on serving plate.

3 Combine ricotta cheese, yogurt, 1 tablespoon lemon juice, sugar, lemon peel and vanilla in small bowl. Spread about ⅓ cup ricotta cheese mixture onto each tortilla.

4 Peel mango. Cut fruit away from pit; chop fruit into ½-inch cubes. Place half of mango cubes in food processor or blender container. Add 2 tablespoons lemon juice, mint and jalapeño pepper; process until puréed.

5 Place remaining mango cubes in small bowl with banana, strawberries and remaining 1 tablespoon lemon juice; toss gently to combine. Spoon ½ cup fruit onto each tortilla; drizzle with about 1 tablespoon sauce. Garnish with mint, if desired.

Makes 4 servings

*Jalapeño peppers can sting and irritate the skin; wear rubber gloves when handling peppers and do not touch eyes. Wash hands after handling.

Nutrients per Serving:

Calories	283 (20% of calories from fat)				
Total Fat	6 g	Carbohydrate	48 g	Iron	2 mg
Saturated Fat	3 g	Dietary Fiber	4 g	Vitamin A	290 RE
Cholesterol	17 mg	Protein	11 g	Vitamin C	50 mg
Sodium	246 mg	Calcium	248 mg		

DIETARY EXCHANGES: 1 Starch/Bread, 1 Lean Meat, 2 Fruit, ½ Fat

INDEX

VOLUME MEASUREMENTS (dry)

⅛ teaspoon = 0.5 mL
¼ teaspoon = 1 mL
½ teaspoon = 2 mL
¾ teaspoon = 4 mL
1 teaspoon = 5 mL
1 tablespoon = 15 mL
2 tablespoons = 30 mL
¼ cup = 60 mL
⅓ cup = 75 mL
½ cup = 125 mL
⅔ cup = 150 mL
¾ cup = 175 mL
1 cup = 250 mL
2 cups = 1 pint = 500 mL
3 cups = 750 mL
4 cups = 1 quart = 1 L

VOLUME MEASUREMENTS (fluid)

1 fluid ounce (2 tablespoons) = 30 mL
4 fluid ounces (½ cup) = 125 mL
8 fluid ounces (1 cup) = 250 mL
12 fluid ounces (1½ cups) = 375 mL
16 fluid ounces (2 cups) = 500 mL

WEIGHTS (mass)

½ ounce = 15 g
1 ounce = 30 g
3 ounces = 90 g
4 ounces = 120 g
8 ounces = 225 g
10 ounces = 285 g
12 ounces = 360 g
16 ounces = 1 pound = 450 g

DIMENSIONS

1/16 inch = 2 mm
⅛ inch = 3 mm
¼ inch = 6 mm
½ inch = 1.5 cm
¾ inch = 2 cm
1 inch = 2.5 cm

OVEN TEMPERATURES

250°F = 120°C
275°F = 140°C
300°F = 150°C
325°F = 160°C
350°F = 180°C
375°F = 190°C
400°F = 200°C
425°F = 220°C
450°F = 230°C

BAKING PAN SIZES

Utensil	Size in Inches/Quarts	Metric Volume	Size in Centimeters
Baking or Cake Pan (square or rectangular)	8×8×2	2 L	20×20×5
	9×9×2	2.5 L	22×22×5
	12×8×2	3 L	30×20×5
	13×9×2	3.5 L	33×23×5
Loaf Pan	8×4×3	1.5 L	20×10×7
	9×5×3	2 L	23×13×7
Round Layer Cake Pan	8×1½	1.2 L	20×4
	9×1½	1.5 L	23×4
Pie Plate	8×1¼	750 mL	20×3
	9×1¼	1 L	23×3
Baking Dish or Casserole	1 quart	1 L	—
	1½ quart	1.5 L	—
	2 quart	2 L	—